Human Rights, Southern Voices

A just international order and a healthy cosmopolitan discipline of law need to include perspectives that take account of the standpoints, interest, concerns and beliefs of non-Western people and traditions. The dominant scholarly and activist discourses about human rights have developed largely without reference to these other viewpoints. Claims about universality sit uneasily with ignorance of other traditions and parochial or ethnocentric tendencies. The object of the book is to make accessible the ideas of four jurists who present distinct 'Southern' perspectives on human rights.

William Twining is Quain Professor of Jurisprudence Emeritus of University College London. He has worked extensively in Eastern Africa, the Commonwealth and the United States. Much of his recent work explores the implications of globalisation for law and legal theory. His previous book, *General Jurisprudence: Understanding Law from a Global Perspective*, is a precursor of *Human Rights: Southern Voices*.

The Law in Context Series

Editors: William Twining (University College London),
Christopher McCrudden (Lincoln College, Oxford),
and Bronwen Morgan (University of Bristol).

Since 1970 the Law in Context series has been in the forefront of the movement to broaden the study of law. It has been a vehicle for the publication of innovative scholarly books that treat law and legal phenomena critically in their social, political and economic contexts from a variety of perspectives. The series particularly aims to publish scholarly legal writing that brings fresh perspectives to bear on new and existing areas of law taught in universities. A contextual approach involves treating legal subjects broadly, using materials from other social sciences, and from any other discipline that helps to explain the operation in practice of the subject under discussion. It is hoped that this orientation is at once more stimulating and more realistic than the bare exposition of legal rules. The series includes original books that have a different emphasis from traditional legal textbooks, while maintaining the same high standards of scholarship. They are written primarily for undergraduate and graduate students of law and of other disciplines, but most also appeal to a wider readership. In the past, most books in the series have focused on English law, but recent publications include books on European law, globalisation, transnational legal processes, and comparative law.

Books in the Series

Anderson, Schum & Twining: *Analysis of Evidence*
Ashworth: *Sentencing and Criminal Justice*
Barton & Douglas: *Law and Parenthood*
Beecher-Monas: *Evaluating Scientific Evidence: An Interdisciplinary Framework for Intellectual Due Process*
Bell: *French Legal Cultures*
Bercusson: *European Labour Law*
Birkinshaw: *European Public Law*
Birkinshaw: *Freedom of Information: The Law, the Practice and the Ideal*
Cane: *Atiyah's Accidents, Compensation and the Law*
Clarke & Kohler: *Property Law: Commentary and Materials*
Collins: *The Law of Contract*
Cranston: *Legal Foundations of the Welfare State*
Davies: *Perspectives on Labour Law*
Dembour: *Who Believes in Human Rights?: The European Convention in Question*
de Sousa Santos: *Toward a New Legal Common Sense*
Diduck: *Law's Families*
Elworthy & Holder: *Environmental Protection: Text and Materials*
Fortin: *Children's Rights and the Developing Law*
Glover-Thomas: *Reconstructing Mental Health Law and Policy*

Goldman: *Globalisation and the Western Legal Tradition: Recurring Patterns of Law and Authority*

Gobert & Punch: *Rethinking Corporate Crime*

Harlow & Rawlings: *Law and Administration*

Harris: *An Introduction to Law*

Harris, Campbell & Halson: *Remedies in Contract and Tort*

Harvey: *Seeking Asylum in the UK: Problems and Prospects*

Hervey & McHale: *Health Law and the European Union*

Holder and Lee: *Environmental Protection, Law and Policy*

Kostakopoulou: *The Future Governance of Citizenship*

Lacey, Wells and Quick: *Reconstructing Criminal Law*

Lewis: *Choice and the Legal Order: Rising above Politics*

Likosky: *Transnational Legal Processes*

Likosky: *Law, Infrastructure and Human Rights*

Maughan & Webb: *Lawyering Skills and the Legal Process*

McGlynn: *Families and the European Union: Law, Politics and Pluralism*

Moffat: *Trusts Law: Text and Materials*

Monti: *EC Competition Law*

Morgan & Yeung: *An Introduction to Law and Regulation, Text and Materials*

Norrie: *Crime, Reason and History*

O'Dair: *Legal Ethics*

Oliver: *Common Values and the Public–Private Divide*

Oliver & Drewry: *The Law and Parliament*

Picciotto: *International Business Taxation*

Reed: *Internet Law: Text and Materials*

Richardson: *Law, Process and Custody*

Roberts & Palmer: *Dispute Processes: ADR and the Primary Forms of Decision-Making*

Scott & Black: *Cranston's Consumers and the Law*

Seneviratne: *Ombudsmen: Public Services and Administrative Justice*

Stapleton: *Product Liability*

Tamanaha: *Law as a Means to an End: Threat to the Rule of Law*

Turpin and Tomkins: *British Government and the Constitution: Text and Materials*

Twining: *Globalisation and Legal Theory*

Twining: *Rethinking Evidence*

Twining: *General Jurisprudence: Understanding Law from a Global Perspective*

Twining: *Human Rights: Southern Voices: Francis Deng, Abdullahi An-Na'im, Yash Ghai and Upendra Baxi*

Twining & Miers: *How to Do Things with Rules*

Ward: *A Critical Introduction to European Law*

Ward: *Law, Text, Terror*

Ward: *Shakespeare and Legal Imagination*

Zander: *Cases and Materials on the English Legal System*

Zander: *The Law-Making Process*

Human Rights: Southern Voices

Francis Deng, Abdullahi An-Na'im, Yash Ghai,
Upendra Baxi

Edited by
WILLIAM TWINING

CAMBRIDGE
UNIVERSITY PRESS

CAMBRIDGE UNIVERSITY PRESS

Cambridge, New York, Melbourne, Madrid, Cape Town, Singapore, São Paulo, Delhi

Cambridge University Press
The Edinburgh Building, Cambridge CB2 8RU, UK

Published in the United States of America by Cambridge University Press, New York

www.cambridge.org
Information on this title: www.cambridge.org/9780521130264

First published 2009

Printed in the United Kingdom at the University Press, Cambridge

A catalogue record for this publication is available from the British Library

ISBN 978-0-521-11321-2 hardback
ISBN 978-0-521-13026-4 paperback

Table of Contents

Acknowledgments

This book has been in preparation for several years. The project crystallized with an invitation to give the annual MacDonald Lecture at the University of Alberta in 2005. The lecture developed into a long article, from that into a proposal for a book, which became the subject of a Symposium at the Transitional Justice Institute of the University of Ulster in June 2008 that was supported by the British Academy and the University of Ulster. This memorable event was attended by all four of the subjects of this reader. Throughout this period Francis Deng, Abdullahi An-Na'im, Yash Ghai and Upendra Baxi have provided material, submitted to interviews, commented on drafts, and debated with each other in public and private. They have co-operated, while respecting my rights as editor, and they have added the warmth of friendship. I am also grateful for comments and suggestions from participants in seminars and symposia at the Universities of Miami, Alberta, Sussex, Warwick, Ulster (in Belfast and Magee), and University College London. I am especially grateful to Fionnuala Ní Aoláin, Christine Bell, Colm Campbell, and Catherine Turner for their encouragement, help, and hospitality at the Transitional Justice Institute and to the Leverhulme Foundation for an Emeritus Fellowship, which supported several visits to Belfast and the final phases of the editorial process. I owe further debts to Terry Anderson, Pratiksha Baxi, Bill Conklin, Jill Cottrell, Marie-Bénédicte Dembour, Conor Gearty, Oscar Guardiola-Rivera, Andrew Halpin, Christopher McCrudden, Jana Promislow, and Carl Wellman. As ever, my wife, Penelope has provided irreplaceable support and assistance.

The following have kindly given permission for republication of copyright material: The Brookings Institution; Cardozo Law Review; Harvard University Press; Interights; The Journal of International Affairs; Oxford University Press (New Delhi); Review of Constitutional Affairs; Syracuse University Press; Transnational Journal of Law and Contemporary Problems; University of Pennsylvania Press; and Abdullahi An-Na'im, Marie-Bénédicte Dembour, and Yash Ghai. Every attempt has been made to secure permission to reproduce copyright material in this title and grateful acknowledgment is made to the authors and publishers of reproduced material.

1

Introduction

A just international order and a healthy cosmopolitan discipline of law need to include perspectives that take account of the standpoints, interests, concerns, and beliefs of non-Western people and traditions. The dominant Western scholarly and activist discourses about human rights have developed largely without reference to these other standpoints and traditions.[1] Claims about universality sit uneasily with ignorance of other traditions and parochial or ethnocentric tendencies. The purpose of this book is to take a modest first step towards de-parochializing our juristic canon by making accessible the basic ideas about human rights of four jurists who present distinct "Southern" perspectives.

Francis Deng justifiably claims to interpret and speak for the traditions and culture of his own people, the Ngok Dinka of the Sudan. He argues that traditional Dinka values are basically compatible, in most respects, with the values underlying the Universal Declaration of Human Rights and like documents. Dinka culture concretizes, supplements, and sometimes conflicts with those more abstract values in the dynamic context of change involving the constant interaction between "tradition" and "modernization".

Abdullahi An-Na'im, a Northern Sudanese and a committed Muslim, argues that a "modernist" interpretation of Islam involves ideas, which are for the most part similarly reconcilable with international human rights norms, but that acceptance of such ideas (their internalization within Islamic belief systems) depends far more on conversations and debates *within* Islam than on cross-cultural dialogue, let alone external attempts at persuasion or imposition. He further argues that coercive enforcement of Shari'a by the state betrays the Qu'ran's emphasis on freedom of religion, voluntary acceptance, and individual interpretation of Islam.

Yash Ghai (Kenya) is sceptical of most claims to universality that are made for human rights; however, adopting a pragmatic materialist stance, he reports that he has found, through practical experience of post-colonial constitution-making, that human rights discourse provides a workable framework for negotiating political and constitutional settlements among politicians and

---

[1] Twining (2009) Ch. 1.

leaders claiming to represent different majority, minority, and ethnic interests in multi-ethnic societies. He is strongly committed to the core values of human rights and social democracy, but he is sceptical about claims invoking "culture" rather than material interests. He is deeply concerned about the paradox involving great progress in the development of human rights norms and the dismal reality of massive human rights violations.

Upendra Baxi (India) argues that as human rights discourse becomes commodified, professionalized by technocrats, and sometimes hijacked by powerful groups, it is in grave danger of losing touch with the experience of suffering and the needs of those who should be the main beneficiaries – the poor and the oppressed. They are the main authors of human rights. To take human rights seriously, is to take suffering seriously.

These thinkers are both significantly similar and strikingly different. They all belong to a single post-colonial generation (three were born, coincidentally, in 1938; An-Na'im is a decade younger, but started early). All four have been concerned with the problems of racism, colonialism, post-independence politics, weak and corrupt regimes, poverty, and injustice in the South. They have given expression to ideas that are rooted in these concerns without claiming to represent any particular constituency. All four were trained in the common law, have spent substantial periods in the United States and the United Kingdom, and write in English. Each has a distinctive voice and says different things. They make a fascinating study in contrasts. How far they agree, complement each other, differ, or disagree is a central question posed by these readings.

All four have been activists as well as theorists, but in different ways. Francis Deng has had a very distinguished career in international diplomacy. Abdullahi An-Na'im has been a human rights activist within the Sudan and several other countries, and a publicist for human rights internationally. Yash Ghai has played a major role in post-independence constitution-making and reform, especially in the South Pacific and Kenya. Upendra Baxi has been an influential publicist, advocate, and campaigner in India and on the international stage, as well as serving as Vice-Chancellor of two Indian universities.

My standpoint is that of a British jurist working in the Anglo-American tradition who is concerned to help to make our culture of academic law less parochial and ethnocentric. The aim of this book is to raise awareness of perspectives, issues, and ideas that are not part of the mainstream of Western discourse about human rights and to provide material for reflection and discussion about central issues in human rights theory. My role as editor is to introduce the authors and let their works speak for themselves.[2] From many potential candidates, I have selected these four jurists mainly for reasons of my limited expertise. They are colleagues and contemporaries. I know each of them personally, I am familiar with their work, and I believe that it deserves to be better known. Three of them are from Sudan and East Africa, where I have

---

[2] My own views on human rights are set out in Twining (1975) and (2009) Ch. 5–7 and 13.

worked, but they all have wide experience of many other parts of the world. The writings included here are accessible just because they are published in English by Western-trained scholars and are mainly addressed to Western academics and human rights activists. This makes them just one potential path away from the parochialism of much Western legal theory and human rights discourse.[3]

Some commentators have queried the idea of "Southern voices" in this context. This raises issues that are considered in Chapter 6, but for present purposes it is enough to equate "Southern" with "the Global South" as in the phrase "the North–South divide".[4]

The focus of this book is on human rights. The claim is that each of the authors has made a distinctive contribution to both the theory and praxis of human rights. "Human rights" is a contested concept with many meanings. Here some standard working distinctions are useful: first, it is important to distinguish between the idea of human rights as moral and political rights and human rights law at international, regional, domestic, and other levels.[5] There are, of course, differing views about the relationship between them. It is also useful to distinguish between human rights theories as substantive moral theories that specify the scope and general content of "universal" human rights and discourse theories that treat "rights talk" as a significant form of thinking, talking, and arguing about basic human values and entitlements. These and several other distinctions are discussed in subsequent chapters. "Human rights" in the present context is used broadly to designate a general area and to cover all of these ideas and much else besides.

The core of the book consists of four chapters introducing the ideas of each of these figures mainly in their own words through a single substantial essay, supplemented by further extracts and quotations. Each chapter contains a brief biographical and interpretive introduction and some suggestions for further reading.[6] The final chapter reports on themes arising from a symposium at the Transitional Justice Institute in Belfast in June 2008 that was attended by all four authors and suggests how the framework developed by Marie Bénédicte Dembour might be used for comparing and contrasting these texts and relating them to mainstream Western theorizing about human rights.

---

[3] On other relevant thinkers and possible future projects see Chapter 6 below.

[4] See below pp. 211–12.

[5] Twining (2009) Ch. 6.2, and Sen (2004) discussed by Baxi (2007) pp. 56–67.

[6] The Bibliography at the end is intended to provide some signposts into an extensive literature. It lists the main relevant writings of the four contributors, selective references to other relevant general literature (including some other similar anthologies), and it includes the references for Chapters 1 and 6 and for the Introductions to Chapters 2–5. The footnote references in the readings in Chapters 2–5 are retained in their original formats and are not listed in the Bibliography.

2

Francis Mading Deng

2.1 Introduction[1]

William Twining

Francis Mading Deng was born in 1938 near Abyei in Kordofan in the West of
the Sudan. His father, Deng Majok, was paramount chief of the Ngok Dinka,
the only Nilotic inhabitants in the Northern Sudan. It is commonly said that
"Abyei is to the Sudan as the Sudan is to Africa", a bridge between the African
and Arab worlds. Deng Majok was an outstanding tribal leader, a national
figure, especially prominent for his bridging role between the Arab North and
the Nilotic South. He was also known as the creator of a huge family through
marrying more wives than any other man in Dinka history.[2] Francis, one of his
senior sons, became both the leading interpreter of Dinka tradition and a

---

[1] This introduction is a shortened version of Twining (2006) pp. 206–22.
[2] Francis Deng's memoir, *The Man Called Deng Majok* (1986b) includes a very frank account of
     debates surrounding his father's polygyny.

committed proponent of human rights, maintaining that they are basically compatible. How could this be?

Francis was the eldest son of Deng Majok's fourth wife. Although he did not groom any of his sons to succeed him, Deng Majok believed in education. The education of Francis Deng is a story of a remarkable journey through different cultures. It began in his father's compound in Abyei and continued in a boarding school for sons of chiefs run on similar lines to a British preparatory school, then at a secondary boarding school in the North, where the great majority of the boys were Muslims. He read law at the University of Khartoum, where he was taught in English, mainly by expatriate teachers, including myself. Although customary law hardly featured in the curriculum, Francis spent some of his vacations in his father's court, reading the court records, interviewing chiefs and elders, and he began a collection of recordings of several hundred Dinka songs.[3]

After graduating from Khartoum in 1962, Francis Deng pursued postgraduate studies in law, first in London, and then at Yale Law School, where he obtained a doctorate in 1967. Before the age of thirty he had been exposed to Dinka, Christian, British colonial, Northern Sudanese, and Islamic ideas as well as to both English and American legal traditions. So it is hardly surprising that one of the central concerns of all his writing has been the problem of identity.

After Yale, Deng worked for five years as a Human Rights Officer in the UN Secretariat and acquired considerable professional expertise in the area, especially in relation to women's rights. Since then he has been a firm, quite orthodox, upholder of the international human rights regime and of basic principles of democracy, both of which he considers to be universal. From 1972 Deng joined the Sudan diplomatic service, in due course serving as Ambassador to the United States, Scandinavia, and Canada. He was Minister of State for Foreign Affairs between 1976–80. Subsequently he has held a number of academic positions, mainly in the United States. He has continued to be involved in public affairs, most notably in efforts to end the civil war in the Sudan. From 1992–2004 he served as a Special Representative of the Secretary-General of the United Nations on internally displaced persons, rising to the status of Under Secretary-General. In this capacity he has had enormous influence in bringing the plight of 25 million people in 40 countries to public attention and in persuading governments that this neglected problem is a matter both of sovereign responsibility and legitimate international humanitarian concern.[4] Since 2007 he has been Special Adviser to the Secretary-General of the United Nations for Prevention of Genocide.

Even when holding responsible full-time public positions, Francis Deng has been a prolific writer. He has produced over thirty books, including two novels.[5]

---

[3] Deng (1973) p. 8.   [4] Cohen and Deng (1998).
[5] His friend, Abdullahi An-Na'im translated one of these, *Cry of the Owl* (1989) into Arabic. This stimulated so much attention and controversy that for a time Deng became known, quite inappropriately, as "the Salman Rushdie of the Sudan".

Many of them deal with the Dinka or with the problems of North–South conflict in the Sudan. Even when writing about broader issues such as human rights, displaced persons, and dispute resolution, he regularly draws on Dinka examples and reaffirms that at the core of his multi-layered identity remains a commitment to Dinka values. A central concern of his work is to reconcile tensions between tradition and modernity, between Dinka culture and universal standards, and between national unity and diversity in a con-flicted Sudan.

In his early writings Francis Deng did not make much reference to human rights, but he has always emphasized human dignity as a basic value. His first book, *Tradition and Modernization: A Challenge for Law Among the Dinka of the Sudan* (1971) was based on his doctoral thesis at Yale, where he was influenced by "the law, science and policy" approach of Harold Lasswell and Myres McDougal. Their emphasis on "dignity" as a core value had immediate resonance for Deng, for whom such concepts as *atheek, cieng,* and *dheng* are at the core of Dinka culture.[6] What "dignity" means in the Universal Declaration of Human Rights and whether the Dinka concepts are exact counterparts are difficult matters of interpretation. For Deng they provide the crucial link between Dinka culture and universal human rights.

Francis Deng has documented this culture in rich detail through inter-views, folk tales, legends, biographies, cases, and historic events. He has recorded and produced many translations of Dinka songs.[7] His early writings bring out the special role played by song in Dinka social relations in relation to courtship, bridewealth, cattle, disputes, war, religious ceremonies, and celebrations.[8]

> Among the Dinka, songs and dance have a functional role in everyday life. They do not deal with constructed situations; they concern known facts, known people, and defined objectives. But, above all they are skills of splendor in which a Dinka finds total gratification and elevation. The vigor and rhythm with which they stamp the ground, the grace with which they run in war ballets, the height to which they jump, the manner of pride and self-approval with which they bear themselves, and the way in which the high-pitched solo receives the loud unified

---

[6] These concepts are explained below at pp. 12–15.   [7] See especially, Deng (1973) and (1974).

[8] "To give some examples of the general significance of songs, the social structure, particularly territorial grouping, is reinforced by age-set group-spirit dramatized in initiation, warfare, and other age-set activities, which without songs would be barren. The concept of immortality through posterity receives a great deal of its support and implementation through songs. Singers not only give genealogical accounts of their families, but also stress and dramatize those aspects, which express their relevance to contemporary society. Young members of competitive families have been known to compose songs or have songs composed for them in reply to each other's allegations about incidents affecting the relative position of their families. In this process a young man may do a special investigation into the history of his family and of the tribe, to find additional evidence to sing about and bolster his family." (*The Dinka and their Songs* (1973) p. 78.) In this book Deng anthologizes ox songs, cathartic songs, initiation songs, age-set insult songs, war songs, women's songs, hymns, fairy-tale songs, children's game songs, and school songs.

response of the chorus combine to give the Dinka a euphoria that is hard to describe. As the singing stops, the drums beat even louder, the dance reaches its climax, and every individual, gorged with a feeling of self-fulfillment, begins to chant words of self-exaltation.

"I am a gentleman adorned with beads
I dance to the drums and level my feet
The girls of the tribe gather before me
The wealth of the tribe comes to me."[9]

Another feature of Dinka culture is the importance of cattle. Cattle are wealth, but they signify much more than that. Cattle constitute bridewealth that ensures continuity through procreation; cattle are prepared for special sacrifices to God, the spirits and ancestors. A great many songs are about oxen or the need for oxen – for marriage, for sacrifice, or just for *dheng*. Young men exalt themselves and their lineage through identification with their personality ox, a castrated bull of little practical value. Cattle are a source of collective pride in their relations with the outside world.[10]

The historical context

Francis Deng's writings need to be viewed in the context of the history of the Sudan. At one time the Dinka were one of the largest peoples in Africa. In the 1956 census they were estimated to number nearly two million, divided into twenty-five independent groups living a semi-nomadic, semi-pastoral life in settlements dispersed over nearly a million square miles within the Sudan. During the period of British rule, they were perceived by outsiders to be strongly religious, immensely proud, exclusive, and resistant to change. Sudan became independent in 1956. During the past half-century, except for a ten-year break (1972–83), a civil war has dominated events.[11] The Dinka have suffered terribly, experiencing repression, massacres, starvation (sometimes deliberately induced), decimation, enslavement, and displacement. Despite this terrible history of death, suffering, and displacement, Francis Deng emphasizes the resilience and vitality of Dinka culture that has formed the basis of their identity.

When Deng writes about reconciling Dinka values with "modernity" he is concerned more with the relationship to human rights norms than to values of the colonial (or Condominium) state. In Deng's writings there is a constant tension between his emphasis on the distinctiveness of Dinka culture and its compatibility with universal values. It is hard to reconcile the Dinka's

[9] Deng (1972) p. 17.   [10] See below pp. 10–19.
[11] A Peace Accord was signed in Nairobi on 9 January 2005. For details, see Sudan Peace Agreements, online: United States Institute of Peace www.usip.org/library/pa/_sudan.html/ (last visited April 2008).

traditional view of cattle with modern economics or a cosmology that venerates ancestors with secular doctrines of human rights. Perhaps the biggest test of Deng's argument about the compatibility of Dinka tradition with human rights is the subject of the status and treatment of women, as it is for many of the world's cultures, traditions, and religions.[12] Deng acknowledges the difficulties and adopts a complex strategy in confronting them. In reading his work it is useful to bear in mind four points: first, Deng is not a cultural relativist. However, following An-Na'im he adopts a cultural approach to human rights and democracy that involves seeing tradition as supplementing and informing abstract values and principles. Second, human rights and the principles of democracy are universal, but only at a very abstract level. *Atheek, cieng*, and *dheng* are conceptions that concretize, localize, and enrich abstract notions of human dignity. Thirdly, the Dinka are changing. But for many the core values embodied in *cieng* and *dheng* have sustained their identity. Fourthly, Deng acknowledges that judged by the standards of human rights norms some aspects of Dinka culture are open to criticism. Dinka culture must change and is changing.

The selection from Deng's writings presented here falls into four parts. First, "The Cow and the Thing called 'What'" brings out the richness, vitality, and self-confidence of Dinka tradition, in which concern with dignity, procreation, cattle, and song are central themes. In the creation myth, when God offers a choice between the Cow and "What", man unhesitatingly chooses the Cow. Deng interprets "What" to refer to curiosity and the search for scientific knowledge and hence a rationalization of Dinka conservatism and backwardness in relation to modern science and technology. He tells the story of how in the face of the twin threats of successive disasters and well-meaning "modernization", the Dinka began to lose faith in their traditions. Nevertheless, when given a fair chance, he suggests that they have proved to be remarkably resilient and adaptable. The second group of readings is taken from a series of articles published in the *Sudan Democratic Gazette*. Addressed to a Southern Sudanese audience, these summarise Francis Deng's views on the relationship between Dinka tradition and "modern" ideas of democracy and human rights. The third section, from a book co-edited with An-Na'im, explores the relationship between culture and modernity in more depth. In his writings Francis Deng's achievement has been to give the Dinka a voice in the outside world. He has also illustrated in a vivid and specific way the complex relationship between long-established traditional values and modern conceptions of human rights.

---

[12] Deng accepts that polygamy is inconsistent with equal respect and that Dinka women have a subordinate role in Dinka cosmology and tradition. He himself is committed to UN values on the status of women. He is monogamous and the Dinka heroes in his two novels are monogamous – indeed, one resists pressures to take additional wives.

READINGS

2.2 The Cow and the Thing Called "What": Dinka Cultural Perspectives on Wealth and Poverty[*]

God asked man, "Which one shall I give you, Black Man; there is the Cow and the thing called 'What,' which of the two would you like?" The man said, "I do not want 'What.'" God said, "But 'What' is better than the Cow!" The man said, "No." Then God said, "If you like the Cow, you had better taste its milk before you choose it finally." The man squeezed some milk into his hand, tasted it, and said, "Let us have the milk and never see 'What.'"

While certain basic indicators of affluence or poverty are globally accepted, whether individuals or groups perceive themselves as rich or poor may not always be a matter of objective determination. Subjective factors attributable to culture may play a vital role in the way people view themselves in terms of wealth and poverty. Building largely on oral literature from the Dinka in southern Sudan, this paper aims to explore the gap between objective poverty and the subjective perception of wealth.

From a policy standpoint, there are both positive and negative implications in the way people are classified or perceive themselves. To be labeled poor is to establish a case for corrective measures toward poverty alleviation, which is positive, but it could also breed apathy, self-pity and dependency. A positive self-perception might breed complacency, which would be negative, but it could also enhance the sense of worth as a resource for self-reliance.

Although it is widely acknowledged that measuring poverty is complex, a commonly used measure is income or consumption among individuals or house-holds. It is also considered relevant to take into account such social indicators as life expectancy, infant mortality and school enrollment.[1] There is a comparative dimension to the determination of poverty by both horizontal and vertical parameters. Horizontal parameters relate to comparisons at the same level of development, while vertical parameters relate to stratified levels of development. Countries or regions may be assessed in relation to others at the same level of development and on a scale of development progression. For example, while the poverty line of U.S.$1 a day is used to make international comparisons of consumption-based poverty, poverty lines are frequently closer to about U.S.$2 dollars a day for middle-income countries.

---

[*] Reproduced from 52 *Journal of International Affairs* 101–30 (1998) by kind permission of the publishers.

[1] The data included in this section is mostly obtained from World Bank, *Poverty Reduction and the World Bank: Progress and Challenges in the 1990s* Washington, DC: World Bank, (1996); World Bank, *World Development Indicators, 1997* Washington, DC: World Bank, (1996); and Michael Walton, "Will Global Advances Include the Poor?" paper prepared for the Aspen Institute Conference on Persistent Poverty in Developing Countries: "Determining the Causes and Closing the Gaps" Broadway, England: December (1997). The author gratefully acknowledges the assistance of Meghan O'Sullivan in bringing to his attention some of the pertinent factors in the definition of poverty.

Global perspectives on poverty imply both integration into the comparative framework and marginalization or exclusion within that framework, which then closely corresponds to a state of poverty as relative deprivation. People are said to be relatively deprived if they cannot obtain, at all or sufficiently, the conditions of life – that is, the diets, standards and services – which allow them to play the roles, participate in the relationships and follow the customary behavior which is expected of them by virtue of their membership of society. If they lack or are denied resources to obtain access to these conditions of life and so fulfill membership of society they may be said to be in poverty.[2]

In the global comparative framework, and by virtually all indicators, the people in sub-Saharan Africa are among the poorest in the world, and the southern Sudanese among the poorest of the poor. Unlike most of Africa, however, the South is less integrated into the global community, being among the least touched by the forces and benefits of modernity. Their marginalization in the modern world is both the result of their cultural outlook and the legacy of British colonial administration. Government policy in southern Sudan was "to build up a series of self-contained racial or tribal units with structure and organization based upon the indigenous customs, traditional usage and beliefs."[3] Part of the motivation for the policy was fear of southern nationalism as the people were introduced to rapid education and modernity.[4] The Nilotics, especially the Dinka and the Nuer, fiercely resisted British rule for two decades. The 1924 rebellion against the British was led by young officers of Dinka background in the Egyptian army. Whatever the motivation, the British administration closed off the South and permitted only the Christian missionaries to pass into southern territory in order to exercise a pacifying influence among the natives. This, combined with Nilotic conservatism, isolated them from modern development.

In order to appreciate Dinka self-perception, their world view and cross-cultural perspectives on their material status, it is necessary to understand the indigenous cultural framework of their values, institutions and patterns of behavior.

The Dinka are the largest ethnic group in the Sudan, numbering several million in a country of around 20 million people and several hundred tribes. Their culture is dominated by cattle (and to a lesser extent by sheep and goats), to which they attach a social and moral significance far beyond their economic value. Although there are no reliable statistics, the Dinka are probably among the wealthiest in cattle on the African continent. The average bridewealth

[2] Quoted in Gerry Rodgers, Charles Gore and Jose B. Figueiredo, eds., *Social Exclusion: Rhetoric, Reality, Responses* Geneva: International Labor Office, (1995) p. 6, no. 3. The author is grateful to Carol Graham for bringing this dimension to his attention.
[3] See Abd Al-Rahim, *Imperialism and Nationalism in the Sudan, A Study in Constitutional and Political Development 1899–1956* Oxford: Clarendon Press, (1969) Appendix B.
[4] See Francis M. Deng and M.W. Daly, *Bonds of Silk: The Human Factor in the British Administration of the Sudan* East Lansing, MI: Michigan State University, (1989) p. 191.

(i.e., what a man pays in marriage) is around 50 cows, while daughters of prominent families are sometimes married with over 100 cows. Bloodwealth (i.e., compensation paid for homicide) is normally estimated to be the equivalent of the average bridewealth as it is intended to be used for obtaining a wife in begetting children to the name of the deceased, or, in the case of a female, to compensate for the loss of potential bridewealth or reproductivity.

Although the Dinka are mainly known to the outside world as devoted owners of cattle, they are also cultivators.[5] As important as cattle are to them, land has an even greater intrinsic value to the Dinka, not only because they depend on it for a wide variety of reasons, including farming, gathering and grazing, but also because it is associated with the ancestors. A Dinka will swear on the land to establish his truthfulness, symbolizing his submission to the judgment of his ancestors. Before drinking or eating, especially in a new setting, one must make an offering to the ancestors by leaving portions on the ground. And before adults can share in the consumption of new crops, festive offerings must first be made to the ancestors. These rituals, which are associated with the value of ancestral land, have a bearing on the rules favoring perpetuity in traditional land tenure.

On balance, however, the Dinka derive their distinctive socioeconomic identity, cultural values and institutions from their preoccupation with cattle. Through the payment of bridewealth, cattle provide the foundation for the family and the continuation of the lineage, as these lines from an ox song indicate:

> Tell the family of Atong
> If they should cease to have cattle
> They will be extinct.[6]

The overriding goal of every Dinka is to marry and produce children, especially sons, "to keep the head upright" after death. The Dinka and their ethnic kindred, the Nuer, are considered "by far the most religious peoples in the Sudan."[7] But their religion does not promise a heaven to come, and although they believe in some form of life hereafter, death for them is an end from which the only salvation is continuity through posterity. What the Dinka fear the most is not death itself, but dying without male progeny, in whom the survival of their individual identities, their source of immortality, is vested. Relatives of a man who dies unmarried assume a moral obligation to marry a woman for him, to live with one of them and beget children to his name. Equally, a man who dies leaving behind a widow of childbearing age bestows a moral obligation on his kinsmen to have one of them cohabit with her to continue bearing children in

---

[5] Stubbs and Morrison, "Land and Agriculture of the Western Dinka," *Sudan Notes and Records*, 21 (1938) p. 251.

[6] Francis M. Deng, *The Dinka and Their Songs* Oxford: Oxford University Press, (1974) p. 241.

[7] Charles and Brenda Seligman, *Pagan Tribes of Nilotic Sudan* London: G. Routledge and Sons, (1932) p. 178.

his name. While in Western law a dead person cannot be defamed, among the Dinka it is a more serious offense to insult or otherwise defame a dead person. It is by respecting the dead that their identity and influence can continue through living memory.

To be sustained after death, respect – a highly esteemed value in Dinka society – must begin in this life. Respect for others is expressed by the word *atheek*, which has various strands of meaning, stemming from the same root. One strand might be called "good manners," which emphasizes self-control and non-aggression.[8] This sense is closest to the English word "respect." The second range of meaning might be summed up as "avoidance." Avoidance between relatives-in-law and between senior son and father are examples. In this sense, *atheek* may apply to situations where the English word "respect" does not. The Dinka conceive of respect in this sense as embodying both voluntary deference and that which is required by the relationship between the parties. It is significant, for instance, that *ryoc*, a verb which means "to fear," is also used to denote "respect." It is difficult to distinguish voluntary respect from mandatory respect, but in certain cases, especially those of avoidance, the evidence is clear. For instance, "respecting" or "avoiding" a menstruating woman is directly connected with fear of spiritual contamination. The same is true of "respecting" clan divinities and emblems. Killing them or being present when acts of violence are committed against them is considered spiritually very dangerous. Respecting a powerful foe out of fear falls into this category.

Seeing respect as both voluntary and mandatory explains the stratified shaping and sharing of respect and its divine and secular manifestations. It is the right of the dead, whose life is perpetuated through younger generations, to be shown respect, for only thus can their participation among the living be adequately immortalized. The giving of respect is a condition for receiving it. If a man shows no respect to people who owe him greater respect, he would be shown only mandatory respect, if any.

Since the values of continued identity and influence through lineage are both individual and communal, they are equally competitive and cooperative. This in turn dictates an emphasis on group solidarity and the resolution of conflicts through mediation and consensus-building. Indeed, despite the war-like profile of the Dinka, their moral values are founded on the ideals of peace, unity, harmony, persuasiveness and mutual cooperation. The pervasiveness of

---

[8] To illustrate: "An ill-mannered or aggressive child, without decorum in the presence of those senior to him in age and status, is said to have no respect. A man who behaves with respect is courteous to his elders and superiors. He will join an assembly of senior men or strangers in a markedly quiet and self-effacing way, gently snapping his fingers to indicate when he wishes to pass, and taking care not to jostle anyone as he takes his place. When approaching a homestead such a man will pause before entering its central courtyard and clap his hands to announce his presence and ask permission to enter. Teasing, joking and horseplay, which are not inappropriate between those who regard themselves as familiar equals and perhaps in some sense rivals, are improper between those who practice *thek* (or *atheek*)." Godfrey Lienhardt, *Divinity and Experience: The Religion of the Dinka* Oxford: Clarendon Press, (1967) p. 128.

violence can be attributed to a generational distribution of roles and functions and the exaggerated sense of dignity young members of the warrior age-sets acquire from their identity and status as warriors and defenders of the society – a role they sometimes play to excess.

By the same token, chiefs, even when young, must be men of peace. One chief, reacting to the assertion that traditional force was the deterrent behind Dinka social order, articulated the delicate balance between the violence of youth and the peacemaking role of chiefs:

> [I]t is true, there was force. People killed one another and those who could defeat people in battle were avoided with respect. But people lived by the way God had given them. There were the Chiefs of the Sacred Spear. If anything went wrong, they would come to stop the … fighting … and settle the matter without blood … Men [chiefs] of the [sacred] spear were against bloodshed.[9]

And in the words of another chief, "There was the power of words. It was a way of life with its great leaders … not a way of life of the power of the arm."[10]

While it was not always easy for the elders to control the overzealous warriors, it was a clearly established principle that the warriors should adhere to the will of their chiefs and elders. When the warriors had to confront aggression and justifiably go to war, they were blessed by their chiefs and instructed by their elders on the ethics of warfare. Trusting in the justice of their cause, they counted on their ancestral spirits and deities to ensure victory against the forces of evil. Among the ethical principles of warfare were that the enemy must not be ambushed or killed outside the battlefield and that a fallen warrior covered by a woman for protection (women accompany men in battle primarily to help the wounded) must be spared, as harming women and children in war was strictly forbidden.

It is particularly noteworthy that despite the lack of police or military forces, civil order was maintained with a very low level of crime other than those incidents associated with honorable fighting. Major Court Treatt, who traveled in Dinkaland in the late 1920s, described the Dinka tribesman as "a gentleman" who "possesses a high sense of honour, rarely telling a lie," and with "a rare dignity of bearing and outlook."[11] And Major Titherington, who served as a colonial administrator among the Dinka also in the late 1920s, wrote of "the higher moral sense which is so striking in the [Dinka]. Deliberate murder – as distinct from killing in fair fight – is extremely rare; pure theft – as opposed to the lifting of cattle by force or stealth after a dispute about their rightful ownership – is unknown; a man's word is his bond, and on rare occasions when a man is asked to swear, his oath is accepted as a matter of course."[12]

---

[9] Francis M. Deng, *Dinka Cosmology* London: Ithaca Press, (1980) p. 58. Quoted in Francis M. Deng, *War of Visions: Conflicts of Identities in the Sudan* Washington, DC: The Brookings Institute, (1995) p. 196.

[10] Deng (1980) p. 42 and Deng (1995) p. 197.

[11] Major Court Treatt, *Out of the Beaten Track* New York: E.P. Dutton & Co. Inc., (1930) pp. 115–116.

[12] Major Titherington, "The Raik Dinka," *Sudan Notes and Records* (1927) p. 159.

Sir Gawain Bell, who served as District Commissioner among the Ngok Dinka in the 1950s, observed, "I can't remember that we ever had any serious crime in that part of the District. Among the Baggara (Arabs) … there was a good deal of serious crime: murders and so forth; and the same applied to the Hamar in the North … The Ngok Dinka were a particularly law-abiding people."[13]

Dinka moral and social values are highly institutionalized and expressed in a concept known as *cieng*, which is fundamental to Dinka moral and civic order. The anthropologist Godfrey Lienhardt wrote: "The Dinka … have notions … of what their society ought, ideally, to be like. They have a word, *cieng baai* (*baai* meaning family, village, tribe or country), which used as a verb has the sense of 'to look after' or 'to order,' and in its noun form means 'the custom' or 'the rule.'"[14] Father Nebel, one of the earliest Catholic missionaries to work among the Dinka, translated morals as "good *cieng*" and benefactor as a man who knows and acts in accordance with *cieng*.[15]

In line with the importance attached to respect as a value, Dinka culture emphasizes a deferential manner that acknowledges in every person a deep sense of worth and dignity. While the Western value system is largely premised on property relations, that of the Dinka is based on kinship, property and welfare ties that complement this shared value system. To Dinka youth, cattlewealth has an aesthetic significance far above its material value. When a man comes of age in his late teens and is initiated into adulthood through the age-set system, he becomes known as *adheng* (gentleman) and his virtue is *dheeng* (dignity). He also becomes known as *apal rak*, meaning that he has stopped milking cows, a function associated with women and uninitiated boys. Indeed, as a gentleman, he can no longer be expected to run the small errands associated with children's services for the adults. He then acquires formal ownership of a "personality ox" as a symbol of his mature identity, cattlewealth, aesthetic esteem and enhanced social status. It is also after initiation that a man becomes known by an ox name based on metaphorical association between his color-pattern and natural phenomena resembling that pattern. These poetic names of metaphoric imagery signify both respect and intimacy and recur frequently in praise songs. The bond between a man and his personality ox is well illustrated by these lines from an ox song:

> My Mijok is essential to me
> Like tobacco to a pipe
> When there is no tobacco
> The pipe goes out;
> His speed and mine are the same.[16]

---

[13] Deng (1995) p. 282.

[14] Godfrey Lienhardt, "Western Dinka," in John Middleton and David Tait, (eds.), *Tribes Without Rulers* London: Routledge and Kegan Paul Ltd., (1958) pp. 106–107.

[15] Arturo Nebel, *Dinka Dictionary* Verona: Missioni Africane, (1936) p. 315.

[16] Deng (1974) p. 119. These and other extracts from songs are reproduced from original translations, occasionally with minor revisions for greater clarity.

Dheeng goes beyond initiation, age-setting and the aesthetics of personality oxen. As a noun, *dheeng* means nobility, beauty, handsomeness, elegance, charm, grace, gentleness, hospitality, generosity, good manners, discretion and kindness. Singing, dancing, initiation ceremonies and celebrations of marriages – indeed, any demonstrations of aesthetic value – are considered *dheeng*. The social background of a man, his physical appearance, the way he walks, talks, eats, drinks or dresses, and the way he behaves toward his fellow men, are all factors in determining his *dheeng*.

A remarkable feature of Dinka culture is that it gives virtually everybody some avenue to dignity, honor and pride. The degree varies, and the means are diverse: there are the sensuous means concerned mostly with appearance, bearing and sex appeal; there are the qualities of virtue in one's relations to others; and there are ascribed or achieved values, material or spiritual, which help determine one's social standing. These ways are interrelated and cannot really be separated. However, only by seeing them as alternatives and by realizing that all ways lead to the same ends can one understand why every Dinka can share in the values of self-esteem, inner pride and sense of dignity.

A good illustration of the self-contained viability, stability and continuity within the Dinka culture is that there are hardly any words in the vernacular language which approximate the concept of "development" in modern usage. The notion of endeavoring to elevate society or individuals to a yet unrealized higher (and better) level of existence through a process called "development" was traditionally foreign to the Dinka. Individual and societal goals, even to the optimum degree, were considered part of experience which was not only achievable, but at one time or another, actually achieved. *Cieng* and related values are seen as part of a heritage that has proved its worth over generations and has become sanctified and elevated, even though it may have negative aspects. Such negative aspects are hardly ever visible to the Dinka. When a Dinka was asked what he thought was negative in his people's ways, he responded with an expressive silence, a puzzled look, a smile and then said, "How can there be anything bad in the Dinka way? If there were, would it not have been abandoned a long time ago?"

Dinka self-perceptions of wealth are reflected in their cultural values, which are intrinsically geared toward a positive self-image. The goal of immortalizing a person in an ancestral chain through remembrance depends largely on continued social esteem and veneration. To the Dinka, poverty implies a demeaning status that is inimical to the exalted image required for honoring the dead through living memory. A corollary of this is the social, moral and spiritual value the Dinka place on cattle as the resource for ensuring the continuity of their lineage through bridewealth. The distribution system itself fosters a degree of social equity through the exchange of cattle in marriage and other reciprocal kinship obligations.

The Dinka always extol their ancestors as the ideal model of their cultural values – material, social, moral and spiritual. No Dinka ever claims to have done better than his forefathers. Traditionally, no Dinka would even entertain such a thought. What one does, and however successful one is, tends to be seen as an effort to live up to the standards set by the forebearers. These lines indicate the extent to which the Dinka brag about their forefathers as the epitome of prosperity:

> My father Ring was called by his father
> He seated him down by his side
> Affectionately rubbed his head
> And left him these words,
> "Son, Ring, there are the cattle."
> He said to him, "O son Ring, there are the cattle
> Cattle are the wealth of man."
> My great father had a cattle-camp
> His house became rich with herds
> The cattle-byres were full.
> My ancestor Akol Kuec is an elephant
> And Thiik Ring is an elephant
> Kiro Riiny is an elephant
> And Ring, my father, is an elephant.[17]

The linkage with God, clan deities and the ancestral spirits is indeed maintained through cattle. As Lienhardt noted, "Cattle and children are gifts from Divinity [i.e., God] and from the clandivinity and they always ultimately belong to Divinity, the clandivinity, and the whole agnatic descent group of which the clandivinity is the tutelary spirit. Any owner's or father's relationship to his cattle or his children is thus a more temporary expression of a transcending relationship between human group, its herd, and its divinity, which persists through the generations ... This aspect of the Dinkas' attitude towards cattle is of ... importance for an understanding of the dedication of cattle to Divinity or other powers."[18] Seen in reverse order, once cattlewealth was given by God to the founding ancestors, who passed it on to successive generations in the lineage, it is seen as a family legacy that continues in perpetuity, and it is a source of great pride.

> Our clan has never been in need
> The clan of Ajong de Monydhang has never been in need of cattle
> From our ancestor, Jok,
> To Achai, our girl with the River Spirits
> Prosperity has remained forever with us.[19]

Among the living, it is the patriarch who is charged with the payment of bridewealth. The dependent members of the family are economically sheltered by him. Their rights are his rights, and it is he who will recover any compensation due to them; their obligations are his obligations, and it is he who

---

[17] Ibid., p. 142.   [18] Lienhardt (1967) p. 23.   [19] Ibid., p. 236.

will assume their liability. His main obligation is to continue his genealogy: he must incur material losses to create a family, to maintain it and to marry his children off. Corresponding to this obligation is the material interest in the members of the family – the son should continue the genealogy by begetting his own children; the daughter should bring wealth to be used for family marriages and maintenance; and the wife should bear him children. Any interference with these interests by third parties calls for material compensation.

Dependent members of the family are subordinated in the control over cattle, so wives and dependent sons preoccupy themselves instead with cattle symbolized by personality oxen, which are bulls castrated from an early age, and therefore of little utilitarian value. This preoccupation may justifiably be called an obsession. For male youth, status is enhanced not only by the man's identification with his personality ox, but by the exaltation of his ancestry and the lineage through which he acquires the ox.

> When I rise to sing [over my ox], gossipers disperse
> I am like my forefathers
> I rise to be seen by my ancient fathers
> I rise to be seen walking with pride
> As it was in the distant past
> Where our clan was born.[20]

Women express their pride by the oxen of their husbands or suitors. A woman singing in praise of her husband's or boyfriend's ox or wealth in general satisfies her ego by occasional reference to him as "I" and thus identifies herself with him and his wealth.

It is devotion to oxen which motivates young men and women to endure the hardships of going to distant camps in search of better grazing, an endeavor that sometimes means suffering from hunger and confronting wild beasts and human foes. In many songs, young men who undergo these hardships refer to the protection and pursuit of good grass and water for their oxen as their motive. In fact, they always herd large numbers of cattle as well. But wealth, from a young man's point of view, is represented by his ox or oxen.

It is at the time of marriage, when a young man needs cattle for bridewealth, that the contest with the father over control of family wealth becomes strikingly manifest. Most songs composed during the cathartic period are pleas to fathers and family elders to provide cattle for marriage, or lamentation over their failure to do so:

> I do not know who to give the seat of my father
> Our words have ended with the times he would
> send me for water
> And the times he would say, "Go and bring a mat

---

[20] Francis M. Deng, *Tradition and Modernization* New Haven and London: Yale University Press, (1971) p. 308.

from the byre"
I would bring them to my father
Is that not the value of a person's son?
People have confused us
I am like the son of a stranger
My father has tapped his chest in refusal
O clan of my father, shall I be only a tribesman?[21]

The payment of cattle as bridewealth itself accounts for the stability of marriage
and the rarity of divorce. Bridewealth is contributed to by a wide circle of a man's
relatives and distributed among a correspondingly large circle of relatives on
the bride's side. If a divorce should occur, unless the marriage has been stabilized
through children (in which case divorce is even less conceivable), bridewealth
cattle and their offspring must be returned. Since some of them would have
been passed on for the bridewealths of other relatives, one divorce could
threaten other marriages. Divorce is therefore viewed as a tragedy to be avoided,
except in the most compelling circumstances of extreme incompatibility.[22]

The distribution system inherent in the institution of bridewealth gives the
Dinka a sense of collective ownership of cattle so that despite differences of
wealth, distinctions are minimized. Since having daughters, through whom a
family acquires wealth, or sons, for whom the bridewealth is to be paid, is a
function of unpredictable events, the system holds the potential for upward
and downward mobility, encouraging egalitarianism and social equilibrium.
A family that is unfortunate enough not to have daughters will often be forced
to pursue claims against kinsmen, who owe obligations of one sort or another.
Kinship obligations, especially those connected with sharing in the bridewealth
of a relative, can be traced and pursued through generations. Claiming compensation for homicide, bodily injuries, sexual offenses (adultery, pregnancy
and abduction), injury to reputation and many other causes, is a frequent
source of litigation and, as such, a source of redistribution. The Dinka are
indeed a very litigious people.

Agok, the White One, counsels me,
Achwil, son of my mother, keep going
A man without a sister must plead his case well
I cannot go, the guinea worm has debilitated my knee.[23]

The values of *cieng* and *dheeng*, which promote social consciousness and
solidarity, also foster reciprocal relationships that bridge economic disparities.
To the Dinka, power and wealth must serve moral and social ends or else they
do not confer *dheeng* on the holder. The word for chief, *beny*, also means "rich"
or "wealthy." A generous man is also praised as *beny*. But a man of wealth who
is stingy or frugal is *ayur*, the opposite of *adheng*. The role of leadership is to see

---

[21] Deng (1974) pp. 171–172.
[22] For examples of reactions to divorce and breach of engagement, see ibid., pp. 219–224.
[23] Ibid., p. 124.

to it that every person is assured access to a minimum standard of living as defined by Dinka cultural norms. The chief does this both by giving to the needy himself and by enforcing kinship obligations of relatives to those in need. The chief himself receives much from his people through voluntary contributions akin to taxation. Since he is almost certain to have the widest circle of kinship ties, his entitlements from those ties are commensurately extensive. By virtue of his position, whatever is owed him is readily offered. His obligation to help therefore corresponds with his privileges. The saying attributed to a chief who was famous for his generosity and hospitality goes:

> What is given goes around
> What is swallowed is wasted.[24]

The outcome of these values and processes is that the Dinka have traditionally seen themselves as members of a society whose reciprocal relationships were mutually beneficial, a people endowed with a land of plenty and blessed with the ideal wealth – cattle. As one Dinka elder proudly expressed it, "You are the Dinka inhabiting this vast territory of rich grassland and the keeper of cattle."[25] Another elder went further: "It is for cattle that we are admired, we, the Dinka … All over the world, people look to us because of cattle. And when they say, Sudan, it is not just because of our color, it is also because of our great wealth; and our wealth is cattle … It is because of cattle that people of other tribes look to us with envy."[26] Yet another elder saw Dinkaland as the source of wealth and sustainability for the country: "One day, should tragedy befall this country, the survival of the black people will start here …. Should we abandon this land with all its blessings, our descendants will blame us."[27]

Dinka pride in their culture, cattlewealth and land has been extensively documented and invoked to explain their conservative attitude. A Christian missionary observed in 1949:

> One of the determinants of the rapid or slow spread of Christianity in the South [Sudan] has been provided by the contrast between semi-nomadic cattle-breeding Nilotic tribes (Shilluk, Nuer and Dinka) and the settled agriculturists. The life of the former is bound up with a cow economy, this animal being a veritable god. They are intensely conservative and very proud of their civilization.[28]

The anthropologist Audrey Butt also wrote of the Nilotics: "They consider their country the best in the world and everyone inferior to themselves. For this reason they … scorn European and Arab culture … They are self-reliant and extremely conservative in their aversion to innovation and interference."[29]

---

[24] Ibid., p. 137.   [25] Deng (1980) p. 46.   [26] Ibid., p. 99.

[27] Francis M. Deng, *The Man Called Deng Majok* New Haven and London: Yale University Press, (1986) p. 227.

[28] John S. Trimingham, *The Christian Church in Post-War Sudan* London and New York: World Dominion Press, (1949) p. 34.

[29] Audrey Butt, *The Nilotes of the Anglo-Egyptian Sudan and Uganda* London: International African Institute, (1952) p. 41.

But Nilotic conservatism has been grossly exaggerated. It has now become apparent that throughout earlier historical phases, they rejected what they regarded as not worth adopting and selected what they considered desirable, assimilating it into their own culture to the point where it eventually lost its foreign character. Their apparent resistance to change was fostered by colonial policies, which kept the tribes isolated and sought to preserve traditional cultures. As a result of intensive cross-cultural interaction and modern education, the process of adopting foreign ways has been accelerated and revolutionized so much that the Nilotics are demonstrating more adaptability to change than could have been predicted only two decades ago. One can hypothesize that the same values of pride and dignity that made them resist change may well provide them with the motivation to enhance their status and self-image through modernization.

The peoples of the Nile Valley have interacted with one another and exerted mutual influences on each other from time immemorial. However, as a result of historical conflicts and animosities between the Muslim-Arabs of the North and the indigenous peoples of the South (especially during the upheavals of the nineteenth century), they have become so alienated from each other that they see little, if anything, in common. Despite an obvious racial and cultural mixture in their features and characteristics, each group sees itself as pure and scorns other groups. Colonialism brought the various groups together within the modern state but kept them apart and introduced modernization selectively and discriminatingly, especially between the North and the South. In the South, limited social services in the fields of education and health care were provided through the Christian missionaries, whose primary objective was proselytization. There was also some exposure to the market economy and labor migration into towns.

Initially, these innovations were resisted as threatening to tradition. Modern medicine was feared as an affront to the ancestral spirits and therefore dangerously counterproductive. Education for women in particular was frowned upon as it was feared that it would morally corrupt the girls and render them worthless for traditional marriage, which embodied the real value of a woman. These lines from a song by a mother, whose husband wanted to send her only daughter to school, indicate the negative sentiment that prevailed against education.

> I am a person tortured, a person bullied
> To give birth to a child now to be siren away
> O our tribe, where shall I go?
> O Dinka, where shall I go?
> An only child like the stand of a drum,
> How can I hear of her in town?
> I heard the name Achol and could not sleep.[30]

---

[30] Deng (1974) p. 237.

Labor migration elicited a mixed response. It provided young men with the opportunity to acquire independent wealth, but paid labor was seen as servility, an indignity that was inappropriate for a "gentleman." This indignity was mitigated by the opportunity to work far away from the Dinka context, in a country where one was unknown. The Dinka saying goes, "Dignity, remain indignity, let us go," which refers to swallowing one's pride in a foreign land. Another saying states that "A nobleman of one tribe does not know a nobleman of another tribe." Despite the mitigating effects of labor migration, the conditions experienced in the urban setting were considered inimical to Dinka values, especially to the solidarity of kinship ties:

> I have become a slave,
> Laboring in a foreign land,
> Cracking my back-bones like the trap of a
> captured bird.
> I worked in the cotton field until my hair turned grey,
> It was not the grey of age;
> It was the bitter pain of the words in our heads,
> As we wasted away in foreign lands.
> O Marial, what I have found, I will not say ...[31]
> In towns, people cultivate with their ears;
> In towns, people depend on market grain ...
> The riches that I hear of in towns;
> People live to old age buying and selling ...
> The family has lost its value;
> Blood ties have been severed in the pockets,
> Even a son of your maternal aunt
> When you ask him for help
> Will first invoke the name of God,
> "May I die, Brother, see my pocket
> If you find a millieme, you are lucky." ...
> In towns people dance to the drums in their pockets
> If one has nothing, one goes with nothing.[32]

The civil war that has raged intermittently over the last four decades between the Arab-Muslim North and the more indigenously African South has been perhaps the most radicalizing and destabilizing factor in Dinka life. And by creating conditions of extreme deprivation and degradation, it has ironically been a source of motivation in the quest for modernizing change. War first broke out in August 1955, four months before independence came on 1 January 1956, as a reaction against anticipated Arab domination. What began as a mutiny in a southern battalion escalated into full-fledged civil war that lasted for 17 years. It was halted by the 1972 Addis Ababa Agreement that granted the South regional autonomy. Hostilities resumed in 1983 when President Gaafar

---

[31] Francis M. Deng, *The Dinka of the Sudan* Prospect Heights, Ill.: Waveland Press, (1984) p. 172.
[32] Ibid., p. 162.

Mohamed Nimeri unilaterally abrogated the agreement, divided the South into three regions and introduced Shari'a (Islamic law) throughout the country. This second phase of the southern struggle has been championed by the Sudan Peoples' Liberation Movement and its military wing, the Sudan Peoples' Liberation Army (SPLM/SPLA), in which the Dinka predominate, being overwhelmingly the largest ethnic group in the South.

Although Nimeri was overthrown in 1985 and multiparty democracy was restored, Shari'a was not repealed as initially promised by the dominant parties and the war continued. A peace agreement between the elected government and the SPLM/SPLA, which might have led to a compromise on the issue of Shari'a, was scuttled when the National Islamic Front, the party most committed to the creation of an Islamic state, conspired with Islamist elements in the army to stage a military coup that overthrew the elected government in June 1989. Since then, the government has moved relentlessly to implement its Islamic agenda. While the northern opposition parties have entered into an alliance with the SPLM/SPLA, and the regime has endeavored to divide the southern liberation movement along ethnic or tribal lines, the war remains predominantly North-South.

It is now estimated that the war has cost the South over two million lives (about a million and a half since the resumption of hostilities in 1983), displaced about four million southerners inside the country and forced half a million into neighboring countries as refugees. Quite apart from its death toll, the war has inflicted on the people of the South unprecedented conditions of deprivation and degradation. Even the life of a refugee, which ensures a reasonable level of protection and assistance from the international community, is a source of great indignity for a people who had grown up thinking of itself and its country as second to none. These lines from a song of lamentation during the first phase of the war are illustrative:

> Gentlemen grind in the land of the Congo;
> The Arab has remained at home
> He has remained in our land.
> We left our herds in the cattle-camps
> And followed Deng Nhial.
> Gentlemen beg in the land of the Congo;
> A Congolese said, "Dinkas are matata."
> I asked Ngor Maker,
> "What does 'matata' mean?'
> Ngor Maker replied,
> "He says we are bad."
> My heart was destroyed
> And I thought of Anger, the daughter of Wol
> Ayalbyor,
> I wish I could see her again.[33]

---

[33] Deng (1984) p. 139 and Deng (1974) pp. 157–158.

The second phase of the war is revealing another side of the struggle of the people of the South. Unlike the first movement, which called for secession, the SPLM/SPLA has postulated the goal of liberating the whole country and creating a New Sudan that would be freed from any discrimination based on race, ethnicity, religion or culture. This is perceived as tantamount to the reversal of Arab-Islamic hegemony in favor of a more African identity for the country. While most people see this as unrealistic, the military strength of the SPLM/SPLA, especially when it received full support from Ethiopia under Mengistu Halle Mariam, gave the objective some credibility. Although most southerners would prefer secession (and the call for a new united Sudan is perceived by many as a euphemistic disguise of separatist aspirations), radical Arab-Islamic elements in the North took the threat from the South seriously and began to counter it by mobilizing the Islamic revival that eventually led to the military coup. Their success in radicalizing Islam politically has exacerbated the polarization of the nation in a militaristic contest for the soul of the country. The competing vision from the South rejects any scheme of power sharing that would give southerners only local control: "What about the Sudan, to whom shall we leave it?"[34]

The Arab is seen as an intruder who must now give way to the true owners of the country:

> Nimeiri, return to your land.
> The country is claimed by its owner
> It is Omdurman which we shall contest
> It is Khartoum which we shall contest
> It is Sudan which we shall contest
> O people, the land is our land.[35]

The confidence of southern freedom fighters reflects only one aspect of the story. In the broader social context, a more tragic process of self-doubt and diminishing self-image appears to be the consequence of violent change and the dehumanizing integration of the indigenous population of the South into the state framework, dominated by the Arab-Muslim North.

As a consequence of their relegation to an inferior status in the modern Sudanese and global contexts, the Dinka now appear to have accepted that their traditional culture and way of life are indeed comparatively inferior. Since their religious thought dictates that everything has an intrinsic meaning, ultimately related to the origin of things and the manifestation of God's will, they have begun to internalize this new awareness into their belief system to give it a convincing explanation. A body of oral literature has begun to emerge in which the Dinka are beginning to rationalize their now inferior position. Even the myth of their original acquisition of cattle as the most noble symbol of wealth is being seen more as an explanation of their scientific and technological back-wardness, attributed to their original choice of the cow in preference to the

---

[34] Ibid., p. 228.   [35] Ibid., p. 229.

thing called "What," which is now perceived to have been given later to the Europeans and Arabs and to have become the source of their material superiority and power. In the following lines, the singer attributes the hardships of urban labor to the inequitable distribution of resources among the races at the time of creation:

> God hates us for the things of the past.
> The ancient things he created with us in the Byre of Creation,
> When he gave the black man the cow
> Leaving behind the Book of his father,
> Our curse goes to the elders of the original land;
> The man who threw the Book away,
> It is he who gave us into slavery.[36]

Another myth explains that the black man was relegated to a status inferior to his white and brown brothers because his mother favored him, forcing their father to plead with God to take care of the disadvantaged children. As one elder commented, "That has remained a curse on us. Our father did not show us the ways of our ancestors fully … Otherwise, we would have known more things than we know."[37]

Lienhardt analyzed the process by which the Dinka, who had taken their superiority for granted, came to accept a significant degree of inferiority. "The Dinka view of age-sets, based upon a cyclical notion of local history, begins to be displaced by a dynamic view of history, accompanied by a philosophy of progress, and with teleological overtones."[38] The new notion of "getting ahead" begins to be directed towards some distant, more universal end, defined in foreign terms and for a society based on foreign models, rather than one conceived by the Dinka.

As the impact of the outside world on the Dinka intensified, traditional pride began to wane, occasionally resurfacing defensively, but otherwise submerged in the quest for self-improvement through development. In a series of interviews conducted in the 1970s with chiefs and elders from different parts of Dinkaland, this change in mindset was striking. The 17-year civil war (1955 to 1972) had just ended with the Addis Ababa Agreement that granted the South regional autonomy. Development was projected as a national ideology that would replace the war psychology. The ruling socialist revolution had abolished native administration in the North and, although it was allowed to continue in the South, chiefs had reason to be apprehensive that they too might be affected. That presumably added to their determination to prove themselves capable of meeting the demands of development.[39]

---

[36] Deng (1995) p. 214.   [37] Deng (1980) p. 269.

[38] Godfrey Lienhardt, "The Dinka and Catholicism," in J. Davis, ed., *Religious Organization and Religious Experience* London and New York: Academic Press, (1982) pp. 89–90.

[39] The accounts quoted here are reproduced, sometimes with minor revisions in the original translation.

Even the principle of continued identity and influence, essentially geared toward a backward-looking veneration of the ancestors and the forefathers, with age as the source of knowledge and wisdom, began to be reconceptualized in a forward-looking emphasis on an educated youth and their contribution to building the future. Chief Arol Kachwol articulated this in terms that delicately balanced tradition and change:

> It is God who changes the world by giving successive generations their turns. For instance, our ancestors, who have now disappeared, by the way their world began and the way they lived, they held the horns of their life. Then God changed things; things changed until they reached us; and they will continue to change. When God comes to change your world, it will be through you and your wife. You will sleep together and bear a child. When that happens, you should know that God has passed to your children borne by your wife the things with which you lived your life.[40]

Arol Kachwol was even more emphatic about the generational change:

> Our stories are gone. New stories will now begin with you. The ancient stories you were asking us about have had their turn. The time has now come for your own stories to begin. So, instead of us being the story-tellers, it is now for you to be the storytellers. It is also for you to bear your children for the stories you are now about to tell.[41]

In response to the question of how he saw the future relations between the North and the South, Chief Arol Kachwol responded: "It is not really for you people to ask us that question ... It is you people who know the good things that will come out of this. And it is you people who know what may go wrong in it ... [I]t is also for you to tell us, 'Our people, this is the way we can make our country go ahead.'"[42]

Chief Ayeny Aleu addressed himself to the prevention and cure of human and animal diseases, the procurement of tractors for cultivating the fields, the provision of potable water and the promotion of education. Chief Thon Wai also spoke on education, agriculture, marketing and health services:

> Let all the chiefs speak about opening schools. Let them speak about cultivating crops. Crops provide food as well as products for sale ... to provide cash which can be used for developing the country ... Diseases are on the increase. There is a disease called *kalazaar* which is killing people and a disease which causes headaches ... diseases which did not exist at the time of our grandfathers. And what brought them? It is because those foreigners came and other foreigners came and people intermingled. All the diseases which were absent are now amidst us. For these we need hospitals.[43]

The chiefs consider their people capable of financing their own development. Chief Thon Wai posed a question and provided the answer: "And with what money will [schools and hospitals] be built? They will be built with the money

---

[40] Deng (1978) p. 50.   [41] Ibid., p. 64.   [42] Deng (1980) p. 61.   [43] Ibid., p. 196.

of the people. The chief must collect the money,… ask his people to build houses and then say to the government, 'We want a doctor to be brought.'[44]

During the period of relative peace following the Addis Ababa Agreement, small scale projects in rural development mushroomed in various parts of the South, including in Dinkaland. A major project that would have had significant impact was the mammoth Jonglei Canal, which was designed to retrieve the waters lost through evaporation in the swampy region known as the Sudd and to provide water for irrigation schemes in northern Sudan and Egypt. Although it was initially opposed by the South because of its feared impact on the environment, the promise of major agricultural schemes for the local people, the Bor Dinka, eventually persuaded the South to accept the project. However, work on the canal was interrupted by the resumption of hostilities in 1983.

Another major development scheme affected by the war is the World Bank-funded rice project in the Malwal Dinka area of Aweil. Located in the transitional grazing areas, the project was initially opposed by the Dinka and only after much demonstration of its utility was it accepted. Rice was used to prepare traditional foods and brew local beer, usually produced from sorghum. Covering an area of one million acres, the project was intended to make the Sudan self-sufficient in rice.[45] Although the project is still productive, its capacity has been considerably reduced by the effects of the war. With the frequent interruption of railroad transportation to the North, marketing has also been adversely affected. Nevertheless, the project demonstrated that the Dinka are receptive to development.

Yet another area of considerable potential for the development of the South (and the Dinka) is the exploration and exploitation of the vast oil resources that have been discovered in that part of the country, but whose production has been so far blocked by the civil war. The discovery of oil indeed contributed to the resumption of hostilities in 1983, as the South resented and strongly opposed the central government plan to take the crude to be refined in the North or moved by pipeline to the Red Sea for exportation. Although the government eventually compromised by agreeing to establish a small refinery in the South and use some of the oil revenues for development projects in the region, oil politics has remained one of the centerpieces in the competition for resources and development opportunities behind the North-South conflict.

So radical have the Dinka become in their commitment to development that according to the chiefs' accounts, there is now a striking willingness to change the traditional Dinka ways, including their attitude toward cattle. According to Chief Makuei Bilkuei:

> I told all my people, 'The North burned down our villages during the war. Everything is now gone … You people are going to remain behind. When

---

[44] Ibid., p. 197.
[45] Information orally provided by Bona Malwal, regional minister of finance and national minister of information and culture at the time of the Addis Ababa Agreement.

I come back from Juba, I want the cattle to be made use of. We have to make use of our cattle.[46]

Chief Ayeny Aleu even opposed high bridewealth: "I spoke to my ... people. I said, 'This costly marriage of the Dinka in which 100 cows must be paid, I have forbidden it ... No girl, whatever she is, should be married for more than 10 and at the very most 20 cows ... What is it that brings 100 cows into marriage?'"[47] Chief Makuei Bilkuei foresaw a time when the Dinka would no longer marry with cattle: "You see, cattle are now in a predicament. There is illness, there's marriage, there is taxation, there are fines; all fall on cattle ... One day the Dinka will accept something other than marriage with cattle."[48]

Among the development activities that generated controversy in Dinka areas was the use of cattle for animal traction. In the Rumbek and Toni areas, people were eventually persuaded through pilot projects to accept the use of cattle for plowing the fields. In other areas, Dinka resistance proved insurmountable. A study of the Jonglei Project Area Development noted:

> The conclusion, drawn from results of application of linear programming in the JPA [Jonglei Project Area] that oxen technology is not appropriate to the JPA, is reinforced by results of interviews that show that the inhabitants of JPA are unlikely to adopt oxen farming.[49]

In a project of integrated rural development among the Ngok Dinka of Abyei, one of the initial members of the project team was a draft animal expert from the United States who had worked with ox plows in Ethiopia and wanted to apply the approach in Abyei. The Ngok Dinka, however, strongly opposed the use of draft animals, preferring tractors as more modern and culturally acceptable. Initially, oxen were used to draw carts for transporting water or silage rather than for the more arduous land-tillage work. But even this provoked strong objections and petitions to local leaders to halt the mistreatment of the revered animals.[50] Eventually, the project was forced to abandon the use of animals for transportation and tillage. Since the Dinka reflect a willingness to use cattle for development, their refusal to use them as draft animals indicates that they are prepared to use them for developmental purposes in ways that are compatible with the dignity of the animals as they see it. Apparently, exchanging cattle for cash is regarded as more dignified than using them as beasts of burden. Acceptance of change still prescribes sensitivity to minimum standards of cultural integrity.

Instead of relying on or taking pride in wealth accrued through bridewealth, it is becoming fashionable to value self-acquired wealth above that which

---

[46] Ibid., p. 201.   [47] Ibid., p. 202.   [48] Ibid.

[49] John Garang de Mabior, *Identifying, Selecting Arid Implementing Rural Development Strategies for Socio-Economic Development on the Jonglei Project Area, Southern Region, Sudan,* dissertation Iowa State University: (1981).

[50] David C. Cole and Richard Huntington, *Between a Swamp and a Hard Place: Development Challenges in Remote Rural Africa* Cambridge: Harvard Institute for International Development, distributed by Harvard University Press, (1997) pp. 159–160.

accrues from status. As Chief Ayeny Aleu conveys, the father's function is increasingly becoming viewed as one of helping his child through education to acquire the necessary skills to stand on his own feet and make his independent wealth. "I have a son in Rumbek Secondary School. I told him, 'In case it ever enters your head to say, "My father has wealth," let me tell you, they are not your cattle; these are my cattle. If you do not make your own wealth, and become a man by your strength, I am not near you; we are not to be relatives. If that happens, don't consider me your father.'"[51]

Development, the chiefs contend, requires considerable self-sacrifice as an investment into a better future. As one chief argued, "Badness is good when you go through it looking forward to goodness. But we have to work for that goodness."[52] In line with their procreational values, the present generation is called upon to sacrifice for the benefit of generations to come: "We have to leave them in a cleared field ... [where] ... no scrubs will pierce their feet and no thorns will hurt their faces and nothing ... will happen to them ... nothing like the things we are now experiencing."[53]

What these views from Dinka chiefs convey are the hopes that national and regional governments will create the necessary infrastructure and opportunities for development. These aspirations have not been realized, primarily because of war conditions of instability, insecurity and social disintegration, but also because of a lack of resources for investment in major development projects.

While these experiences indicate the need to be sensitive to specific cultural values and concerns, the Dinka commitment to development is now beyond doubt. Since the war has brought most of the development process to a grinding halt, much of their commitment to development remains an aspiration. Should conditions permit, the Dinka possess a strong ambition for accelerated development. And while they expect the government to support their development, they also expect a great deal from themselves. In the accounts of the chiefs, what is demanded of the individual is total dedication to the reconstruction and development of the country. In the words of Chief Thon Wai: "What we call the country is built by a man who does not sleep. A man who sleeps is not a man; he is bad. But a man who stands up and works hard and knows the work of the morning and the night, he makes night and day one thing; he is a good man."[54]

Whether it is a manifestation of characteristics hitherto hidden by their isolationism, the result of the impact of the civil war or simply adaptability to their present circumstances, the Dinka are demonstrating a degree of commitment to development that would surprise the observers of the 1950s. Development appears to be both an objective pursuit and a normative value – a material and moral defense against current insecurities. At the initial stage, the Dinka focus appears to be on the provision of social services, such as education and health, but the long-term objective is the transformation of society in modern terms, sadly impossible under the prevailing war conditions.

[51] Ibid., p. 203.   [52] Ibid., p. 193.   [53] Ibid.   [54] Ibid., p. 204.

The civil war that has raged intermittently in southern Sudan for over four decades has devastated the country and resulted in one of the worst humanitarian tragedies and indignities of modern times. To the world, the Dinka are now known not for their cattlewealth, cultural pride and general self-esteem, but rather for their destitution, starvation and even the indignity of slavery.

In response, the Dinka not only yearn for peace and security but have become keenly aware of the need to improve their lot and try to engage in development, previously alien to their culture, but now voiced with an almost obsessive sense of purpose. And yet, not once did any of the chiefs and elders interviewed describe their condition as one of poverty. Quite the contrary, what comes through is a paradoxically positive determination to overcome their predicament, with considerable self-confidence that they possess the human and material resources to do so. There is of course something unreal about this, for what the Dinka would need to generate meaningful growth goes beyond their cattlewealth. Nonetheless, it is important that they have accepted the use of their cattle for procuring the necessary cash to finance their development. And above all, they are confident about their human resources, especially if adequately prepared through education. It is that self-confidence in both the conversion of cattle to the cash economy and the mobilization of human resources that makes the Dinka positive self-perception a significant potential asset for development. The Dinka now demonstrate willingness to give up the cow in pursuit of the thing called "What." What they need is a conducive environment of peace, security and the power to determine their own destiny.

Will a downward slide in self-perception lead the Dinka to recognize that they are poor, or will they sustain a positive self-image, even as they recognize their underdevelopment and the need to improve their lot by modern standards? The answer to this question will probably depend on the outcome of the civil war and the post-war strategy for reconstruction and development. If the South succeeds in achieving self-determination, whether within the framework of a united Sudan or through separation, and if their program of reconstruction and development is culturally oriented as a process of self-enhancement from within, then it is possible that Dinka tradition will not only sustain a positive self-image in the process but will also be a vital factor in regional development. Appreciating these options is essential to the conceptualization, formulation and implementation of appropriate development policies and strategies.[55]

---

[55] For arguments in favor of a culturally oriented approach to development see Francis M. Deng, "Crisis in African Development: A Social and Cultural Perspective," in The Rockefeller Brothers' Fund, Annual Report New York: The Rockefeller Brothers' Fund, (1984); Francis M. Deng, "Cultural Dimensions of Conflict Management and Developments: Some Lessons from the Sudan" in Ismail Serageldin and June Tabaroff (eds) Culture and Development in Africa Washington, DC: The World Bank, (1994), Technical Paper 225, p. 466; Afterword in Cole and Huntington: and Francis M. Deng and Terrence Lyons (eds) African Reckoning: A Quest for Good Governance Washington, DC: The Brookings Institution Press (1998).

A final question that should be considered is whether the distinction made between objective indicators of poverty and subjective perceptions of a given people is valid beyond the Dinka context. While there is no basis for venturing an answer to the question, it would be difficult to resist the assumption that the Dinka cannot be unique. What is perhaps somewhat uncommon about the Dinka situation is the degree to which they have been relatively isolated from modernity until very recently. They are therefore still connected to their indigenous culture to a significant extent. The premise of this paper is that notions of wealth and poverty are only meaningful within a given cultural context. Attitudes similar to those of the Dinka have been observed among pastoral peoples throughout Africa, and, while the poverty of the continent is taken for granted, there are voices throughout Africa that resist this blanket classification, invoking the wealth of the continent in untapped natural resources, vibrant indigenous cultures and dynamic human potential. For policy purposes, a positive self-image is in itself a vital resource for self-reliant development. To be constructive, development policies and strategies must be appropriately contextualized to make effective use of people's values and institutions behind a positive self-image.

2.3 Human rights, universalism and democracy

(a) Traditional institutions and participatory democracy in Africa*

Although African societies were characterised by significant differences in their political systems, they all shared characteristics that might be described as a participatory form of democracy. Despite their hierarchical structures, traditional political systems were generally governed by broad participation through group representation. Extended families chose their heads who together formed a council of elders. Decisions were made through a process of extensive consultation and by consensus. It is generally recognised that the chief had no right to impose his wishes on the council of elders. Instead, elders would deliberate until they agreed on the outcome. As one observer commented, "The moral order was robustly collective. Majority rule, winner-take-all, or other forms of zero sum games were not acceptable alternatives to consensus decision making."

This decision-making process is particularly pronounced in what anthropologists call the segmentary lineage system in which the autonomy of the various components is emphasised down to the level of the family and even the individual. The Somalis and the Nilotics of Southern Sudan and East Africa belong to this category. Relations between groups are seen as a balance of power, maintained by competition at alternating levels. While relations are

---

* From *Sudan Democratic Gazette* April 1998, pp. 9–11. This is the third of a series of articles published about the same time as "The Cow and the thing called 'What'". The first two articles summarised the thesis in "The Cow" and (b)–(e) below are the subsequent articles in the series.

competitive at one level, in another situation, groups that previously competed would unite against the more distant group.

In view of the manner in which the segmentary lineage systems function, it should not be surprising that Somali society, one of the most illustrative of this system, was susceptible to the manipulation of the clan rivalry by Siad Barre. Nor should the assertiveness of the autonomous identity of the clans under their warlords that led to the destruction of the central authority and the collapse of the modern Somali state be surprising either. The manner in which the Somalis joined ranks to resist foreign intervention, when it went beyond relief supplies and took sides in their internal conflicts, demonstrated the way in which, "the formerly competitive groups merge in mutual alliance against an outside group."

In Sudan, while the Sudan People's Liberation Movement and its Army (SPLM/SPLA) has been fighting on behalf of the non-Arab, non-Muslim peoples of the South against Arab Muslim domination, it has also suffered severely from internal factionalisation between and within the Dinka – and the Nuer. Their propensity for division, despite their common cause, emanates from the individualised, yet collective quest for identity and influence, the essence of the segmentary lineage system. As the late Godfrey Lienhardt explained, the Nilotics: "positively value the unity of their tribes, and of their descent groups, while also valuing the autonomy of their component segments which can lead to fragmentations." Underlying this contradiction is the ambition of every individual to belong to a large descent group, but also to found his own descent group, by which he will be remembered. "These values of personal autonomy and of co-operation, of the inclusiveness and unity of any wider political or genealogical segments and the exclusiveness and autonomy of its several subsegments are from time to time in conflict."

Evans-Pritchard, describing the system among the Nuer, noted, "There is … always a contradiction in the definition of a political group, for it is a group only in relation to other groups … The political system is an equilibrium between opposed tendencies towards fission and fusion, between the tendency of all groups to segment, and the tendency of all groups to combine with segments of the same order … an equilibrium between … contradictory, yet complementary, tendencies."

Clearly, this is a system that resists domination, especially by an outside power. But it is also susceptible to divisive manipulation by enemies. Indeed, as in the case of Somalia, the central Government in Khartoum has exploited with relative success, the contradictions of the Nilotic segmentary lineage system to weaken the Southern liberation movement, causing devastatingly violent confrontations between increasingly fragmentary factions.

Despite Nilotic egalitarianism and sense of independence, leadership is of critical importance to their value system. Chiefs of the Sacred Spears among the Dinka, or of the Leopard Skin among the Nuer, were indispensable to the maintenance of peace and public order. However, a chief among them is not a ruler in the Western sense, but a spiritual leader whose power rests on divine enlightenment and wisdom. In order to reconcile his people, the chief should be a model of virtue, righteousness, "a man with a cool heart", who must depend on persuasion and consensus building rather than on coercion and dictation. Godfrey Lienhardt wrote: "I suppose anyone would agree that one of the most decisive marks of a society we should call in a spiritual sense 'civilised' is a highly developed sense or practice of justice, and here, the Nilotics, with their intense respect for the personal independence and dignity of themselves and of others, may be superior to societies more civilised in the material sense ... The Dinka and Nuer are a warlike people, and have never been slow to assert their rights as they see them by physical force. Yet, if one sees Dinka trying to resolve a dispute, according to their own customary law, there is often a reasonableness and a gentleness in their demeanour, a courtesy and a quietness in the speech of those elder men superior in status and wisdom, an attempt to get at the whole truth of the situation before them."

It can be argued that the emphasis placed on the ideals of peace, unity, mediation, and persuasion amongst the Nilotic societies emanates from the pervasiveness of violence. Internal violence can in turn be attributed to generational distribution of roles and functions and the exaggerated sense of dignity young members of the warrior age-sets acquired from their identity and status as warriors, as defenders of the society from aggression, a function they over-zealously displayed to excess, resorting to violence at the slightest provocation.

By the same token, chiefs, even when young, must be men of peace. Chief Arol Kachwol, reacting to the assertion that the Dinka were traditionally a chiefless people in whose society force was the deterrent behind the social order, articulated the delicate balance between the violence of youth and the peacemaking role of chiefs: "It is true, there was force. People killed one another and those who could defeat people in battle were avoided with respect. But people lived by the way God had given them. There were the Chiefs of the Sacred Spear. If anything went wrong, they would come to stop the ... fighting ... and settle the matter without blood ... Men of the sacred spear were against bloodshed." And in the words of Chief Giir Thiik, "There was the power of words. It was a way of life with its great leaders ... not a way of life of the power of the arm."

While it was not always easy for the elders to control the over-zealous warriors, it was a clearly established principle that the warriors should adhere to the will of their chiefs and elders. When they had to confront aggression and justifiably go to war, they were blessed by their chiefs, instructed by their war leaders on the ethics of warfare, and trusting in the justice of their cause, count on their ancestral spirits and deities to ensure their victory against the forces of evil.

The lesson to be drawn from this aspect of tradition is two-fold. First is the clear division of roles between warriors and civilian leaders. The fusion of the two in the modern state system in which the Government becomes synonymous with police and military force, has undermined this division and forced youth to extend their military prowess into political ambition. The second is the control the chiefs and the elders wielded on the warrior age-sets, which is not dissimilar to the civilian control of the military in modern liberal democracies. Here is an instance in which reform might be inspired by, and predicated on, authentic indigenous values and institutions.

(b) Globalisation and localisation of democracy in the African context*

While indigenous values and institutions will continue to influence Africa's political thought and practice, the challenge of democracy must be placed in the global context. Globalisation, now intensified by the victory of capitalism over Marxist socialism and by the leaps and bounds of technological revolution, has been an on-going historical process. In Africa, it was dramatised by the colonial incorporation of the continent into the imperial economies and power structures of Europe. But the realities on the ground also pull Africa in the opposite direction of localisation. The independence movement was a reversal of colonial globalisation. That process is being extended internally through local demands for self-determination, pluralistic democracy, human rights, and good governance.

The contradictory pulls of globalisation and localisation present several challenges for the state and the international community. While the centrepiece remains the state, a relic of European intervention, the internal challenge of localisation demands a more effective use of indigenous cultural values and institutions for nation building and self-reliant development. Externally, state linkage to regional and international contexts raises questions about the objectives and the scope of sovereignty. While sovereignty stipulates the basis of relations with the outside world, it should be predicated on domestic legitimacy. Inherently, these processes pose serious dilemmas for the African state. On the one hand, state borders, though artificially drawn and continue to be porous, have been made sacrosanct. On the other hand, the normative legitimacy of the state internally is at best contested. The obvious policy implication of these dilemmas is to harmonise between the demands of localisation and the external forces and standards of globalization.

Universal quest for democracy

By both the local and the global standards, Africa is now facing a call for democracy. This is posing a formidable challenge for pluralistic states, especially those acutely divided on racial, ethnic or religious grounds. Because it has become closely associated with elections, and Africans tend to vote on the basis of their politicised ethnic or religious identity, democracy risks becoming a

---

* From *Sudan Democratic Gazette* May 1998, pp. 11–12. This is the fourth in the series of articles referred to above.

dictatorship of numbers. This enables an automatic majority to impose its will on the minority with impunity. For this reason, the suitability of democracy for the continent is being questioned by some, both within and outside the continent. But, of course, Africans cannot accept dictatorship as the alternative. The increasing assault on democracy is based on a narrow definition that places overwhelming emphasis on the procedural aspect, reflected in elections, then uses the negative consequence of this narrow definition to question democracy as a policy objective. A balanced approach should draw a distinction between the principles of democracy and the institutional mechanisms for their application.

Principles of democracy

Among the principles of democracy that have gained universal validity are that governments rule in accordance with the will of the people and adhere to the rule of law, separation of powers, the independence of the judiciary, and respect for fundamental rights and civil liberties. These principles should be safeguarded by transparency, freedom of expression (and of the press), access to information, and accountability to the public. Given the tendency of Africans to vote according to their ethnic or tribal identities, democracy will also have to mean more than electoral votes. In the context of ethnic diversity, devolution of power through decentralisation down to the local level, combined with some method of ensuring the representation of those who would otherwise be excluded by the weight of electoral votes, would be necessary. In any case, democracy, however defined or practiced, implies accommodation of differences and a special responsibility for the protection of minorities.

Democracy in the context of diversity

In many African countries, the situation is complicated by the fact that the country is usually a conglomerate of many ethnic groups. This makes it difficult, if not impossible, to speak of majority and minority. Given the fact that these are countries still in the process of nation building, groups that find themselves threatened with a minority status would rather resist affiliation into such a stratifying national framework. Their preference may be to exit if they have the capacity for resistance. This would pose a serious challenge to the legitimacy of the regime, if not the state itself. The result is likely to be a call either for secession or for a major restructuring of the political system. But although the electoral system should make allowance for the protection and participation of minorities in the short run, the goal in the long run must be to transcend these differences and apply democracy on a non-racial, non-ethnic and non-religious basis – a truly uniting concept of nationhood.

Ultimately, the only sustainable unity is one based on mutual understanding and agreement. Unfortunately, the constitutional framework for national unity in modern Africa is not the result of consensus. Except for the post-apartheid

South Africa, Africans won their independence without negotiating an internal social contract that would forge and sustain national consensus. Of course, the leaders of various factions, ethnic or political, negotiated a framework that gave them the legitimacy to speak for the country in their demand for independence. In virtually every African country, independence was preceded by dialogue and negotiation among various groups, parallel to negotiations with the colonial powers. But these were tactical moves to rid the country of the colonial rule and were in any case elitist negotiations that did not involve the grass roots. In contrast, the South African negotiations involved a broad-based network of political organisations and elements of civil society.

The failure of crafted constitutions

Typically, the constitutions which African countries adopted at independence were drafted for them by the colonial masters. Contrary to the authoritarian modes of governance adopted by the colonial powers, these constitutions were laden with idealistic principles of liberal democracy to which Africans had not previously been introduced. The regimes built on them were in essence foreign conceptualisations with no indigenous roots and therefore lacked legitimacy. In most cases, they were soon overthrown with no remorse or regrets from the public.

But these upheavals involved only a rotation of like-minded élites, or worse, military dictators, intent on occupying the seat of power vacated by the colonial masters. They soon became their colonial masters' images. In the overwhelming majority of countries, the quest for unity underscored the intensity of disunity, sometimes resulting in violent conflicts. Many of these conflicts intensified in the post-Cold War era. It can be argued that the gist of these crises is that the ethnic pieces that were welded and kept together by the colonial glue, reinforced by the Cold War bi-polar control mechanisms, began to pull apart and reassert their autonomy or demand the total restructuring of the state to be more representative. African states must respond to the demands of justice, equity and dignity by the component elements or risk disintegration and collapse.

Toward an African model of democracy

The main point is to realise that there are no instantaneous solutions to the dilemmas of democracy in the pluralistic African context. Lasting solutions will have to evolve and in the process of their evolution, conditions on the ground will have to be part of the equation. What this means is that while democracy, broadly defined in terms of normative ideals or principles, is universally valued, it needs to be contextualized. This should put into consideration the African reality and make effective use of indigenous values, institutions and social mores. Democracy should be home-grown in order to be sustainable. However, this must not be allowed to degenerate into a pretext for relativistic authoritarianism that is inimical to traditional African political thought and practice.

In traditional Africa, rulers governed with the consent of the people who participated broadly in their own self-administration, were free to express their will; and held their leaders to high standards of transparency and accountability. In that sense, indigenous societies were more democratic than most modern states in Africa. In any case, indigenous communities are not only part of the African reality, but constitute by far the largest portions of its social structures and community processes, often linking the rural and the urban contexts of participation. It is imperative that they be factored into the equations of the modern political concepts, institutions, and processes.

(c) Universalism versus relativism in cultural contextualisation of human rights*

Along with the issue of democracy, discussed in the last two essays in this series, a concept that poses a challenge for reinterpreting traditional cultures and using them as a benchmark for evaluating the performance of governments in Africa is that of human rights. As a normative concept, human rights principles are rooted in the quest for human dignity. While there is considerable variation of cultural perspectives on the norms of human dignity, the principles involved in human rights protection have become largely adopted by the international community and enshrined in the International Bill of Rights.

These principles are not without controversy relating to both normative formulation and enforcement mechanism. It is indeed ironic that a concept which derives from the universal pursuit of "the dignity and worth of the human person", to quote the preamble of the United Nations Charter, or in the language of the Universal Declaration of Human Rights, "the recognition of the inherent dignity and of the equal and inalienable rights of all members of the human family", should be an ideological battle-field between those labelled as universalists and their relativist protagonists.

Universalism

While universalism seems self-evident, relativism, whether based on culture, religion, or differences in public policy priorities, is a reality dictated by conditions on the ground, and cannot be dismissed lightly. The challenge is to debate the arguments on both sides with the view to fostering understanding and narrowing the ideological gap toward optimal or functional consensus. Combined with the weight of global public opinion, such a debate can serve the multiple purpose of promoting the ideals of international human rights, appreciating justified concerns in specific cultural contexts and countervailing the opportunistic exploitation of cultural relativism by offending authorities.

---

* From *Sudan Democratic Gazette* June 1998, pp. 9–11.

This approach necessitates disaggregating the clusters of universalists and relativists. It is perhaps relatively easy to group together all those inspired by the ideals of universal dignity of all human beings and its articulation in international human rights instruments as representing the global agenda of humankind. But even here it is often argued that those who support universality may be driven more by vested political interests than by altruism of the ideals. The selective application of human rights principles by those espousing universality raises questions of objectivity or partiality based on the interests of the powers concerned. Clarifying these sets of objectives would help expose any hidden motives and promote the integrity of the human rights agenda.

Relativism

When it comes to those collectively labelled the relativists, the composition of the agents and the perspectives involved become more complex. The context in which relativism is invoked is by no means monolithic. As much as there are those who would plead the defence of relativism, there are those who seek the protection of universalism against the relativists. In other words, the victims of human rights violations in the context of the nation-state look and appeal to the principles and mechanisms of universalism to provide them with international protection against their own national or local authorities. On the other hand, not all relativists are offenders: some may indeed be motivated by competing ideals within their own cultural contexts or at least by a different order of policy priorities.

On the assumption that all cultures recognize the inherent dignity of the human person and postulate various norms and procedures for its pursuit, it is useful to understand how local cultures seek to achieve this otherwise global objective. Ultimately it is possible to conceive relativism as a local reinforcement and enrichment of universalism to explore the weakness of each tradition in approximating the ideals, or to appreciate the sources of genuine conflicts between the local and the universal standards.

Indeed, some of those who argue that international human rights, as now articulated, are Western in origin do not necessarily object to them on that account, but merely wish to underscore the opportunity for all major cultural blocs of the world to negotiate the normative content of human rights law and the purpose for which the discourse should be legitimately deployed.

As the Sudanese human rights scholar and advocate, Abdullahi Ahmed An-Na'im has argued, to be legitimate, the universality of human rights must rely on the norms and institutions of the particular cultures involved. If meaningful and lasting changes in attitudes and practices are to be achieved, the proposed reinterpretation has to be undertaken from within the culture by those who, while promoting universal norms, are sensitive to the integrity and authenticity of the local cultures. Their arguments in favour of universal human rights standards need to be consistent with the internal logic of the culture, yet be guided by the postulates of international consensus on the scope and implications of human rights. In An-Na'im's words: "With internal cultural legitimacy, those in power could no longer argue that national sovereignty is demeaned through compliance with standards set for the particular human rights as an external value. Compliance with human rights standards would be seen as legitimate exercise of national sovereignty and not as an external limitation." The critical issue then is whether cross-cultural analysis can be used to transform notions of human dignity into human rights principles on which there is universal agreement.

Cross-fertilization

While it is important to make a case for cross-fertilisation and mutual reinforcement in human rights standards and their implementation, it should also be acknowledged that a certain degree of tension is inevitable between the demands of cultural relativism, on the one hand, and those of universalism, on the other. The premise of this tension is the inherent right of people within a given community or society to live in accordance with the values and institutions of their own culture and to promote respect for human rights on the basis of that culture. On the other hand, all cultural groups are required to live up to the highest standards which the community of humankind postulates as universal norms of human rights by which all the varied cultural traditions can be judged. Unless certain standards are recognized as universal, serious violations may be condoned because they happen to be tolerated or sanctioned by the cultural tradition of the society or the community in question.

Human rights ideals represent a goal that no nation or society has as yet achieved, an aspiration that is pursued with varying degrees of approximation. But the sequence of requirements begins with the definition of fundamental standards, which in turn begins with the Universal Declaration of Human Rights. Both in terms of its content and its process of development and promulgation, the Universal Declaration is the most comprehensive and authoritative international document on human rights. Any legal system which can claim legitimacy must adhere to the basic elements of its principles. As one policy analyst put it, "a legal system worthy of the name must protect all individuals against murder, robbery, rape, enslavement, and torture, and no state claiming legitimacy can validly quarrel with that set of commitments." Although crimes of this sort cannot be absolutely prevented, whenever they occur or threaten to occur on a massive and sustained scale all societies have valid reason for active concern.

Of course, adoption of international norms does not always guarantee their enforcement. The political will and the capacity of international agents to act are pivotal determinants of the effectiveness of the human rights system. On the other hand, norm-setting is a prerequisite to enforcement. The fact that international practice has not yet lived up to the norms underscores the need to develop a more effective mechanism of enforcement.

(d) Cultural constraints on the universality of human rights*

The fifth essay in the series focused on the effect of the structural inequities of the Dinka value system on the non-discriminatory nature of the universal notions of human rights. A related cultural constraint on the universality of human dignity from the Dinka perspective is its ethnocentrism and the way it impacts on adaptability to changing conditions and respect for all peoples, irrespective of their race, ethnicity, culture or gender.

In the traditional Dinka value system, the idealized view of the ancestral past reinforces the present to shape the future. The Dinka never claim to do better than their fathers, even if they indeed do better. After all, the continued participation of the forebears in the affairs of the living is largely dependent on their being remembered for their virtues, in turn dependent on continued exaltation and glorification.

Until recently, when the coming of modernity began to have a visible effect on the Dinka, the notion of development, now widely accepted among them, was nonexistent. The role of leadership was to maintain peace, unity, harmony and stability, not "progress." When a man succeeds to a position of leadership and proves himself a worthy leader, he is said to have established control over the situation, *dom baai*. If there are particular problems that need solutions, such as conflicts between community members or when God and the ancestral spirits have, for one reason or another, been provoked into punishing the community with natural disasters, then the leader has the duty to take appropriate measures to resolve the conflicts, propitiate the supernatural powers, and restore a state of unity, harmony, and functional prosperity. That is *guier baai*. When that state is achieved, the task of the leader is to ensure that it is stabilised and maintained, *muk baai*.

Related to Dinka conservatism is also cultural exclusiveness. Because of the family orientation of the system, values become minimal in relations with foreigners. Of course, all peoples seek or ought to seek immortality through the principles of *koc e nhom* – procreation. And all peoples have their own *cieng*, whether or not they live up to the standards of the ideals of unity and harmony in accordance with the Dinka *cieng*. Nor is the notion of human dignity as embodied in *dheeng* a Dinka prerogative. But in all these areas the Dinka believe that their conceptualisation of the principles involved and the behavioural ways of applying them are superior to those of others.

Of course, pride in race and culture are shared to an even greater degree by the Arabs. It would indeed surprise most Northern Sudanese to learn that the Nilotics regard themselves as "the chosen" people, and their race and culture, preferred models of human dignity. It is no exaggeration to say that the North-South incompatibility may not be due so much to the differences as to the similarities of otherwise parallel systems of values and institutions. One major difference worth emphasis is that the Nilotics, like the Jews, but unlike the

* From *Sudan Democratic Gazette* August 1998, pp. 8–9.

Arabs, do not wish to impose their culture and beliefs on others. The ethno-centrism of Nilotic self-image is based on feelings of distinctiveness as a people rather than on assumptions of dominating superiority over others. Having been dominated by foreign rulers and having seen the technological superiority of others over them, the Nilotics have developed sentiments of human worth that are in the realm of moral and spiritual rather than material values.

As the South became incorporated in the modern context of the nation-state, more opportunities arose for individual members to move on in the path of "progress" through education, employment, and labour migration. Southerners, specifically the Nilotics who had been the most resistant to change, realised the inferiority of their situation as judged by the new criteria. Many of them began to adjust rapidly to the demands of modernity. One can indeed hypothesise that the same values of pride and dignity that had made them resist change may well provide them with the motivation to enhance their status and self-image through radical change. Change was despised when it did not offer convincing evidence of self-improvement, and it was embraced when it became the obvious way toward dignity by the new standards.

After all, the Dinka never saw the model represented by the Arab North, specially with its bent towards the enslavement of black Africans, as something worth emulating as an incentive for change. This is indeed an area in which the Dinka have always claimed moral superiority over the Arabs, believing that God created the Dinka differently from the Arabs. Referring to the allegation that slavery was practiced by all societies, Arabs and Africans alike, one elder, Bulabek-Malith, observed in protest: "A human being created by God was never made a slave by the black man meaning Dinka; it was the Arabs who made them slaves ... Slavery is not known to us ... To capture people to become slaves among us is unknown ... A person known to his relatives is the man who stays among us. And he is not treated like a slave; he becomes a member of the family."

Chief Biong Mijak observed that to call slavery a universal practice "is a lie ... Even our ancestors tell us they never captured Arab children. People kill themselves in war, face to face, but we do not go and capture people ... We have something God gave us from the ancient past, from the time our ancestors came leading the people ... War has always occurred but we have war ethics that came with us from the ancient past. We never ambush ... we kill face to face. It is the Arabs who treat us as slaves and capture us in secrecy."

Dinka reaction to development in the pluralistic world of the nation-state and its conflicting array of positives and negatives is equally contradictory. On the one hand, they are beginning to reinterpret their value systems to become more universally valid. For instance, the following lines of a song that was composed during the peaceful period of the Addis Ababa Agreement stress the universality of human equality, irrespective of race or religion:

No one was bad when God created us
No one was bad when the Creator made us

No one was bad when we emerged from
the Byre of Creation;
We were all equal
I swear by death, we were all children of
the one Adam;
Both Mohamed and Deng – Arab and
Dinka
I swear by death, we were all children of
the one Adam;
The Black Sudan and the Brown Sudan.

The Dinka have become increasingly disillusioned by their position in the modern world and in particular their subordination to the dominant Arab Muslim North. This has created a situation in which they have to reinterpret their relative inferiority in the modern context, while nevertheless upholding their distinctive moral ideals. As the Dinka see the need to pursue their traditional pride and human dignity by the new modern criteria, they reflect a willingness to change in sharp contrast to their reputed conservatism. At the same time, fear of assimilation by the Arab Muslim North has aroused in them an intense desire to preserve their traditional ways. "If you, our children, have survived," implored Chief Biong Mijak, "hold to the ways of our ancestors very firmly. Let us be friends with the Arabs, but each man should have his own way." Another elder, Chief Makuei Bilkuei, remarked: "Why don't we promote our own ways? Why do we take Arab ways without our own plan? ... What have you people done to promote our own ways with the Arabs?" "God did not create at random," Chief Biong Mijak concluded. "He created some people brown and some black. We cannot say we want to destroy what God has created ... God would get angry if we spoiled his work." Chief Makuei Bilkuei gave a dramatic account of his resistance to Arab Islamic influence: "God has refused my speaking Arabic. I asked God, 'Why don't I speak Arabic?' And he said, 'You will turn into a bad man.' ... I said, 'There is something good in Arabic!' And he said, 'No, there is nothing good in it.'"

The experience of the Dinka suggests that they clearly had notions of human rights that formed an integral part of their value system: its overriding goals for life, its ideals for relationships between people, and its sense of human dignity. However, the logic of this value system stratified people according to descent, age, gender and culture creating inequities that were recognized but endured, since dissidents lacked alternatives. The system was also conservatively oriented away from change and development and its effectiveness diminished as people moved away from the family and the lineage-oriented concept of the community.

With the emergence of the nation-state, new opportunities for education and employment, and Western ideas of democracy and equality, the old structures and their underlying cultural values became exposed to reassessment and scrutiny. The result was that, while certain traditional values and practices continued to be upheld, new values and patterns of behaviour developed that postulate universal standards for the promotion and protection of human rights. However, the competition for power and resources in the pluralistic context of the state has generated tensions and conflicts that have triggered egregious violations of human rights. By both indigenous and internationally recognised standards, Sudan today has one of the worst human rights records in the world.

(e) Dinka moral values and human rights principles*

To argue for the principle of universality is not to deny the significance of the cultural context for the definition, the scope, and the degree of protection of human rights. It is indeed by seeing human rights concretely manifested in a particular context that we can fully appreciate their form and content in the comparative framework of universality. It is with these cross-cultural dynamics and potentials in mind that this essay approaches the subject of human rights among the Dinka by presenting the concept in terms of the fundamental values of Dinka society, how they condition the social structures and patterns of behaviour and the level of success of traditional ideas and practices in approximating universal standards.

As explained earlier, the overriding goal of Dinka society is *koc e nhom*, a concept of procreational immortality which aims at perpetuating the identity and influence of every individual male. Respect for the dignity of any person is central to this principle. Another principle which is essential to the Dinka value system is *cieng*, a concept of ideal human relations, which fosters deferential treatment and commands unity and harmony. Although the continuity of the lineage is a common objective, the values of unity and harmony are beneficial to all in varying degrees. Dinka social morals ensure the mutual interest of all the members by providing them with varied avenues to individual and collective pride, honour and dignity, expressed in *dheeng*, a concept of normative and aesthetic dignity. Although *dheeng* relates to social relations, it should not be confused with *cieng*; *cieng* provides standards for evaluating conduct, while *dheeng* classifies people according to that conduct; *cieng* requires that one should behave in a certain way. While *dheeng* labels one virtuous for behaving in that way; *cieng* is a normative concept, a means; while *dheeng* is a concept of status, an end.

The Dinka believe their value system to be ordained and ultimately sanctioned by God and the ancestral spirits. Despite the martial culture of the Dinka as herders and warriors, killing, even in fair fight, is believed to be spiritually contaminating and dangerous and must be redressed according to certain ritual practices. Killing by stealth or ambush is considered particularly depraved and requires even more elaborate procedures of redress and rites of atonement. Theft was hardly heard of in traditional society and, when it occurred, was met

* From *Sudan Democratic Gazette* September 1998, pp. 10–11.

with degrading sanctions that were severely damaging to one's social standing. Virtually every wrong threatens the wrongdoer with misfortune and even death. As Godfrey Lienhardt observed, "Divinity [God] is held ultimately to reveal truth and falsehood, and in doing so provides a sanction for justice between men. Cruelty, lying, cheating, and all other forms of injustice are hated by Divinity, and the Dinka suppose that, in some way, if concealed by men they will be revealed by Him … The Dinka have no problem of the prospering sinner, for they are sure that Divinity will ultimately bring justice." As one chief expressed it: "Even if a right is hidden, God will always uncover the right of a person. It may be covered for ten years, and God will uncover it for ten years, until it reappears … If a man is not given his right, God never loses sight of the right."

These moral and spiritual principles are also applied to guide and control the exercise of political and legal authority. Dinka law is not a dictate of the ruler with coercive sanctions. Rather, it is an expression of the collective will of the community, inherited from the ancestors, generally respected and observed, sanctioned largely through persuasion or, if need be, spiritual sanctions.

Until the advent of colonial rule, there were no police or prisons; the effectiveness of leaders depended largely on the moral force of their character; which was, in turn, dependent on the degree of adherence to the values subsumed in the overriding principles that guided Dinka society. The introduction of the coercive use of the police and imprisonment were extremely resented by the Dinka as inimical to their notions of human dignity – *dheeng* – and became a popular subject of protest and lamentation songs.

Contrary to general assumptions, the lineage system placed considerable emphasis on the individual as a crucial element in the ancestral line and therefore as a vital spark in the collective interest of the community. The individual's sense of justice was as important to the group as was the interest of the group to the individual. The society ultimately rested on the sum total of the cooperation of the individuals. Sanctions against the individual were resorted to only when the individual disregarded the community sense of right and wrong, and after a lengthy attempt at persuasion.

By and large, the benefits from these principles accrued according to one's relative position in the social hierarchy or structure as determined by descent, leadership position, age, or gender, even though certain obligations toward fellow human beings are universally prescribed. The dignity of every human being was sacrosanct. …

Here I give a few examples of the kind of rights that accrued in accordance with the priorities of the value system. Marriage, for instance, being directly related to the goal of procreational immortality, was the right of every individual; it imposed the duty on a man's family to provide the requisite social and material means for marrying – even if the individual should be dead. And so great was the demand for marriage that every woman was married sooner or later. Any man whose family was too poor to acquire a wife for him could approach a wealthier person and ultimately the chief to offer him help. A woman who ran the risk of "remaining in the cattle camp", a euphemism for an "old maid", would be offered to a man on the understanding that a modest bridewealth would be paid in the future, especially when the success of the marriage was assured by her bearing children.

The sanctity of life and of the human body was well established and appropriate measures were taken to remedy any violation. Even in tribal fights, for which the Nilotic people are known, war ethics dictated that an enemy outside the battlefield must not be attacked; an injured warrior, physically sheltered by a woman for protection, must not be killed or subjected to any torture.

During emergency situations of need, the more fortunate were compelled to assist their less fortunate kinsfolk with relief provisions. Where famine threatened a family with starvation, the victims were entitled to seize the property of a relative, and if necessary, of anybody, so as to relieve hunger, on the implied understanding that appropriate compensation would eventually be provided when conditions went back to normal. The same principle applied where illness threatened death and required an animal sacrifice to ancestral spirits to bring relief. If a family had no animal to sacrifice, relatives were called upon to assist. And if the pressures of the situation required acting promptly, the relatives of the sick person were authorised to seize any animal within easy reach for the sacrifice, on the understanding that they would, in due course, compensate the owner. Within his means as the head of the tribe, the chief was ultimately responsible for providing the needy with relief against famine or illness.

Although Dinka cultural values, in particular the emphasis placed on procreational continuity, idealised human relations, and the dignity of the individual in the communal context, engendered the elements of human rights principles, the system had built-in shortcomings embodied in structural inequities, resistance to change, and a condescending view of the outside world.

2.4 A cultural approach to human rights among the Dinka*

The underlying postulate presented here takes issue with the view, widely held in the West and accepted or exploited in developing countries, that the concept of human rights is peculiarly Western. Such a view is not only empirically questionable but also does a disservice to the cause of human rights. Whether or not they are articulated, respected, or violated, human rights are, and ought to be, viewed as universally inherent in the very notion of humanity; to hold otherwise would be a contradiction in terms. To arrogate the concept to only

* From An-Na'im and Deng (eds.) *Human Rights in Africa: Cross-cultural Perspectives* (1990) Washington DC: Brookings Institution, pp. 261 and 269ff. reproduced here by kind permission of the copyright holders.

certain groups, cultures, or civilizations is to aggravate divisiveness on the issue, to encourage defensiveness or unwarranted self-justification on the part of the excluded, and to impede progress toward a universal consensus on human rights.

To argue for the principle of universality is not to deny the significance of the cultural context for the definition, the scope, and the degree of protection of human rights. In a world that is paradoxically shrinking and proliferating at the same time, it is by seeing human rights concretely manifested in a particular context that we can fully appreciate their form and content in a comparative framework. To understand the diversity of the cultural contexts and their relevance to the conceptualization and protection of human rights is to enhance prospects for cross-cultural enrichment in defending and promoting human rights.

The potential in this regard lies in the hypothesis that every culture has humanitarian ideals or principles that could contribute to the redefinition and promotion of universal standards as the latter are adapted to local and national contexts. In practical terms, societies or cultures do not retain or alter their entire systems of values and institutional practices in the process of change, but rather selectively adopt from, adapt to, and integrate into new situations of cross-cultural interaction. In this process, old and new ideas and practices are favored, modified, or rejected, depending on their appeal and degree of compatibility with preferred values and modes of behavior ...

Implications for human rights

Dinka cultural values and patterns of behavior have both positive and negative implications for the protection of human rights. Positively, semblances of rights were observed before the modern nation-state. But the same principles that guaranteed respect for those rights limited the scope of their realization, both in terms of the substance and of the people benefited.

There can be hardly any doubt that some notions of human rights are defined and observed by the Dinka as part of their total value system. Respect for human dignity as they see it is an integral part of the principles of conduct that guide and regulate human relationships and constitutes the sum total of the moral code and the social order.

By and large, responsibility in the observance of these principles is apportioned according to one's relative position in the social hierarchy or structure as determined by descent, leadership position, age, or gender, even though certain obligations toward fellow human beings are universally prescribed. How else, but as indigenous principles of human rights, can we interpret these words from a Dinka chief, describing his people's moral values?

> If you see a man walking on his two legs, do not despise him; he is a human being. Bring him close to you and treat him like a human being. That is how you will secure your own life. But if you push him onto the ground and do not give him

what he needs, things will spoil and even your big share, which you guard with care, will be destroyed ... Even the tree which cannot speak has the nature of a human being. It is a human being to God, the person who created it. Do not despise it.[1]

Needless to say, what is said about men in this context applies to women with equal moral force.

Another chief, referring to what he saw as the disdain the Arab-Muslim North has toward the people of the South, said:

Our brothers [the northerners] thought that we should be treated that way because we were in their eyes like fools. I have never heard of a man being such a fool. A human being who speaks with his mouth cannot be such a fool. Whatever way he lives, he remains a human being. And whatever he does must be thought of as the behavior of a human being.[2]

Rights accruing from the value system*

...

All these customs might be labeled positive economic and social rights. The so-called negative civil and political rights were implicit in the values that political and legal authorities were to observe in their exercise of power. This was ensured particularly by the lack of police force behind the authority of the chief, except for the power to curse, which by its moral and spiritual nature could be effective only against a deserving wrongdoer. These are only examples of what the Dinka would consider the rights of belonging to a lineage or a clan: the proper way to live together in good *cieng*, and with the dignity *(dheng)* that every Dinka expects as a birthright. The ultimate responsibility for ensuring their protection rests with the chief, as the father of all.

Shortcomings of the value system

There are, however, severe constraints on the Dinka cultural system of values in terms of objective universal human rights standards. One set of negative effects derives from the inequities inherent in the logic of the lineage system and its stratification on the basis of descent, age, and sex. Another set of negative characteristics lies in the conservative nature of the system and its resistance to change or cross-cultural assimilation. And yet another shortcoming of the system lies in the fact that its human rights values weaken as one goes away from the structural center of Dinka community.

---

[1] Deng, *Africans of Two Worlds* (1978), p. 65.
[2] Deng, *Africans of Two Worlds*, pp. 64–65.
* For examples of rights in relation to marriage, sanctity of life and of the human body, and the equivalent of social and economic rights in emergencies see above pp. 43–4.

Inequities in the system

The problem lies not only in the injustices of the system but also in the fact that those who are less favored by it tend to react to the inequities, thereby creating paradoxes in the social system. For instance, although women are the least favored by the ancestral values, society depends on them not only as sources of income through the custom of marriage with cattle wealth but also as mothers who perform the educational role of inculcating ancestral values in their children at an early age. Yet women have no legitimate voice in the open channels of decisionmaking and can participate only through indirect influence on their sons and husbands. But because of the close association between mothers and children and the considerable influence wives have over their husbands, women are regarded as most influential in the affairs of men. Nevertheless, because of their general subordination, and especially because of the inequities of polygyny, women are known for jealousies, divisiveness, and even disloyalty to clan ideals. Their influence, especially on the children, must therefore be curtailed.

The Dinka reconcile these conflicting realities by recognizing the love and affection for the mother as functions of the heart, while those feelings for the father are functions of the mind. One's feelings for the mother are recognized as natural, but should not be openly displayed and indeed should be controlled, concealed, and only discreetly expressed. Since the father is the symbol of family unity and solidarity, love and affection for him are recognized as objective and should be actively fostered, encouraged, and openly displayed. Although a Dinka will address his mother by name, he should always address his father deferentially as "father" and observe the highest standards of filial piety toward him.

As a result of these contradictions, the position of women among the Dinka is a complex one in which deprivations and inequities are compensated by devices that ensure a degree of conformity and stability, despite ambivalences.

The position of male youth is equally fraught with paradoxes, though less threatening to the system. Youth, especially men, are tomorrow's beneficiaries of the ancestral ideals and their succession to their elders is considered as only a function of time and patience. The process by which they get to that objective is regulated by a system of age-grades or age-sets, which every Dinka joins at about the age of sixteen to eighteen. Initiation into the age-set entails elaborate rituals and in some tribes an operation of cutting the forehead with deep marks that cicatrize and become quite prominent. This operation is perhaps the most painful ritual in Dinka society.

After graduating from initiation, a man becomes a member of his age-set, a corporate entity that provides a lifelong comradeship and mutual dependency on the members. They move from being warriors to being family men, and on to being tribal elders with a legitimate voice in public affairs. Young women are also classified into age-sets that correspond with male age-sets, for whom they play a supportive role. But in most Dinka tribes, women are not subjected to the painful physical operation that men must endure to qualify as adults.

Although the young men are the ultimate beneficiaries of the values of ancestral continuity, they are subordinated in a way that is only ameliorated by considerable compensation devices, in essence a division of functions and roles. For instance, while the choice or at least the consent of the father for a marriage partner is pivotal and all the social and legal formalities of marriage are performed by him, a young man and his age-mates preoccupy themselves with the aesthetics of courtship and winning the girl's love or consent. Indeed, although the power of decisionmaking lies with their father, the cooperation of the young couple is essential, if only as a practical consideration. Furthermore, although the control of family wealth lies with their elders, the youth preoccupy themselves with the aesthetics of cattle-complex, including displaying and singing over "personality oxen", which are usually adorned with objects of beautification and with which young men identify themselves as symbols of their virility and wealth. Young men particularly relish the euphoric life of the cattle camps to which they move in search of grazings and water and in which they otherwise engage themselves in courtship, singing, and dancing. But perhaps one of the most critical divisions of functions between the generations is that while the elders are the peacemakers who will endeavor to settle disputes amicably and restore unity and harmony through mediation and reconciliation, male youth age-sets, supported by their female counterparts, are essentially warriors whose role is to defend society against the aggression of wild animals, cultivate the fields of the chiefs, and build their houses, or otherwise perform other community services that require physical courage, strength, and endurance.

Although the roles of the elders and the youth are complementary, their relationships are fraught with tension and potential conflict, which are inherent in the nature of procreational stratification. After all, it is the son who will step into the shoes of the father, and among the Dinka the eldest son does in fact inherit his father's shoes. According to the custom of levirate, the son inherits his father's junior wives of child-bearing age and begets children with them as sons and daughters of his dead father – his own half-brothers and half-sisters. While this relationship must await the father's death, the potential is threatening to the father and can be a cause of conflict.

Generational competition for young women and overall dominance is implicit in a custom known as *biok*, in which the dominant warrior age-set provokes the newly graduated age-set into a play fight that can result in severe casualties. Since fighting is perhaps the most conspicuous way in which youth warrior age-sets assert their power and foster their subjective sense of identity and dignity, they tend to be aggressive and find cause for war in the slightest provocation. Consequently, their role is fundamentally counter to that of the peacemaking elders. The Dinka reputation as warlike largely emanates from this disposition of its youth. By the same token, these compensational devices sublimate the energies of youths in activities that might seem rebellious but that never threaten the foundations of the social system of which they are the eventual heirs.

The sublimation of aggressive dispositions in young men is remarkably evident in the way they sharpen the horns of their bulls and encourage them to fight. Castrated bulls, which are used as personality oxen, symbolize the qualities of gentleness and submissiveness on the one hand and of aggressiveness and physical courage on the other. In their ox songs, young men and women praise their oxen or the oxen of their husbands or boyfriends for their aggressiveness and valor even as they criticize them for the same.

To a young man or woman, an ox symbolizes wealth. The pride in one's family wealth is usually expressed in ox songs and in relations to one's ox. The hardships of herding in distant camps are always justified by young men in terms of slaving for the love of one's personality ox. Thus by owning an ox or a few oxen, a young man feels as rich as his father who controls the herd. The fact that oxen, though castrated and subdued, are pivotal in the aesthetics of cattle is symbolic of the fact that young men, though subordinated to elders, occupy a high position in the aesthetics of Dinka society.

The significance of aesthetic values as compensational or alternative avenues to material *dheng* is evident in Dinka terminology. A man is said to be *alueth*, a liar (though not in the usual sense of the word), if he is not particularly good at singing or dancing, not really handsome or wealthy, or otherwise not socially known, but puts on an impressive show of being a good singer or dancer, bears himself with such exaggerated style as though strikingly handsome, shows excessive hospitality as though wealthy, or is otherwise pompous in any *dheng* situation.

At the same time, a man who is distinguished in singing, dancing, handsomeness, wealth, or any attribute of *dheng* and acts in accordance with his awareness of, and pride in, this distinction is also referred to as *alueth* – liar. Every young man and woman is considered essentially vain by virtue of a preoccupation with aesthetic values. And to the Dinka this is not really a criticism; quite the contrary, it is a paradoxical compliment or praise.

Singing is seen in the same light. To compose a song is "to create" a song (*cak dit*); to tell a lie is also "to create" words (*cak wel*). *Cak* is also applied to God's act of creation, and although it might be pushing the analogy too far to consider such a creation "telling a lie," there is the common denominator of making something that was formerly nonexistent. In the case of songs, "telling a lie" may indicate the usual exaggeration and distortion, but this does not discredit the positive values of song, which give to young men and women the standard values used by elders to embody the acceptable ideals of the system. Songs mean much to all Dinkas of both sexes and of all ages; otherwise, their significance to youth would be much less meaningful. It is, however, significant that this is the group most conspicuously preoccupied with them. So ritualized, mystified, and glorified are the values of young people that their forms and their effect on society are more conspicuous and attention drawing than those of their elders. The result is a purposeful, proud, gratified, and socially integrated youth, delighted with the pleasures of today yet aspiring to the utilitarian promises of later age. Generally satisfied with their status, they conform to the fundamental norms of the system, the dictates of their male elders.

Resistance to change or cross-cultural assimilation.

The Dinka value system is essentially backward-looking in that the idealized view of the ancestral past forms and reinforces the present value system so as to facilitate the future. The Dinka never claim to have done better than their fathers, and even if they have, they never voice pride in that achievement. On the contrary, they tend to glorify the achievements of the forefathers; after all, the continued participation of the forebears in the affairs of the living is largely dependent on their being remembered for positive virtues, in turn dependent on continued exaltation and glorification.[3] A frequently heard comment among the Dinka is that "in the past, people listened to each other and words would unite and flow in one direction."

Until recently, when the coming of modernity began to have a visible effect on the Dinka, the notion of development, now widely accepted among them, was nonexistent. This is quite apparent from the principles that the Dinka associate with the role of leadership. When a man succeeds to a position of leadership and proves himself a worthy leader, he is said to have established control over the situation, *dom baai*. If there are particular problems that need solutions, such as conflicts between community members or when God and the ancestral spirits have, for one reason or another, been provoked into punishing the community with natural disasters, then the leader has the duty to take appropriate measures to resolve the conflicts, propitiate the supernatural powers, and restore a state of unity, harmony, and functional prosperity. That is *guier baai*. When that state is achieved, the task of the leader is to ensure that it is maintained, *muk baai*. The notion of endeavoring to elevate society or individuals to a yet unrealized higher and better level of existence through a process similar to "development" was, I believe, foreign to the Dinka. Individual and societal goals, even to the optimum degree, were considered part of experience, achievable and, indeed, at one time or another, actually achieved. Godfrey Lienhardt provides an insight into the Dinka perspective in this respect:

> To traditional Dinka, that idea of progress was quite foreign. There was little evidence that life had ever been different from what it was today, nor, until the coming of the Europeans, that it was ever going to change in the future. But by the

---

[3] In these lines from an ox song, for instance, a relative whose good conduct supposedly attracted a man with high-quality cattle to marry her (as a result of which he, the singer, acquired his ox) is praised with reference to the old Dinka ways: "The girl named after my grandmother, mother of Deng de Bong, / her conduct is as good as that of the ancient Dinka." Deng, *The Dinka and Their Songs*, p. 113.

1940s, it had become apparent to many thoughtful Dinka that in lacking education their people were lacking some of the essential skills for political survival in the modern Sudan, and they came to accept the idea that they were in some ways which put them at a disadvantage in the modern world, backward. This idea was suggested to them, with no disrespect for their own culture, by missionaries and government officials alike, since both were anxious that the Dinka should be able to speak for themselves in councils of state outside their own homeland when the Sudan became independent.[4]

Cultural exclusiveness

Because of the family orientation of the system, Dinka cultural values tend to weaken as the community widens, and they become minimal in relations with foreigners. The Dinka do not believe the principles of *koc e nhom*, *cieng*, or *dheeng* apply only to the Dinka. All peoples seek or ought to seek immortality through procreation; and all people have their own *cieng*, whether or not they live up to the objective standards of the ideal *cieng* as the Dinka see it. Nor is the notion of human dignity as embodied in *dheeng* a Dinka prerogative. But in all these areas the Dinka believe that their conceptualization of the principles involved and the behavioral ways of applying them are superior to those of others – the foreigners. As they see it, the best possible procreation is one that ensures the continuation of the Dinka race, religious beliefs, and cultural patterns …[*]

The implications of the Dinka value system for the respect and protection of human rights among the Dinka are complex. On the one hand, there would seem to be a high regard for the human being and human dignity in the moral code of the Dinka as defined by their value system. On the other hand, that value system stratifies those within it according to descent, age, and sex. The Dinka also have a condescending view of the world beyond them. Although non-Dinkas are critically appraised by the yardstick of the Dinka code, they are considered almost by definition incapable of living up to those standards and are also recognized as disadvantaged in their sharing the benefits of Dinka cultural values. Traditionally, the Dinka code not only stratified and discriminated internally but also was essentially circumscribed to exclude non-Dinkas, whose behavior was inadequate since it was not in accordance with Dinka ideas. Whether the Dinka attributed these inferior qualities to an inherent incapability or to a choice to remain morally depraved is not clear.

Conclusion

The experience of the Dinka suggests that they clearly had notions of human rights that formed an integral part of their value system: its overriding goals for

---

[4] Godfrey Lienhardt, "The Dinka and Catholicism," in J. Davis, ed., *Religious Organization and Religious Experience* (Academic Press, 1982), p. 88.

[*] See further above pp. 14–15.

life, its ideals for relationships between people, and its sense of human dignity. However, the logic of this value system stratified people according to descent, age, and sex in a way to create inequities that were recognized but tolerated, since dissidents lacked alternatives. The system was also conservative and oriented away from change and development. Furthermore, the effectiveness of the value system diminished as people moved away from the family and the lineage-oriented sense of the community.

With the emergence of the nation-state, new opportunities for education and employment, and Western ideas of democracy and equality, the old structures and their underlying cultural values became exposed to reassessment and scrutiny. The result was that, while certain ideals and practices continued to be expressed and given wider application, new values and patterns of behavior developed that redefined standards for the promotion and protection of human rights. And yet the competition for power and national resources in the pluralistic context of the nation-state has generated tensions and conflicts leading to gross violations of human rights.

With regard to the Sudan, a cross-cultural approach to developing new ethical values, which uses coexisting or interactive value systems and practices, would not only form a bridge between cultural contexts but would also enrich the process of universalization in the promotion and protection of human rights. This is essentially a function of education, cross-cultural communication, and practical cooperation. Although the long-term result may be viewed as a composite, integrated whole, expressed in some form of universal instruments, in reality the process will continue to reflect an eclectic multiplicity of contents and levels, a complex combination of unity of purpose and diversity of means. As one elder said on a different but related issue: "Man has only one head and one neck, but he has two legs to stand on."[5]

2.5 Suggestions for further reading[1]

In addition to the collections of Dinka songs, folk tales and interviews with elders referred to above, Francis Deng's general account, *The Dinka of the Sudan* (1972), is recommended. His biography of his father, *The Man Called Deng Majok* (1986b) is remarkably frank and quite moving. *War of Visions* (1995) is Deng's fullest account of conflict in the Sudan. One of his novels, *Cry of the Owl* (1989) was translated into Arabic by Abdullahi An-Na'im and created a sensation in Sudan. His latest book, *Talking it Out: Stories in Negotiating Human Relations* (2006) is part memoir, part scholarly reflections on negotiation and mediation. John Ryle *et al.* (1982) is a vivid popular account of Dinka life around 1980.

---

[5] Chief Giir Thiik, quoted in Deng, *Dinka Cosmology*, p. 44.
[1] For further references and full citations see the Bibliography (below pp. 222ff.).

3

Abdullahi An-Na'im

3.1 Introduction

William Twining

I am arguing for secularism, pluralism, constitutionalism and human rights from an Islamic perspective because I believe this approach to these principles and institutions is indispensable for protecting the freedom for each and every person to affirm, challenge or transform his or her cultural or religious identity.[1]

On 18 January 1985 Mahmud Mohamed Taha was publicly executed in Khartoum on the grounds that he was an apostate and a heretic. Taha was the leader of a small radical modernizing movement in the Sudan, known as the

---

[1] *The Future of Shari'a Project* (2005a) Ch. 1, para. 15.

Republican Brothers (or Republicans), founded in the late 1940s during the struggle for independence. For the previous two years the Republicans had been peacefully protesting against human rights violations that resulted from President Ja'far Nimeiry's programme of Islamicization that had begun in 1983. Their protest had included bringing several unsuccessful suits in the courts alleging that the introduction of a traditionalist version of Islamic law (Shari'a) was unconstitutional because it involved discrimination against women and non-Muslims.

Taha and some of his followers had been interned in 1983. They were released about eighteen months later, but Taha and some others were re-arrested in January 1985. Apostasy was not then an offence under Sudanese law. Taha was originally charged and tried for offences under the Penal Code and the State Security Act. However, the appellate court, without any serious trial of the issue, or even a pretence of due process, convicted Taha of heresy and apostasy and sentenced him to death. The President swiftly confirmed the sentence, which was immediately carried out. This blatantly political and unlawful killing shocked many ordinary Sudanese, Northerners as well as Southerners who were opposed to Islamicization. It was without precedent and quite contrary to Sudanese ways of handling political disagreements. Instead of representing a great victory for Islam, as Nimeiry proclaimed, Taha's execution strengthened the opposition to his regime, which was overthrown in a peaceful revolution in April 1985, only three months after Taha's death. Human rights activists proclaimed Taha to be a martyr and established Arab Human Rights Day to commemorate the anniversary of his death.[2]

Among Taha's followers was Dr Abdullahi An-Na'im, who at the time was an Associate Professor of Law at the University of Khartoum. An-Na'im had joined the Republicans in the late 1960s when he was still a law student. After graduating from Khartoum in 1970, he went to England for postgraduate work, first in Cambridge and then in Edinburgh, where he obtained a doctorate in criminology in 1976. He returned to Sudan to teach and practise law and to resume his association with the Republicans. An-Na'im was one of Taha's most loyal followers and soon became a leading spokesman for his ideas. In 1983, with Taha and others, he was interned without charge for about eighteen months. They were released in late 1984, but Taha was arrested again, tried, and executed. Having unsuccessfully campaigned for Taha's reprieve An-Na'im left the Sudan in 1985, resolved to promote and develop the ideas of his master. He has remained in exile ever since (except recently for occasional visits), first holding some short-term appointments, including being Executive Director of Africa Watch from 1993–95. Since 1995 he has been a Professor of Law at Emory University at Atlanta. An-Na'im is now well-known, not only as Taha's most prominent follower, but also as a distinguished Islamic jurist and human rights activist in his own right.

An-Na'im has always been an activist as well as a scholar. He was involved in Taha's Islamic Reform Movement from the late 1960s. He has always

---

[2] Mayer (1994), p. 387.

emphasised the importance of implementation and enforcement of human rights. He has been active in many committees, non-governmental organizations as well as projects to promote human rights values at grass roots levels. All of his "advocacy for social change" is based on his two central ideas: a liberal modernist interpretation of Islam and the need to strengthen the cultural legitimacy and effectiveness of international human rights standards.

An-Na'im has published several books and over fifty articles. He has written about public law, family law, international law, constitutionalism, and many particular topics. His views on human rights need to be read in the context of his broader interests. His intellectual development is marked by several stages, but he has remained faithful to the basic methodology and conclusions of his teacher. He first promulgated Taha's own ideas in both Arabic and English. His first major book, *Toward an Islamic Reformation* (1990) built explicitly on Taha's ideas, but developed them in more detail in respect of political structure, criminal justice, civil liberties, human rights, and international law.

In the second stage he developed the thesis of "cultural legitimization".[3] He argues that human rights standards will only be plausible to a given constituency if members believe that they are sanctioned by their own cultural traditions. Legitimacy can mainly be attained by dialogue and struggle *internal* to that culture. Dialogue between cultures is also important in order to achieve an overlapping consensus on human rights and the necessary conditions for peaceful co-existence, but it is secondary.

In a third stage, culminating in his recent book, *Islam and the Secular State: Negotiating the Future of Shari'a* (2008), An-Na'im explores the relationship among Islam, state, and society. The objective "is to ensure the institutional separation of Islam and the state, despite the organic and unavoidable connection between Islam and politics".[4] It challenges "the dangerous illusion of an Islamic state that can enforce Shari'a principles through the coercive power of the state".[5] This work develops a number of themes: that human agency has been central to the development of Shari'a, and is necessary for its continuing interpretation and for motivation for social and cultural change; that whatever the state or other authority tries to enforce in the name of Shari'a is necessarily secular;[6] that the separation of Islam and the state does not involve relegation of Islam to the private domain, for it still has a role in the formation of public policy and

---

[3] Especially An-Na'im and Deng (1990), An-Na'im (1992) and (1993).

[4] An-Na'im (2005a) at Ch. 1; cf. An-Na'im (2008) at pp. 1–9.

[5] Ibid., Ch. 1. Cf. "The categorical repudiation of the dangerous illusion of an Islamic state to coercively enforce Shari'a principles is necessary for the practical ability of Muslims and other citizens to live in accordance with their religious and other beliefs." (ibid.)

[6] If, as is widely assumed, "secularism" implies hostility to religion or its decline or exclusion of all considerations drawn from belief in God, this is naturally opposed to an Islamic point of view. But, more narrowly interpreted as a principle for mediating between different religious beliefs through separation of religion and state, it is necessary for ensuring a stable basis for co-existence and co-operation in conditions of pluralism of beliefs (now almost universal) and for facilitating "the unity of diverse communities in one political community". See below pp. 91–8.

legislation; but this role needs to be performed through civic reason rather than coercion.[7]

The selection of readings in this chapter follows the stages of An-Na'im's intellectual development. First, Taha's views and method are explained and applied specifically to the subject of human rights. The second reading outlines his idea of "cultural legitimation" with particular reference to Islamic punishments. The third section briefly introduces his recent work on secularism and the future of Shari'a without the idea of an Islamic state.

An-Na'im's method, following Taha, is to contrast the Medina version of the Shari'a (and the Mecca texts that were intended to be universal) with "enlightened" international standards and his liberal theory of human rights. He is critical of the tendency for some to play down or be evasive about conflicts between the historical Shari'a and international human rights norms. For example, some governments in Muslim countries sign up to international human rights conventions, but do not abide by them; others enter vague reservations. Islamic Declarations of Human Rights are silent on key issues relating to the position of women, non-Muslims, and religious freedom.[8] An-Na'im criticizes the selective nature of many reforms of family law in Muslim countries.[9] Conversely, he argues that the Shari'a needs to be radically reformed because it is inconsistent with human rights standards, especially in respect of discrimination against women and non-Muslims,[10] freedom of religion, and slavery.[11]

---

[7] Ibid. "[B]y civic reason I mean that the rationale and the purpose of public policy or legislation must be based on the sort of reasoning that the generality of citizens can accept or reject. Citizens must be able to make counter-proposals through public debate without being open to charges about their religious piety." (An-Na'im (2008) at pp. 7–8. An-Na'im uses "civic reason" in order to distinguish his concept from Rawls' specific idea of "public reason" (discussed ibid. at pp. 97–101).)

[8] An-Na'im (2001). For forceful critiques of some Islamic Declarations see Mayer (1991/1999) and Bassam Tibi (in Lindblom and Vogt (1993)) at pp. 80–81. For a detailed analysis of the 1990 Cairo Declaration on Human Rights see Mayer (1994).

[9] See especially An-Na'im (2002). He also criticizes Dr Hassan al Turabi, the leader of the Islamic National Front in Sudan, for being vague and evasive on the status and role of women, while claiming that Islam treats all believers equally (An-Na'im (1990) pp. 39–42). Some are more candid: for example, Sultanhussein Tabandeh indicates clear inconsistencies between the Shari'a and the Universal Declaration of Human Rights in arguing that Muslims are not bound by the latter (Sultanhussein Tabandeh (1970) 171–2).

[10] An-Na'im is unequivocal about his own position on the treatment of women and non-Muslims. In a response to Susan Okin he stated: "I am not suggesting, of course, that either minority or majority should be allowed to practice gender discrimination, or violate some other human right, because they believe their culture mandates it. In particular, I emphasize that all women's rights advocates must continue to scrutinize and criticize gender discrimination anywhere in the world, and not only in Western societies. But this objective must be pursued in ways that foster the protection of all human rights, and with sensitivity and respect for the identity and dignity of all human beings everywhere." An-Na'im in Okin *et al.* (1999). On religious toleration see An-Na'im (1990) pp. 175–77, (2008) pp. 117–25 and below pp. 75–7.

[11] An-Na'im's treatment of slavery is a good example of his approach. See below pp. 67–9, 71–5. Recently, An-Na'im has emphasized a continuing role for a re-interpreted Shari'a: "Thus Shari'a does indeed have a most important future in Islamic societies and communities for its foundational role in the socialization of children, sanctification of social institutions and

An-Na'im's views are, not surprisingly, controversial in the Muslim world. In internal debates within Islam he is in danger of being dismissed as an extremist, as the disciple of Taha who was condemned as an apostate, and as an open subscriber to "Western liberal values". Clearly his overt challenges to a number of cherished beliefs may be felt to be shocking. However, his views are not as extreme as may appear at first sight. His account of history is close to that of many respected scholars. There is a long tradition of liberal interpretation within Islam.[12] All Muslim countries have accepted the form of the nation state, most with "modern" constitutions. Most of these states are signatories of the bulk of human rights conventions, with surprisingly few reservations. Many of the reforms that An-Na'im advocates have been adopted in several, sometimes most, Muslim countries, but in a more piecemeal fashion than he suggests. His special contribution is to provide a coherent religious justification for reforms that have been, or might be, made in the name of "modernization" or "secularization".

An-Na'im is controversial, but there is a danger that he could be perceived as the darling of Western liberals, a liberal Muslim who is importing "enlightened" ideas into Islam. But his message to non-Muslims is not so comfortable. First, participants in a debate need to be prepared to learn as well as to teach. There is much in the Islamic tradition from which Westerners can learn, for instance in relation to commercial morality and social welfare (*zakah*).[13] There is also the problem of ignorance. Before rushing to judgement non-Muslims need to try to understand the internal logic of views that may seem strange or abhorrent to them; they need to be aware of the ways in which such views are contested and debated within the culture of Islam; they should not exaggerate the gap between Islamic beliefs and the values embodied in international human rights norms at this stage in their history; and, above all, before labelling some practice as "barbaric" they need to consider how some of their own practices appear to members of other cultures. They also need to be aware of the extent of the leeways for interpretation within traditions such as that of Islam, as is vividly illustrated by recent scholarship on law reform in Malaysia and other predominantly Muslim countries.[14] Finally, An-Na'im does not feel a need

relationships, and the shaping and development of those fundamental values that can be translated into general legislation and public policy through democratic political process. But it does not have a future as a normative system to be enacted and enforced as such as public law and public policy" (2005) Ch. 1. See now An-Na'im (2008) Ch. 7.

[12] John Bowen has suggested that contemporary "liberal" or "modernizing" interpreters of Islamic law fall into three main groups: those who justify a liberal position by selective interpretation of the Qur'an itself; those who draw selectively on different schools and use *ijtihad* to justify contemporary interpretations based on the whole range of sources, the Qur'an, the *hadith*, and the received tradition of secondary Muslim Jurisprudence; and those, like An-Na'im, who emphasize the distinction between general principles and historically contingent precepts and treat the latter as non-binding. An-Na'im may seem radical to many orthodox Muslims because his and Taha's approach require treating large parts of the Qur'an, the *hadith*, and medieval learning as not being relevant to contemporary conditions (communication to author December 2008). See further, Bowen (2003).

[13] See Khurshid Ahmed (2003). On Islamic Banking, Siddiqi (1997). On *Zakah* see Abdelkader (2000).

[14] E.g. Horowitz (1994). An-Na'im (2008) contains extended discussions of attempts at law reform in Egypt, India, and Indonesia.

to be defensive about his religion. At the symposium in Belfast he emphasized that his concern goes beyond questions of compatibility with the existing regime to construct a coherent Islamic vision of human rights that can contribute to future developments at the global level.

READINGS

3.2 Context and methodology: the Second Message of Islam*
The main implications of the Second Message

For the benefit of readers who may not be familiar with Islamic history, the main relevant features of that history may be briefly stated here in order to put Ustadh Mahmoud's work in context. The Prophet Mohamed was born in Mecca, a town in western Arabia, around 570 A.D. At the age of forty he began receiving revelation, the Qur'an, which is believed by Muslims to be the literal and final word of God. For thirteen years the Prophet preached the faith to his own tribe, Qurysh, and other Arabs who used to frequent Mecca as a leading religious and commercial center at the time. Then, in the face of the growing hostility of Qurysh, culminating in a plot to kill the Prophet himself, in 622 A.D. Mohamed and his few followers migrated to Medina, another town in western Arabia. The Qur'an continued to be revealed for a total of twenty-three years, thirteen years in Mecca and ten years in Medina, up to the Prophet's death in 632 A.D. Throughout this period, the Prophet continued to explain and apply the Qur'an in response to the concrete needs of the growing Muslim community. The record of what the Prophet is believed to have said and done during that period was subsequently called *Sunnah*, the second source of Islam.[1]

The first Islamic state was established in Medina through an alliance between the migrants and their supporters in Medina, together with the Christian and Jewish tribes of the area. During that initial period, Christians and Jews, known as *Ahl al-Kitab*, People of the Book, were treated with tolerance and respect as equal partners in the charter which regulated their relationship with the Muslims.[2] Provided they submitted to the Prophet as ruler of the community, they were to enjoy protection of their persons and property and allowed to practice their religions. When the Jews violated that charter, according to Muslim historical records, the Prophet punished them and severely restricted

---

* From Abdullahi An-Na'im, Introduction to Mahmoud Mohamed Taha, *The Second Message of Islam* (1987) at pp. 19–24. Reproduced with permission of Syracuse University Press.
[1] As will be explained in the text of this book, Ustadh Mahmoud makes a distinction between two levels of *Sunnah*, one level pertaining to Shari'a as promulgated for use by the community at large, while the other level pertains to the Prophet's own superior standards of conduct.
[2] For a translation of this charter see M. Watt, *Islamic Political Thought* (Edinburgh: Edinburgh University Press, 1968), pp. 130–34.

their rights.[3] The growing popularity of Islam and the consequent strength of the Muslim state enabled the Prophet to march back into Mecca unopposed and consolidate his rule over most of Arabia before his death in 632 A.D.

Following the Prophet's death, his leading companion, Abu Bakr, was chosen, with some difficulty, as his successor. Differences as to who was entitled to succeed the Prophet as ruler of the Islamic state led to strife and civil war within a couple of decades, and they continue to divide Muslims to the present day. The Shi'a sect of modern-day Iran and other parts of the Muslim world derive their origins from the party which supported Ali, the Prophet's cousin and son-in-law, as leader of the Muslims.

Although the Qur'an itself was recorded during the reign of Osman, the third *Khalifa* or successor of the Prophet, the second source of Islam, the Sunnah, was not recorded until the second and third centuries of Islam. For the first few generations, Muslims accepted the moral and religious authority of the Prophet's companions, *sahabah*, and their successors, *tabi'in*, with their assumed knowledge of the oral traditions of the Prophet. With the recording of Sunnah and the development of *usul alfiqh*, the science of Islamic jurisprudence for deriving general principles and specific rules from the fundamental sources, the scene was set for the articulation and tabulation of the general principles and detailed rules of Shari'a. The leading surviving schools of orthodox Islamic jurisprudence were founded in the second and third centuries of Islam. Al-Tabari, who is generally recognized as the last founder of an independent school of Islamic jurisprudence, died in 923 A.D.

In this way, the law which came to be known as Shari'a was created through the interpretation by jurists of the fundamental sources of Islam, mainly the Qur'an and Sunnah, during the eighth and ninth centuries A.D. From the tenth century up to the present time, Muslim jurists have confined themselves to the study and elaboration of the work of those early masters. Even the intermediate reformers, such as Ibn Taymiya, who died in 1328 A.D., and the modern reformers of the last and present centuries, such as Mohamed Abdu and Jamal al-Din al-Afghany, have accepted the main principles set by the established orthodox schools of Islamic jurisprudence and complied with the acceptable processes of reform as determined by the early jurists.

Without going into the theological arguments which are the subject of [his] book, the main thesis of Ustadh Mahmoud regarding the evolution of Islamic law may be summarized as follows. Islam, being the final and universal religion according to Muslim belief, was offered first in tolerant and egalitarian terms in Mecca, where the Prophet preached equality and individual responsibility between all men and women without distinction on grounds of race, sex, or social origin. As that message was rejected in practice, and the Prophet and his

---

[3] This episode is discussed in, for example, B. Lewis, *The Arabs in History* (New York: Harper and Row, 1960), p. 40ff., and F. Gabrielli, *Muhammad and the Conquest of Islam* trans. by V. Luting and R. Linell (New York: World University Library, McGraw-Hill Co., 1968), pp. 64–80.

few followers were persecuted and forced to migrate to Medina, some aspects of the message changed in response to the socioeconomic and political realities of the time. Migration to Medina *(hijrah)* was not merely a tactical step, but also signified a shift in the content of the message itself. The difference is clearly shown in close examination and comparison of the Qur'anic texts and Sunnah dating from the Mecca stage and those following the migration to Medina. Texts from both periods are contained in the fundamental sources of Islam, namely the Qur'an and Sunnah; the difference is in the level of the audience being addressed and the society and particular class of texts was supposed to regulate.

Historical Islamic Shari'a law as known to the Muslims today was based on texts of the second stage. In the Medina stage God was responding, through the Prophet in the Qur'an and Sunnah, to the potential and actual needs of human society at that stage of its development. To that end, some aspects of the earlier level of revelation and Sunnah were subjected to repeal or abrogation (*naskh*) from the legal point of view, although they remained operative at a moral/persuasive level. This much is readily accepted by most Muslims, although some may object to the candid language in which these developments were discussed by Ustadh Mahmoud. What is revolutionary in his thinking, however, is the notion that the abrogation process (*naskh*) was in fact a postponement and not final and conclusive repeal. Once this basic premise is conceded, a whole new era of Islamic jurisprudence can begin, one that allows for the development of complete liberty and equality for all human beings, regardless of sex, religion, or faith. As it stands now, historical Islamic Shari'a law does in fact discriminate on grounds of sex and religion.

Under historical Shari'a rules of personal status, for example, a man has the right to marry up to four wives and the right to divorce any of them at will. There is no need for him to comply with any procedural or substantive requirements, or even to reveal his reasons. In contrast, a woman can only obtain a divorce by judicial decree within very strict and limited causes for divorce. Furthermore, women under Shari'a law suffer a variety of civil limitations, such as disqualification from holding certain types of public office and from testifying in certain types of judicial proceedings, even when their own rights are at issue.

Religious discrimination under historical Shari'a law derives from the fact that Shari'a classifies people in terms of their religious beliefs and apportions civil and political rights accordingly.[4] Muslims, at one end of the scale, enjoy the full range of rights accorded to a citizen by Shari'a. An unbeliever, at the other end, has no rights whatsoever, except under temporary license or safe-conduct (*aman*). Non-Muslim believers, mainly Christians and Jews, may be offered a

---

[4] See generally, Majid Khadduri, *War and Peace in the Law of Islam* (Johns Hopkins University Press, (1955)), chapters 14 and 17 and H. A. R. Gibb and J. H. Kramers, eds., Shorter *Encyclopedia of Islam* (Leiden: E. J. Brill, (1953)), pp. 16–17, 75–76, 91–92, 205–206 and 542–544.

compact of *dhimma*, whereby they enjoy security of person and property, and a degree of communal autonomy in matters of personal status, in exchange for payment of a special personal tax (*jiziah*). A person who is "tolerated" within a Muslim state under a compact of *dhimma* also suffers a variety of civil disqualifications in relation to competence to hold public office or testify in judicial proceedings. The fact that Shari'a does not treat women and non-Muslims equally with male Muslims is beyond dispute. Beside seeking to justify such discrimination in apologetic terms,[5] modern Muslim scholars claim that some of the objectionable rules may now be reformed by reviving the techniques of creative juristic reasoning (*ijtihad*). None of these scholars, however, claims that such reform can possibly remove all discrimination against women and non-Muslims, because *ijtihad* itself has its limitations. In particular, *ijtihad* is not permitted in any matter governed by an explicit and definite text of the Qur'an or Sunnah.[6] It therefore follows that any discriminatory rule that is based on an explicit and definite text – and some of the most obviously discriminatory rules are in fact based on such texts of Qur'an or Sunnah – is not open to reform through *ijtihad* or any other technique known to historical Shari'a.

This presents the modern Muslim with a real and serious dilemma: either implement historical Shari'a with its discrimination against women and non-Muslims, or discard Shari'a in public life and seek to establish a secular state. Both options are untenable in the modern Muslim world. The realities of domestic and international relations make implementation of the first option impracticable, while the religious obligation of Muslims to conduct every aspect of their public as well as private life in accordance with Islamic teachings would not permit the second.[7] The only way out of this dilemma, argued Ustadh Mahmoud, is to evolve Islamic law to a fresh plane rather than waste time in piecemeal reform that will never achieve the moral and political objective of removing all discrimination against women and non-Muslims in Islamic law.

Starting with the premise explained and substantiated in … *The Second Message of Islam*, namely, that historical Shari'a is not the whole of Islam but merely the level of Islamic law that suited the previous stage of human development, Ustadh Mahmoud proposed to shift certain aspects of Islamic law from their foundation in one class of texts of the Qur'an and Sunnah and place them

---

[5] The term "Muslim apologetics" was coined by Professor W.C. Smith. (See his book, *Islam in Modern History* [Princeton University Press, (1967)].) For critical review of these reform efforts see also H.A.R. Gibb, *Modern Trends In Islam* (Chicago University Press, 1947) and Malcolm Kerr, *Islamic Reform* (University of California Press, (1966)).

[6] The Sunnah which provides authority for the exercise of *ijtihad*, the Prophet's instruction to Ma'adh ibn Jabal when he appointed him governor of Yemen, describes *ijtihad* as a last resort, to be exercised only when no explicit and definite ruling can be found in the Qur'an or Sunnah.

[7] On this religious obligation, see, for example, Qur'an chapter 4 verse 59 and chapter 33 verse 36. 8.

on a different class of texts of the Qur'an and Sunnah. The limitations of reform noted above are removed by reviving the earlier texts, which were never made legally binding in the past, and making them the basis of modern Islamic law. Explicit and definite texts of the Qur'an and Sunnah that were the basis of discrimination against women and non-Muslims under historical Shari'a are set aside as having served their transitional purpose. Other texts of the Qur'an and Sunnah are made legally binding in order to achieve full equality for all human beings, regardless of sex or religion. This shift is made possible through examining the rationale of abrogation (*naskh*) in the sense of selecting which texts of the Qur'an and Sunnah are to be made legally binding, as opposed to being merely morally persuasive.

In *The Second Message of Islam*, Ustadh Mahmoud explained his main thesis for the evolution of modern Islamic law. In other writings and throughout his life, he articulated and developed this fundamental principle, which provides the ideological basis for his position on a wide range of social or political issues. The principle of the evolution of Islamic Shari'a law, as the Arabic term may be translated, was not Ustadh Mahmoud's only contribution. More fundamental to his work, in my view, is his essentially religious view of the universe and the role of humans in the cosmic order of things ...

3.3 Shari'a and basic human rights concerns*

... As used in this chapter, the term *human rights* refers to those rights recognized by and promoted through international law and institutions. Thus, although fundamental constitutional rights and international human rights are both concerned with the same type of claim or entitlement, the former deals with these claims and/or entitlements in the context of a domestic legal system while the latter deals with them in the context of the international legal system.

In accordance with the fundamental purpose of this book – to enable Muslims to exercise their right to self-determination without violating the rights of others to the same – this chapter will attempt to identify areas of conflict between Shari'a and universal standards of human rights and seek a reconciliation and positive relationship between the two systems. The hypothesis of this chapter ... is that if they implement historical Shari'a, Muslims cannot exercise their right to self-determination without violating the rights of others. It is possible, however, to achieve a balance within the framework of Islam as a whole by developing appropriate principles of modern Islamic public law.

Stating the objectives of the chapter in this way raises the initial question of the relevance of so-called universal human rights to Shari'a, or for that matter to

---

* From Abdullahi An-Na'im, *Toward an Islamic Reformation* (1990) Ch. 7 (pp. 161–77, 179–81), reproduced with kind permission of Syracuse University Press.

Islam itself. Why should universal human rights be a criterion for judging Shari'a and an objective of modern Islamic public law?

Universality of human rights

Article 1.3 of the Charter of the United Nations … imposes on all members of the United Nations the obligation to cooperate in promoting and encouraging respect for human rights and fundamental freedoms for all without distinction as to race, sex (gender), language, or religion. But the charter did not define the terms *human rights* and *fundamental freedoms*. That task was undertaken by the United Nations in a series of declarations, conventions, and covenants drafted and adopted since 1948.[1] The U.N. human rights documents and regional documents of Europe, the Americas, and Africa[2] all have the same premise – that there shall be universal standards of human rights which must be observed by all countries of the world, or countries of the region in the case of regional documents.

There is some debate as to the genuine universality of some of these standards,[3] and there are some serious problems of enforcement. This does not mean, however, that there are no universal and binding standards or that enforcement efforts should be abandoned. The position adopted here is that there are certain universal standards of human rights which are binding under international law and that every effort should be made to enforce them in practice. Thus the principle of respect for and protection of human rights has been described as *jus cogens*, that is, such a fundamental principle of international law that states may not repudiate by their agreement.[4] This would, of course, be true of respect for and protection of human rights in principle. It is easier to give examples of human rights of this stature, such as the prohibition of genocide and slavery, than to define the concept in a categorical fashion. Nevertheless, such a definition, or at least a criterion by which human rights may be identified, will be attempted below.

[1] See generally *United Nations Action in the Field of Human Rights*, U.N. Doc. ST/HR/2/Rev.1, U.N. sales no. E.79.XIV.6 (1980); and B.G. Ramcharan, ed., *Human Rights Thirty Years after the Universal Declaration of Human Rights* (The Hague: Martinus Nijhoff, 1979).

[2] These are the European Convention for the Protection of Human Rights and Fundamental Freedoms of 1950, the American Convention on Human Rights of 1969, and the African Charter on Human and Peoples' Rights of 1981.

[3] See, for example, Jack Donnelly, "Human Rights and Human Dignity: An Analytic Critique of Non-Western Conceptions of Human Rights," *American Political Science Review* 76 (June 1982): 303; and Rhoda Howard and Jack Donnelly, "Human Dignity, Human Rights and Political Regimes," *American Political Science Review* 80 (September 1986): 801.

For a survey of the main problems and theories in justification and support of universal standards of human rights, see Jerome J. Shestack "The Jurisprudence of Human Rights," in Theodore Meron, *Human Rights in International Law: Legal and Policy Issues* (Oxford: Clarendon Press, 1985), p. 69.

[4] Warwick McKean, *Equality and Discrimination under International Law* (Oxford: Clarendon Press, 1983), pp. 280–81.

The main difficulty with working to establish universal standards across cultural, and particularly religious, boundaries is that each tradition has its own internal frame of reference because each tradition derives the validity of its precepts and norms from its own sources. If a cultural, especially religious, tradition relates to other traditions at all, it is likely to do so in a negative and perhaps even hostile way. To claim the loyalty and conformity of its members, a cultural or religious tradition would normally assert its own superiority over other traditions.[5]

Nevertheless, there is a common normative principle shared by all the major cultural traditions which, if construed in an enlightened manner, is capable of sustaining universal standards of human rights. That is the principle that one should treat other people as he or she wishes to be treated by them. This golden rule, … the principle of reciprocity, is shared by all the major religious traditions of the world. Moreover, the moral and logical force of this simple proposition can easily be appreciated by all human beings of whatever cultural tradition or philosophical persuasion.

It is not easy to place oneself in the exact position of another person, especially if that other person is of a different gender or religious belief.[6] The purpose of the principle of reciprocity, as applied to the present argument, is that one should try to achieve the closest possible approximation to placing oneself in the position of the other person. Assuming that one is in the exact position of the other person in all material respects, including gender and religious belief or other convictions, what basic human rights would one demand?

It should be emphasized that reciprocity is mutual so that when one identifies with another person, one would ascribe equivalent reciprocity to the belief system of the other person. Thus, when person X accepts the status or belief of person Y for the purposes of conceding Y's right to the same treatment which X would demand for himself, X would assume that Y accepts the same principle of reciprocity toward X by conceding to X the same rights he would demand for himself. In other words, X should not be entitled to deny Y's rights on the grounds that Y is unlikely to afford X the same rights because Y's belief system does not impose that obligation upon Y. If Y's belief system in fact fails to accord X the same rights, the answer would be for X to insist on reciprocity from Y rather than abdicate his obligation to afford Y the same rights he would claim for himself.

The problem with using the principle of reciprocity in this context is the tendency of cultural, and particularly religious, traditions to restrict the application of the principle to other members of its cultural or religious

---

[5] Official spokesmen of the Islamic Republic of Iran have voiced their belief that they are bound by Islamic law and not international human rights standards. See a collection of these statements in Edward Mortimer, "Islam and Human Rights," *Index on Censorship* 12, no. 5 (1983), pp. 5–6.

[6] The same would be true of other differences such as race or ethnicity, language, and so on. But because Shari'a does not sanction discrimination on any other grounds except gender and religion, this chapter will focus on these two grounds of discrimination.

tradition, if not to a certain group within the given tradition.[7] The historical conception of the principle of reciprocity under Shari'a did not apply to women and non-Muslims to the same extent that it applied to Muslim men.[8] In other words, by granting women and non-Muslims a lower status and sanctioning discriminatory treatment against them, Shari'a denies women and non-Muslims the same degree of honor and human dignity it guarantees to Muslim men.

This general problem will have to be addressed within each cultural tradition. In the case of Islam, for example, one must be able to establish a technique for reinterpreting the basic sources, the Qur'an and Sunna, in a way that would enable us to remove the basis of discrimination against women and non-Muslims* … In the remainder of this chapter, I hope to explain the inadequacy of Shari'a as a basis for human rights in the Muslim context and propose an alternative Islamic foundation for universal human rights.

Without going into the details of arguments that may be too closely identified with a particular cultural tradition,[9] one can make the following basic trans-cultural justification for universal standards of human rights. The criteria I would adopt for identifying universal human rights is that they are rights to which human beings are entitled by virtue of being human. In other words, universal standards of human rights are, by definition, appreciated by a wide variety of cultural traditions because they pertain to the inherent dignity and well-being of every human being, regardless of race, gender, language, or religion.[10] It follows that the practical test by which these rights should be identified is whether the right in question is claimed by the particular cultural

---

[7] In the context of the modern nation-state, this tendency is reflected in general intolerance of minorities, whether religious or otherwise. Thus it has been said that "the ideals of national unity manifested by a central concentration of power; by a common language, culture and religion; and by economic and geographical limits, all so fundamental to the self-identification of the new states, tended also to express themselves in intolerant and repressive attitudes toward those who were perceived or perceived themselves as 'others.'" (Patrick Thornberry, "Is There a Phoenix in the Ashes? International Law and Minority Rights," *Texas International Law Journal* 15 [Summer 1980]: 421).

[8] Although this is the unavoidable conclusion of the briefest survey of the relevant principles and rules of Shari'a, it is rarely admitted by contemporary Muslim writers on the subject.

One of the rare exceptions in modern Muslim writings is Sultanhussein Tabandeh, *A Muslim Commentary on the Universal Declaration of Human Rights* (London: F.T. Goulding and Co., 1970), pp. 17–20 and passim, where the author states clearly and defends the exclusion of women and non-Muslims from the full range of human rights under Shari'a.

* See below pp. 75–7, 94–5. The technique is illustrated in detail with regard to constitutionalism, criminal justice, and international relations in Chapter 3 of *Toward an Islamic Reformation* (not included here (ed.)).

[9] For example, the theories surveyed by Shestack, "Jurisprudence of Human Rights," pp. 85ff., appear to be primarily based on the Western tradition. In fact, the available literature on the philosophical notions of "rights" and "universal human rights," reviewed in ibid., pp. 70–85, is not very useful for our purposes because it is primarily based on Western cultural tradition.

[10] Oscar Schachter, in his editorial comment "Human Dignity as a Normative Concept," *American Journal of International Law* 77 (1983): 853, has suggested that it may be philosophically significant to derive human rights from the inherent dignity of human beings. But as Schachter himself has shown the term *human dignity* has its own definitional problems.

tradition for its own members. Applying the principle of reciprocity among all human beings rather than just among the members of a particular group, I would argue that universal human rights are those which a cultural tradition would claim for its own members and must therefore concede to members of other traditions if it is to expect reciprocal treatment from those others.

In content and substance, I submit that universal human rights are based on the two primary forces that motivate all human behavior, the will to live and the will to be free.[11] Through the will to live, human beings have always striven to secure their food, shelter, health, and all other means for the preservation of life. Moreover, people have always striven to improve the quality of their lives through the development and manipulation of available physical resources and through political struggle to achieve the fair and equitable distribution of wealth and power among the members of the particular community. At one level, the will to be free overlaps with the will to live, in that it is the will to be free from physical constraints and to be secure in food, shelter, health, and other necessities of a good life. At another level, the will to be free exceeds the will to live in that it is the driving force behind the pursuit of spiritual, moral, and artistic well-being and excellence.

The right to seek the satisfaction of the legitimate claims of these two forces is granted by every cultural tradition to its own members and must therefore, in accordance with the principle of reciprocity, be granted to the members of other traditions. This is, in my view, the basis of the universality of certain minimum human rights. By applying this simple criterion, we can identify those rights, claims, and entitlements that ought to be protected as human rights even if they are not identified as such by any formal document.

Relevant standards of human rights

Our primary concern here is to establish cross-cultural foundations for the universality of human rights. Consequently, other major and important issues, such as the relationship between strategic goals and tactical means, the question of hierarchy and trade-offs between different sets of rights, and the legitimacy of permitting derogations from certain obligations in times of emergency are not discussed [here].

Being consistent with its own historical context, Shari'a restricted the application of the principle of reciprocity in relation to women and non-Muslims. … [T]he inadequacy of the public law of Shari'a can only be understood and supplemented through a consideration of the impact of the historical context within which Shari'a was constructed by the founding jurists of the eighth and ninth centuries out of the original sources of Islam. In that historical context, it was natural for the Muslim jurists to restrict the "other person" in

---

[11] Here I am adopting the analysis of Ustadh Mahmoud Mohamed Taha, *Second Message of Islam*, pp. 80ff.

the reciprocity rule to other Muslim men. This is a common feature of all historical cultural traditions and is also reflected in attitudes and policies of modern nation-states. It is for this aspect of the historical interpretation of the principle of reciprocity ... that this principle can sustain universal human rights "if it is construed in an enlightened manner." An enlightened construction would extend the "other person" to all human beings, regardless of gender, religion, race, or language.

If such an enlightened construction is to be effective in changing Muslim attitudes and policies, two conditions must be satisfied. First, the proposed broad construction of the other person has to be valid and credible from the Islamic point of view. This can be done only through Islamic arguments that repudiate the historical restrictive construction and support the alternative broader construction. Second, other cultural and religious traditions must undertake a similar process of enlightened construction. It seems to me that the historical restriction of the other person to male members of one's own culture was unavoidable when other cultural traditions practiced similar exclusion of women and nonmembers of the particular culture. It would therefore seem to follow that we need to overcome historical hostility and resentment through concurrent action, each working within his or her own cultural tradition toward the same goal.

In the following outline of the relevant universal human rights, it is useful to quote international custom and treaties that recognize these rights because they establish norms that are binding on Muslim states under international law. In quoting these documents, however, it is not suggested that the given rights are accepted as universal simply because they are recognized as such by the documents. Rather, the rights are recognized by the documents because they *are* universal human rights, that is, rights to which every human being is entitled by virtue of being human.

Slavery is one of the most serious impediments on both the will to live and the will to be free. Although it has been practiced by every major human civilization throughout history, slavery, in the sense of institutionalized and legal ownership of human beings as chattel, has finally come to be universally condemned and outlawed by both domestic and international law.[12] More effort is needed to eradicate all shades and forms of economic exploitation and degradation reminiscent of slavery. In the present context, however, we are concerned with slavery as a legal institution.

---

[12] Myres S. McDougal, Harold D. Lasswell, and Lung-chu Chen, *Human Rights and World Public Order* (New Haven: Yale University Press, 1980), pp. 473–508; and V. Nanda and C. Bassiouni, "Slavery and the Slave Trade: Steps towards Eradication," *Santa Clara Law Review* 12 (1972): 424.

Article 8 of the Supplementary Convention of the Abolition of Slavery, the Slave Trade, and Institutions and Practices Similar to Slavery of 1956 requires states party to the convention to communicate to the secretary general of the United Nations copies of any laws, regulations, and administrative measures enacted or put into effect to implement the provisions of this convention. This documentation is to be used by the Economic and Social Council of the United Nations as a basis for further Recommendations on this subject.

The abolition of slavery may well be the first example of the acceptance of an international human right as a limitation on domestic jurisdiction.[13] In other words, the antislavery movement established a precedent for recognizing the principle that the violation of a universal human right by one country is the legitimate concern of other countries.[14] As a result of this movement, a series of international agreements was concluded, culminating in one of the most widely ratified conventions condemning and prohibiting slavery under international law.[15] Moreover, several major international treaties have since reiterated the prohibition of slavery and required signatory states to outlaw and eliminate its practice in their domestic jurisdictions.[16]

Another early example of international cooperation in the field of human rights is the movement to eliminate the persecution of and discrimination against religious minorities.[17] Besides the moral abhorrence of such practices, persecution and discrimination on grounds of religion were perceived to be among the major causes of international conflict and war.[18] Consequently, a number of international treaties declared such persecution and discrimination a violation of human rights.[19]

A third area of emerging universal human rights, as defined above is the prohibition of discrimination on grounds of gender. Although this right did not receive international attention as early as the other two rights, it has now come to be recognized as a universal human right under a variety of international conventions.[20]

---

[13] McKean, *Equality and Discrimination under International Law*, pp. 116–21.

[14] Henkin et al., *International Law*, p. 982.

[15] The main current slavery convention was signed on September 25, 1926, and entered into force on March 9, 1927 (60 L.N.T.S. 253). More recent international treaties on the subject include the Supplementary Convention of the Abolition of Slavery, the Slave Trade and Institutions and Practices Similar to Slavery, which was signed on September 7, 1956, and entered into force on April 30, 1957 (18 T.I.A.S. No. 6418, 266 U.N.T.S. 3).

[16] See, for example, Article 5 of the African Charter on Human and Peoples' Rights and Article 8 of the International Covenant on Civil and Political Rights. This last article is exempt by Article 4 of the convention from derogation, that is, no state party to the convention may ever derogate from its obligation to prohibit slavery and the slave trade and servitude under any circumstances. Moreover, Articles 6 and 7 of the International Covenant on Economic, Social and Cultural Rights, providing for the right to work, render slavery obsolete.

[17] Arcot Krishnaswami, *Study of Discrimination in the Matter of Religious Rights and Practices* (New York: United Nations, 1960), pp. 11–12; and Francisco Capotorti, *Study of the Rights of Persons Belonging to Ethnic, Religious and Linguistic Minorities* (New York: United Nations, 1979), pp. 1–3.

[18] This was true among states professing different sects within the same religion as well as among those adhering to different religions. Thus various European peace treaties since the seventeenth century have provided for the protection of Protestants within Catholic territory and vice versa. See Thornberry, "Is There a Phoenix in the Ashes?" p. 426 and accompanying notes.

[19] See, for example, Articles 1.3 and 55(c) of the U.N. Charter, Article 2 of the African Charter, and Article 2 of the Civil and Political Rights Covenant.

   For a comprehensive survey and analysis of current treaty-based guarantees against such discrimination since the end of World War II see Capotorti, *Study of the Rights of Persons Belonging to Ethnic, Religious and Linguistic Minorities*, pp. 26–41.

[20] The principle of non-discrimination provided for in the articles cited in the previous note apply equally to discrimination on grounds of gender. Moreover, several specialized

The principle of nondiscrimination does not preclude all differential treatment on grounds such as race, gender, or religion. In this respect, I would agree
with the proposition that one has to judge the nature of differential treatment
in light of its purpose. "If the purpose or effect is to nullify or impair the
enjoyment of human rights on an equal footing, the practice is discriminatory."[21] In this way, one would accept action that has the purpose or effect of
enhancing rather than impairing the enjoyment of human rights on an equal
footing.[22] It is not necessary to go into these issues in detail in this context.
What is being affirmed here is that discrimination on grounds such as gender
and religion violates human rights.

[Section on "Problems of implementation and enforcement" omitted.]

Shari'a and human rights

During the formative stages of Shari'a (and for the next millennium at least)
there was no conception of universal human rights anywhere in the world.
Slavery was an established and lawful institution in many parts of the world
throughout this period. Until the nineteenth century, moreover, it was normal
throughout the world to determine a person's status and rights by his religion.
Similarly, up to the twentieth century, women were not normally recognized
as persons capable of exercising legal rights and capacities comparable to those
enjoyed by men. Full citizenship and its benefits were to be restricted to the
men of certain ethnic or racial groups within a particular polity in the same
way that status and its benefits were restricted by Shari'a to Muslim men. The
most that Shari'a could do, and did in fact do, in that historical context was to
modify and lighten the harsh consequences of slavery and discrimination on
grounds of religion or gender.[23]

Once again, to argue that Shari'a's restrictive view of human rights was
justified by the historical context and that it was an improvement on the
preexisting situation is not to say that this view is still justified. On the contrary,
my position is that since Shari'a's view of human rights was justified by the

---

conventions specifically apply to the rights of women, such as the Convention on the Political
Rights of Women of 1953 (193 U.N.T.S. 135). The most comprehensive of this class of
international treaties is the Convention on the Elimination of All Forms of Discrimination
against Women of 1979.

[21] Vernon Van Dyke, *Human Rights, Ethnicity and Discrimination* (Westport, Conn.: Greenwood
Press, 1985), p. 194.

[22] This differential treatment, known as affirmative action or positive discrimination, has its own
problems in practice. See, for example, Marc Galanter, *Competing Equalities* (Berkeley and Los
Angeles: University of California Press, 1984), for an explanation of these problems as they have
arisen through the recent application of this principle in the Indian context.

[23] As was explained in Chapter 4, the status of *dhimma* under Shari'a guaranteed non-Muslims
security of person and property and a degree of communal autonomy.
    Shari'a also recognized for women an independent legal personality, including the full capacity
to hold and dispose of property in their own right and certain minimum right in family law and
inheritance. See generally, Jane I. Smith, "Islam," in Arvind Sharama, ed., *Women in World
Religions* (Albany: State University of New York Press, 1987), p. 235.

historical context, it ceases to be so justified in the present drastically different context. By the same token that Shari'a as a practical legal system could not have disregarded the conception of human rights prevailing at the time it purported to apply in the seventh century, modern Islamic law cannot disregard the present conception of human rights if it is to be applied today.

In an early short piece, Khadduri said: "Human rights in Islam, as prescribed by the divine law [Shari'a] are the privilege only of persons of full legal capacity. A person with full legal capacity is a living human being of mature age, free, and of Moslem faith. It follows, accordingly, that non-Moslems and slaves who lived in the Islamic state were only partially protected by law or had no legal capacity at all."[24] While accepting this statement as a substantially accurate presentation of the position under Shari'a,[25] I would add the following qualification with respect to the status of Muslim women: although it is true that they have full legal capacity under Shari'a in relation to civil and commercial law matters, in the sense that they have the requisite legal personality to hold and dispose of property and otherwise acquire or lose civil liabilities in their own independent right, Muslim women do not enjoy human rights on an equal footing with Muslim men under Shari'a. Moreover, in accepting Khadduri's statement of the position under Shari'a, I would also reiterate my often-stated position that this aspect of Shari'a is not the final word of Islam on the subject. As I shall argue at the end of this chapter, an alternative formulation of Islamic public law which would eliminate these limitations on human rights is both desirable and possible.

When we consider writings by contemporary Muslim scholars, we find that most of the published expositions of human rights in Islam are not helpful because they overlook the problems of slavery and discrimination against women and non-Muslims.[26]

One of the better discussions of human rights in Islam, which shows sensitivity to gender discrimination, is that by Riffat Hassan entitled "On Human Rights and the Qur'anic Perspectives".[27] The problem with this article is that it is selective in its choice of the Qur'anic perspectives. In overlooking some relevant verses of the Qur'an, the author fails to confront those Qur'anic perspectives which are not consistent with her vision of the Qur'anic perspectives

---

[24] Majid Khadduri, "Human Rights in Islam," *Annals of the American Academy of Political and Social Science* 243 (1946): 79.

[25] In a recent substantially revised version of this paper Khadduri omitted the above-quoted statement. Though emphasizing the need for reform and compliance with current international standards of human rights, Khadduri's revived version does not dispute the accuracy of the statement from his 1946 paper. See Majid Khadduri, *The Islamic Conception of Justice* (Baltimore: Johns Hopkins University Press, 1984), p. 233.

[26] See, for example, Ali Abdel Wahid Wafi, "Human Rights in Islam," *Islamic Quarterly* 11 (1967): 64; Khalid M. Ishaque, "Human Rights in Islamic Law," *International Commission of Jurists Review* 12 (1974): 51; and Isma'il al-Fariqu, "Islam and Human Rights," *Islamic Quarterly* 27 (1983): 12.

[27] Riffat Hassan, "On Human Rights and the Qur'anic Perspectives," *Journal of Ecumenical Studies* 19 (1982): 51.

on human rights. As will be suggested at the end of this chapter, the only effective approach to achieve *sufficient* reform of Shari'a in relation to universal human rights is to cite sources in the Qur'an and Sunna which are inconsistent with universal human rights and explain them in historical context; while citing those sources which are supportive of human rights as the basis of the legally applicable principles and rules of Islamic law today.

In contrast to the generally evasive approach of the majority of Muslim writers on human rights issues, a few other Muslim writers have adopted a more honest and candid approach. A good example of this approach is Sultanhussein Tabandeh's *Muslim Commentary on the Universal Declaration of Human Rights*. This short book has the merit of clearly indicating the inconsistencies between Shari'a and the 1948 Universal Declaration of Human Rights in relation to the status of women and non-Muslims.[28] Tabandeh notes these inconsistencies to argue that Muslims are not bound by the Universal Declaration of Human Rights in these respects, whereas I am suggesting that it is Shari'a which should be revised, from an Islamic point of view, to provide for these universal human rights. I welcome the clear statement of the inconsistencies between Shari'a and universal human rights as part of my argument for Islamic law reform. It should be recalled, however, that the proposed reform must maintain its Islamic legitimacy if it is to be effective in changing Muslim attitudes and policies on these issues.

For our purposes here, we need not go into an exhaustive statement of all human rights because there are no fundamental problems with Shari'a except for slavery and discrimination on grounds of gender and religion. It is more to the point to focus on those human rights standards which are violated by Shari'a, the prohibition of slavery and discrimination on grounds of gender and religion.

Slavery

It is obvious that Shari'a did not introduce slavery, which was the norm throughout the world at the time. Shari'a recognized slavery as an institution but sought to restrict the sources of acquisition of slaves, to improve their condition, and to encourage their emancipation through a variety of religious and civil methods.[29] Nevertheless, slavery is lawful under Shari'a to the present day.[30] It is unlikely today that institutionalized slavery will be formally

---

[28] Tabandeh, *Muslim Commentary on the Universal Declaration of Human Rights*, pp. 18–20 and 35–45.

[29] Rahman, *Islam*, p. 38; and Khadduri, *War and Peace in the Law of Islam*, p. 130. For a comprehensive treatment of slavery in Shari'a and in history see R. Brunschwig, "'Abd" in *Encyclopedia of Islam*, new ed., 1:24–40. See also Reuben Levy, *The Social Structure of Islam* (Cambridge: Cambridge University Press, 1957), p. 73–85.

[30] Modernist arguments that slavery should have been abolished by Shari'a will be considered below.

sanctioned in any Muslim country.[31] If the right conditions under which slaves may be acquired should arise today and someone was made a slave under those conditions, Shari'a would protect the "rights" of both the master and the slave in the same way it did thirteen centuries ago. In this respect, one would appreciate the candid and honest statement of the situation under Shari'a by Tabandeh, who noted the absence of any possibility of finding confirmation of the legality of the enslavement of any person today, and then proceeded to say:

> Nonetheless, should the legal condition for the enslavement of anyone be proven (because he had been taken prisoner fighting against Islam with a view to its extirpation and persisted in invincible ignorance in his sacrilegious and infidel convictions, or because there did exist legal proof that all his ancestors without exception had been slaves descended from a person taken prisoner conducting a warfare of such invincible ignorance) Islam would be bound to recognize such slavery as legal, even though recommending the freeing of the person and if possible his conversion, in this modern age.[32]

In accepting this as an accurate statement of Shari'a, I am not accepting this aspect of Shari'a as the final and conclusive law of Islam. In this light, it would be lawful, from Shari'a's point of view, if slavery is reestablished in a modern Islamic state ... [H]owever, there is the possibility of replacing these dated and archaic aspects of Shari'a with modern and humane principles of Islamic law. Such an enlightened construction would prohibit slavery as a matter of *Islamic* law. Thus it is Shari'a and not Islam that "would be bound to recognize such slavery" under Tabandeh's statement.

To make an Islamic argument for the prohibition of slavery, we first need to know the circumstances under which slavery is permitted by Shari'a and its rules regarding the treatment and emancipation of slaves.

There is no verse in the Qur'an which directly sanctions the enslavement of any person, but many verses do so by implication when, for example, the Qur'an speaks of a Muslim's right to cohabit with his slave concubine, which clearly presupposes the existence of such slave women. The same can be said of Sunna on the subject.[33] The only way a person who is born free may be brought into slavery under Shari'a is through military defeat in a war sanctioned by Shari'a.[34] According to the founding jurists, subjecting the vanquished unbelievers to slavery is one of the options open to Muslims under Shari'a. Thus the Shafi'i school allowed the imam four options in dealing with prisoners of

---

[31] I am not concerned here with secret slavery and semislavery, which exist in many parts of the world.

[32] Tabandeh, *Muslim Commentary on the Universal Declaration of Human Rights*, p. 27.

[33] For reports of Sunna and other early traditions showing the free practice of slavery during the Prophet's time see Khadduri, *Islamic Law of Nations*, pp. 80ff.

[34] This, of course, does not cover the purchase of slaves, which is treated by Shari'a jurists as part of the law of sale. See Brunschwig, "'Abd".

war: immediate execution, enslavement, or release with or without ransom. The Maliki school restricted the options to execution, enslavement, or release with ransom, and the Hanafi school reduced them further to either execution or enslavement.[35]

Once a person is brought into slavery through military conquest or is born to slave parents, he or she remains a slave until emancipated. While a slave, he or she may be employed in whatever manner deemed fit by his or her master but must be treated with kindness and compassion as required by Shari'a.[36] That does not preclude the sale of slaves in principle, but it may place some limitations on the conditions under which the sale is concluded, such as a requirement not to separate a mother and child when they are sold as slaves.[37]

Shari'a encouraged the emancipation of slaves through a variety of methods. The emancipation of slaves is designated by verses 9:60 and 2:177 of the Qur'an as one of the prescribed items of expenditure of the official treasury or private charity. Moreover, the emancipation of a slave is prescribed by some verses of the Qur'an, such as verses 4:92 and 58:3, as religious penance and atonement for some sins, and recommended by others, such as verses 2:177 and 90:11–13, as a most meritorious act. Verse 24:33 of the Qur'an encourages a Muslim to grant the wish of a slave who wants to contract with the master for emancipation in exchange for the payment of a certain sum of money or performance of certain services.

Given the entrenched position of slavery throughout the world at the time, Islam had no choice but to recognize the institution of slavery in that historical context and do its best to improve the conditions under which slaves were to endure their unfortunate status. It can also be argued that Islam was aiming at the elimination of slavery by restricting its incidence and encouraging its termination. But since there was no internal mechanism by which slavery was to be rendered unlawful by Shari'a, it continued to be lawful under that system of law up to the present day.

Riffat Hassan quoted with approval the argument made by G. A. Parwez to the effect that since the Qur'an restricted the source of slavery to prisoners of war, and then prescribed in verse 47:4 that prisoners of war were to be set free either for ransom or as a favor, it follows that "the door for future slavery was thus closed by the Qur'an forever. Whatever happened in subsequent history was the responsibility of the Muslims and not of the Qur'an."[38] Similarly, it is

---

[35] Khadduri and Liebesny, *Law in the Middle East*, pp. 355–56. For a documented account of these options and differences of opinion among the jurists in matters of detail see Khadduri, *War and Peace in the Law of Islam*, pp. 26–30.

[36] For example, verse 4:36 of the Qur'an instructs Muslims to "do good" and to treat their parents, relatives, and orphans, slaves, and others well.

[37] Khadduri, *War and Peace in the Law of Islam*, pp. 131–32.

[38] Hassan, "Human Rights and the Qur'anic Perspectives," p. 59.

sometimes argued by modern Muslims that verse 47:4 of the Qur'an prohibits the enslavement of captives after a war with Muslims. The relevant part of this verse may be translated as follows: "When you meet the unbelievers [in battle], smite at their necks [kill them]. Once you have thoroughly subdued them, then [hold] and bind [them]. Thereafter [practice] either generosity [by freeing them without compensation] or [for] ransom, until war is terminated."

These arguments are, in my view, examples of selective citation of Shari'a sources leading to serious distortion and confusion. When we consider that both the Qur'an and Sunna did recognize and regulate slavery in a number of ways, that the Prophet himself and leading Companions had slaves, and that all the founding jurists of Shari'a took the existence of slavery for granted and elaborated rules for its regulation, we cannot dismiss the matter as the alleged failure of generations of Muslims to implement the intention of the Qur'an to abolish slavery. Despite the apparent limitation by verse 47:4 of the options open to Muslims over their captives, it is a historical fact that Muslim armies, during and after the Prophet's time, have continued to exercise the option to enslave their captives. Moreover, it should be emphasized that the founding jurists of Shari'a did not perceive this verse as excluding the option of enslavement of captives.[39] This verse may now be used in an argument for prohibiting enslavement as a matter of Islamic law, but this possible construction of the verse should not be confused with the position under Shari'a as it has been established by early Muslim practice and authoritatively stated by the founding jurists.

I believe that the early Muslims were correct in interpreting the Qur'an and Sunna as recognizing the institution of slavery *in the historical context* of early Islam. In the current historical context and with a new principle of interpretation such as the one proposed in the present study, the basic premise of the argument by modern Muslims against slavery may now be used to abolish slavery under Islamic law in an authoritative manner. Although those arguments cannot be accepted to alter the legal and historical fact that Shari'a recognized slavery, and continues to do so to the present day, they provide a very significant indication of the eagerness of modern Muslims to abolish slavery in Islamic law. Modern Muslims should welcome the evolutionary approach proposed by Ustadh Mahmoud Mohamed Taha. As applied to slavery, for example, that principle would conclude that though Shari'a implemented the transitional legislative intent to permit slavery, subject to certain limitations and safeguards, modern Islamic law should now implement the fundamental Islamic legislative intent to prohibit slavery forever.

When slavery was eventually abolished in modern Muslim states, in some cases as late as the 1960s and after, that result was achieved through secular

---

[39] In his explanation of this verse, Ibn Kathir does not mention any implication of prohibition of the enslavement option. Rather he quotes Shafi'i's statement of the four options open to the ruler over captives of war: execution, enslavement, or release with or without ransom.

law and not Shari'a.[40] Given the formal abolition of slavery in all Muslim countries, some may argue that it is no longer an issue. I disagree and believe that slavery is a fundamental human rights issue for Muslims until it is abolished in Islamic law.

In my view, it is utterly abhorrent and morally indefensible for Shari'a to continue to sanction slavery today, regardless of the prospects of its practice. Moreover, the fact that slavery is permissible under Shari'a does have serious practical consequences not only in perpetuating negative social attitudes toward former slaves and segments of the population that used to be a source of slaves but also in legitimizing forms of secret practices akin to slavery. In the Sudan, for example, images of slavery under Shari'a and Islamic literature continue to support negative stereotypes of Sudanese from the southern and western parts of the country, which were sources of slaves until the late nineteenth century. Moreover, recent news reports indicate that Muslim tribesmen of southwestern Sudan feel justified in capturing non-Muslims from southern Sudan and keeping them in secret slavery.

Discrimination on grounds of gender and religion

A similar analysis applies to discrimination against women and non-Muslims under Shari'a. Both types of discrimination were the norm at the time.[41] While accepting such discrimination in principle, Shari'a restricted its incidence and reduced its scope.[42] Nevertheless, when viewed in modern perspective, principles of Shari'a sanctioning serious and unacceptable discrimination on grounds of gender and religion are, in my view, untenable today.

According to Shari'a, non-Muslims may live within a Muslim state either under the status of *dhimma* for non-Muslim subjects or the status of *aman* (pledge of security or safe-conduct) for non-Muslim aliens.[43] ... [P]ersonal and private law matters for non-Muslims within an Islamic state were left to their own personal law and communal arrangements for administration. Should the matter involve a Muslim, Shari'a would apply.

---

[40] Slavery was abolished in Bahrain in 1937, Kuwait in 1947, and Quatar in 1952. See
      C. W. W. Greenidge, "Slavery in the Middle East," Middle Eastern Affairs (December 1956): 439.
[41] Levy, *Social Structure of Islam*, pp. 91–134 and passim, for comparisons between various aspects
      of the status of women before and during the early Islamic period.
[42] On the relative improvement in the status of women introduced by Shari'a see Sayed Ameer Ali,
      The Spirit of Islam (London: Christophers, 1922), pp. 222–57; Fazlur Rahman, "Status of Women
      in the Qur'an," in Guity Nashat, ed., *Women and Revolution in Iran* (Boulder, Colo.: Westview
      Press, 1983), p. 37; and Coulson, *History of Islamic Law*, pp. 14–15.
[43] On the acquisition of the status of *aman* and its consequences see Hamidullah, *Muslim Conduct
      of State*, pp. 201–2; Khadduri and Liebesny, *Law in the Middle East*, pp. 361–62; and Shihata,
      "Islamic Law and the World Community," pp. 108–9. Other examples of discrimination under
      the public law of Shari'a on grounds of religion were given in the chapters on constitutionalism
      and criminal justice (chapters 4 and 5) of *Toward an Islamic Reformation*.

Discriminatory Shari'a rules of personal and private law include the following:

- A Muslim man may marry a Christian or Jewish woman, but a Christian or Jewish man may not marry a Muslim woman.[44] Both Muslim men and women are precluded from marrying an unbeliever, that is, one who does not believe in one of the heavenly revealed scriptures.[45]
- Difference in religion is a total bar to inheritance. Thus a Muslim may neither inherit from nor leave inheritance to a non-Muslim.[46]

Examples of discrimination on grounds of gender in family and private law include the following:[47]

- A Muslim man may be married to up to four wives at the same time but a Muslim woman can only be married to one man at a time.[48]
- A Muslim man may divorce his wife, or any of his wives, by unilateral repudiation, *talaq*, without having to give any reasons or justify his action to any person or authority. In contrast, a Muslim woman can obtain divorce only by consent of the husband or by judicial decree for limited specific grounds such as the husband's inability or unwillingness to provide for his wife.[49]
- In inheritance, a Muslim woman receives less than the share of a Muslim man when both have equal degree of relationship to the deceased person.[50]

We are not concerned here with the historical justification of these instances of discrimination on grounds of religion or gender. Reasonable people may differ in their view of the historical sufficiency of any justifications that may be offered for any particular instance of discrimination. For example, it may be argued that economic and social conditions of seventh-century Arabia did not justify some or all of the discriminatory rules cited above. It is my submission, however, that regardless of differences over the historical sufficiency of justifications, these instances of discrimination against women and non-Muslims under Shari'a are no longer justified.

---

[44] Although this is the position of all major schools of Islamic jurisprudence, it is not based on direct Qur'anic prohibition of such marriages. Rather, it is based on the derivative argument that since verse 4:34 of the Qur'an entitles the husband to exercise authority over his wife while stating, as in verse 4:141, that a non-Muslim may never exercise authority over a Muslim, it follows that a man from the People of the Book, such as a Christian or Jew, may never marry a Muslim woman.

This reasoning will be repudiated at the end of this chapter through the application of the evolutionary principle of construction of Islamic sources.

[45] This was the construction given by the founding jurists to verses 2:21, 5:5, and 9:10 of the Qur'an.

[46] Schacht, *Introduction to Islamic Law*, p. 170.

[47] On the contrast between Shari'a view of the status and rights of women and that envisaged by Article 16 of the Universal Declaration of Human Rights see Tabandeh, *Muslim Commentary on the Universal Declaration of Human Rights*, pp. 35–67.

[48] Verse 4:2 of the Qur'an. See Coulson, *History of Islamic Law*, pp. 18–19.

[49] This is the construction given by the founding jurists to verses 2:226–32 of the Qur'an. Look under *talaq* in H.A.R. Gibb and H.H. Kramers, eds., *Shorter Encyclopedia of Islam* (Leiden: E.J. Brill, 1953), pp. 564–67.

[50] Verses 4:11 and 4:176 of the Qur'an.

It should be emphasized here that such unacceptable discrimination exists despite the modern reforms of personal law in several Muslim countries … [T]hese efforts cannot achieve the desired degree of reform because of the internal limitations of reform within the framework of historical Shari'a. Moreover, the limited benefits achieved through these modern reforms are constantly challenged and threatened by more fundamental principles of Shari'a which remain intact in the jurisprudence and legal practice of the countries that introduced those reforms.

In light of the preceding discussion, the following conclusions seem justified. First, in continuing to recognize slavery as a lawful institution, even if only in theory, Shari'a is in complete violation of a most fundamental and universal human right. It is very significant that slavery was abolished in the Muslim world through secular law and not Shari'a and that Shari'a does not object to the reinstitution of slavery under its own conditions regarding the source of slaves and conditions for their treatment. Although the vast majority of contemporary Muslims abhor slavery, it remains part of their religious law.

Second, discrimination on grounds of religion and gender under Shari'a also violates established universal human rights. Discrimination on grounds of religion has been found to be one of the major causes of international conflict and war because other countries that sympathize with the persecuted non-Muslim minority are likely to be prompted into acting in support of the victims of religious discrimination, thereby creating a situation of international conflict and possibly war. More important, it is my submission that discrimination on grounds of either gender or religion is morally repugnant and politically untenable today.

These are, in my view, the most serious points of conflict and tension between Shari'a and universal human rights as defined in the present study.

[Section on "Current Muslim ambivalence on human rights" omitted.]

Universal human rights in Islam

Once again … we come to the same conclusion. Unless the basis of modern Islamic law is shifted away from those texts of the Qur'an and Sunna of the Medina stage, which constituted the foundations of the construction of Shari'a, there is no way of avoiding drastic and serious violation of universal standards of human rights. There is no way to abolish slavery as a legal institution and no way to eliminate all forms and shades of discrimination against women and non-Muslims as long as we remain bound by the framework of Shari'a. … [T]he traditional techniques of reform within the framework of Shari'a are inadequate for achieving the *necessary* degree of reform. To achieve that degree of reform, we must be able to set aside clear and definite texts of the Qur'an and Sunna of the Medina stage as having served their transitional purpose and implement those texts of the Meccan stage which were previously inappropriate for practical application but are now the only way to proceed.

A similar approach is proposed for achieving the reconciliation of Islamic law with the full range of universal human rights identified through the criteria indicated earlier in this chapter. The key to the success of this part of the effort is to convince Muslims that the other person with whom they must identify and accept as their equal in human dignity and rights includes all other human beings, regardless of gender and religion. This would require an explanation of why the verses of antagonism which instructed Muslims to be *awliya*, friends and supporters, of each other and disassociate themselves from all non-Muslims, should not apply today. It would also require showing that verse 4:34 of the Qur'an, which establishes general male guardianship over women, and other verses which establish specific instances of discrimination against women, should not be implemented today.

In accordance with the logic of the evolutionary principle proposed by Ustadh Mahmoud Mohamed Taha, the texts of the Qur'an emphasizing exclusive Muslim solidarity were revealed during the Medina stage to provide the emerging Muslim community with psychological support in the face of the violent adversity of non-Muslims. In contrast to these verses, the fundamental and eternal message of Islam, as revealed in the Qur'an of the Mecca period, preached the solidarity of all humanity. In view of the vital need for peaceful coexistence in today's global human society, Muslims should emphasize the eternal message of universal solidarity of the Qur'an of the Mecca period rather than the exclusive Muslim solidarity of the transitional Medina message. Otherwise, Muslims would only provoke counter exclusive solidarity by non-Muslims, thereby repudiating the prospects for peaceful coexistence and cooperation in promoting and protecting universal human rights.

The application of this evolutionary principle of interpretation to specific instances of discrimination against women and non-Muslims can be illustrated by the rule of Shari'a prohibiting marriage between a Muslim woman and a non-Muslim man. This rule is based on the combined operation of the guardianship of the man, in this case the husband, over his wife, and that of a Muslim over a non-Muslim. Since a non-Muslim husband may not be the guardian of his Muslim wife, Shari'a prohibits such a marriage. If either form of guardianship, of a husband over his wife or of a Muslim over a non-Muslim, is repudiated, there would be no justification for prohibiting marriage between a Muslim woman and a non-Muslim man. The evolutionary principle of Ustadh Mahmoud would repudiate both types of guardianship.

The evolutionary principle will also repudiate another possible rationale of the prohibition of marriage between a Muslim woman and a non-Muslim man, namely the assumption that a wife is more susceptible to influence by her husband than vice versa. In other words, it appears to be assumed that if such a marriage is permitted, it is more likely that the non-Muslim husband will draw his Muslim wife away from Islam than that she will draw him to Islam. This rationale is, of course, part of the wider sociological phenomenon, namely, the lack of confidence in a woman's integrity and good judgment. Educational and other efforts are needed to repudiate this sociological phenomenon in all its manifestations. Besides its immediate practical impact, legal reform can also be an effective tool of education and leadership. This task can be begun by removing, through the application of the evolutionary principle of Ustadh Mahmoud, all aspects of the law which discriminate against women, thereby encouraging and sustaining a positive view of women.

3.4 Cultural legitimation: Towards a cross-cultural approach to defining international standards of human rights: The meaning of cruel, inhuman, or degrading treatment or punishment*

An intelligent strategy to protect and promote human rights must address the underlying causes of violations of these rights. These violations are caused by a wide and complex variety of factors and forces, including economic conditions, structural social factors, and political expediency. For the most part, however, human rights violations are due to human action or inaction – they occur because individual persons act or fail to act in certain ways. They can be the overlapping and interacting, intended or unintended, consequences of action. People may be driven by selfish motives of greed for wealth and power, or by a misguided perception of the public good. Even when motivated by selfish ends, human rights violators normally seek to rationalize their behavior as consistent with, or conducive to, some morally sanctioned purpose. Although their bid to gain or maintain public support may be purely cynical, such an attempt is unlikely unless they have reason to believe that their claim of moral sanction is plausible to their constituency.

It is not possible in this limited space to discuss the multitude of factors and forces that contribute to the underlying causes of human rights violations in general. I maintain that the lack or insufficiency of cultural legitimacy of human rights standards is one of the main underlying causes of violations of those standards. In this chapter, I argue that internal and cross-cultural legitimacy for human rights standards needs to be developed, while I advance some tentative ideas to implement this approach. The focus of my supporting examples will be the right not to be subjected to cruel, inhuman, or degrading treatment or punishment. Insiders may perceive certain types of punishment, for example, as dictated or at least sanctioned by the norms of a particular cultural tradition, whereas to outsiders to that culture, such measures constitute cruel, inhuman, or degrading treatment. Which position should be taken as setting the standards for this human right? How can the cooperation of the proponents of the counter-position be secured in implementing the chosen standards?

---

* Extracts from "Toward a Cross-Cultural Approach to Defining International Standards of Human Rights" from Abdullahi An-Na'im (ed.) (1992) *Human Rights in Cross-Cultural Perspectives: A Quest for Consensus* (pp. 19–21, 28–30, 32–43), reproduced by kind permission of the University of Pennsylvania Press.

My thesis does not assume that all individuals or groups within a society hold identical views on the meaning and implications of cultural values and norms, or that they would therefore share the same evaluation of the legitimacy of human rights standards. On the contrary, I assume and rely on the fact that there are either actual or potential differences in perceptions and interpretations of cultural values and norms. Dominant groups or classes within a society normally maintain perceptions and interpretations of cultural values and norms that are supportive of their own interests, proclaiming them to be the only valid view of that culture.

Dominated groups or classes may hold, or at least be open to, different perceptions and interpretations that are helpful to their struggle to achieve justice for themselves. This, however, is an *internal* struggle for control over the cultural sources and symbols of power within that society. Even though outsiders may sympathize with and wish to support the dominated and oppressed groups or classes, their claiming to know what is the valid view of the culture of that society will not accomplish this effectively. Such a claim would not help the groups the outsiders wish to support because it portrays them as agents of an alien culture, thereby frustrating their efforts to attain legitimacy for their view of the values and norms of their society.

Cross-cultural perspectives on human rights

The general thesis of my approach is that, since people are more likely to observe normative propositions if they believe them to be sanctioned by their own cultural traditions, observance of human rights standards can be improved through the enhancement of the cultural legitimacy of those standards.[1] The claim that all the existing human rights standards already enjoy universal cultural legitimacy may be weak from a historical point of view in the sense that many cultural traditions in the world have had little say in the formulation of those standards. Nevertheless, I believe not only that universal cultural legitimacy is necessary, but also that it is possible to develop it retrospectively in relation to fundamental human rights through enlightened interpretations of cultural norms.

Given the extreme cultural diversity of the world community, it can be argued that human rights should be founded on the existing least common denominator among these cultural traditions. On the other hand, restricting international human rights to those accepted by prevailing perceptions of the values and norms of the major cultural traditions of the world would not only limit these rights and reduce their scope, but also exclude extremely vital rights. Therefore, expanding the area and quality of agreement among the cultural

---

[1] See generally Abdullahi Ahmed An-Na'im, "Problems and Prospects of Universal Cultural Legitimacy for Human Rights," in *Human Rights in Africa: Cross-Cultural Perspectives*, ed. A. An-Na'im and F. Deng (Washington, D.C.: Brookings Institution, 1990), 331–67.

traditions of the world may be necessary to provide the foundation for the widest possible range and scope of human rights. I believe that this can be accomplished through the proposed approach to universal cultural legitimacy of human rights.

The cultural legitimacy thesis accepts the existing international standards while seeking to enhance their cultural legitimacy within the major traditions of the world through internal dialogue and struggle to establish enlightened perceptions and interpretations of cultural values and norms. Having achieved an adequate level of legitimacy *within* each tradition, through this internal stage, human rights scholars and advocates should work for *cross-cultural* legitimacy, so that peoples of diverse cultural traditions can agree on the meaning, scope, and methods of implementing these rights. Instead of being content with the existing least common denominator, I propose to broaden and deepen universal consensus on the formulation and implementation of human rights through internal reinterpretation of, and cross-cultural dialogue about, the meaning and implications of basic human values and norms ...

Alison Renteln is one of the few human rights scholars sensitive to issues of cultural legitimacy. She suggests a cross-cultural understanding that will shed light on a common core of acceptable rights.[2] Her approach seems to be content with the existing least common denominator, however, a standard I find inadequate to assure sufficient human rights throughout the world. In my view, a constructive element is needed to broaden and deepen cross-cultural consensus on a "common core of human rights." I believe that this can be accomplished through the internal discourse and cross-cultural dialogue advocated here.

Cultural relativity and human rights

Culture is defined in a variety of ways in different contexts.[3] A wide array of definitions is available in the social sciences.[4] In this chapter, culture is taken in its widest meaning – that of the "totality of values, institutions and forms of behavior transmitted within a society, as well as the material goods produced by man [and woman] ... this wide concept of culture covers *Weltanschauung* [world view], ideologies and cognitive behavior."[5] It can also be defined as

---

[2] Alison D. Renteln, "The Unanswered Challenge of Relativism and the Consequences for Human Rights," *Human Rights Quarterly* 7 (1985): 514–40; and "A Cross-Cultural Approach to Validating International Human Rights: The Case of Retribution Tied to Proportionality," in *Human Rights Theory and Measurements*, ed. D.L. Cingranelli (Basingstoke, Hampshire, and London: Macmillan, 1988), 7. See generally her recent book, *International Human Rights: Universalism Versus Relativism* (Newbury Park, Calif., London, and New Delhi: Sage Publications, 1990).

[3] See, for example, T.S. Eliot, *Notes Toward the Definition of Culture* (London: Faber and Faber, 1948); Raymond Williams, *Keywords: A Vocabulary of Culture and Society* (New York: Oxford University Press, 1976), 76–82.

[4] See generally, for example, A.L. Kroeber and C. Kluckhohn, eds., *Culture: A Critical Review of Concepts and Definitions* (New York: Vintage Books, 1963).

[5] Roy Preiswerk, "The Place of Intercultural Relations in the Study of International Relations," *The Year Book of World Affairs* 32 (1978): 251.

"an historically transmitted pattern of meanings in symbols, a system of inherited conceptions expressed in symbolic form by means of which men [and women] communicate, perpetuate and develop their knowledge and attitudes towards life."[6]

Culture is therefore the source of the individual and communal world view: it provides both the individual and the community with the values and interests to be pursued in life, as well as the legitimate means for pursuing them. It stipulates the norms and values that contribute to people's perception of their self-interest and the goals and methods of individual and collective struggles for power within a society and between societies. As such, culture is a primary force in the socialization of individuals and a major determinant of the consciousness and experience of the community. The impact of culture on human behavior is often underestimated precisely because it is so powerful and deeply embedded in our self-identity and consciousness.

Our culture is so much a part of our personality that we normally take for granted that our behavior patterns and relationships to other persons and to society become the ideal norm. The subtlety of the impact of culture on personality and character may be explained by the analogy of the eye: we tend to take the world to be what our eyes convey to us without "seeing" the eye and appreciating its role.[7] In this case, the information conveyed by the eye is filtered and interpreted by the mind without the individual's conscious awareness of this fact. Culture influences, first, the way we see the world and, further, how we interpret and react to the information we receive.

This analogy may also explain our ethnocentricity, the tendency to regard one's own race or social group as the model of human experience. Ethnocentricity does not mean there is no conflict and tension between a person and his or her own culture, or between various classes and groups within a society. It rather incorporates such conflict and tension in the ideal model, leading us to perceive the conflict and tension we have within our own culture as part of the norm. For example, some feminists in one cultural tradition may assume that women in other cultures have (or ought to have) the same conflicts and tensions with their societies and are seeking (or ought to seek) the same answers.

A degree of ethnocentricity is unavoidable, indeed indispensable. It is the basis of our acceptance of the validity of the norms and institutions of our culture, an acceptance that ultimately is a matter of material and psychological survival.[8] Even the most radical "dissidents" rely on their culture for survival. In fact, their dissent itself is meaningful to them only as the antithesis of existing cultural norms and institutions. Rigid ethnocentricity, however, breeds intolerance and hostility to societies and persons that do not conform to our models and expectations. Whether operating as initial justification or as subsequent

---

[6] Clifford Geertz, *Interpretation of Culture* (New York: Basic Books, 1973), 89.
[7] I am grateful to Tore Lindholm for suggesting this useful analogy.
[8] Melville J. Herskovits, *Cultural Dynamics* (New York: Knopf, 1964), 54.

rationalization, the tendency to dehumanize "different" societies and persons underlies much of the exploitation and oppression of one society by another, or of other classes within a society by one class of persons in the same society.

The appreciation of our own ethnocentricity should lead us to respect the ethnocentricity of others. Enlightened ethnocentricity would therefore concede the right of others to be "different," whether as members of another society or as individuals within the same society. This perspective would uphold the equal human value and dignity of members of other societies and of dissidents within society. In sociological terms, this orientation is commonly known as cultural relativism, that is to say, the acknowledgment of equal validity of diverse patterns of life.[9] It stresses "the dignity inherent in every body of custom, and … the need for tolerance of conventions though they may differ from one's own."[10]

Cultural relativism has been charged with neutralizing moral judgment and thereby impairing action against injustice.[11] According to one author, "[It] has these objectionable consequences: namely, that by limiting critical assessment of human works it disarms us, dehumanizes us, leaves us unable to enter into communicative interaction; that is to say, unable to criticize cross-culturally, cross-sub-culturally; intimately, relativism leaves no room for criticism at all … behind relativism nihilism looms."[12] Some writers on human rights are suspicious of a cultural relativism that denies to individuals the moral right to make comparisons and to insist on universal standards of right and wrong.[13]

As John Ladd notes, however, relativism is identified with nihilism because it is defined by its opponents in absolute terms.[14] I tend to agree with Clifford Geertz that the relativism/antirelativism discourse in anthropology should be seen as an exchange of warnings rather than as an analytical debate. Whereas the relativists maintain that "the world being so full of a number of things, rushing to judgment is more than a mistake, it's a crime," the antirelativists are concerned "that if something isn't anchored everywhere nothing can be anchored anywhere."[15] I also agree with Geertz's conclusion:

> The objection to anti-relativism is not that it rejects an it's-all-how-you-look-at-it approach to knowledge or a when-in-Rome approach to morality, but that it imagines that they [these approaches] can only be defeated by placing morality

---

[9] See generally, Ruth Benedict, *Patterns of Culture* (Boston: Houghton Mitfflin, 1959) and Herskovits, *Cultural Dynamics*, chap. 4.

[10] Melville Herskovits, *Man and His Works* (New York: Knopf, 1950), 76.

[11] Elvin Hatch, *Culture and Morality: The Relativity of Values in Anthropology* (New York: Columbia University Press, 1983), 12.

[12] I.C. Jarvie, "Rationalism and Relativism," *British Journal of Sociology* 34 (1983): 46.

[13] Rhoda E. Howard and Jack Donnelly, "Introduction," in *International Handbook of Human Rights*, ed. R.E. Howard and J. Donnelly (Westport, Conn. Greenwood Press, 1988), 20.

[14] John Ladd, "The Poverty of Absolutism," *Acta Philosophica Pennica* (Helsinki) 34 (1982): 158, 161.

[15] Clifford Geertz, "Anti Anti-Relativism" (Distinguished lecture) *American Anthropologist* 86 (1984): 265.

beyond culture and knowledge beyond both. This ... is no longer possible. If we wanted home truths, we should have stayed at home.[16] ......

I would emphasize that, in this age of self-determination, sensitivity to cultural relativity is vital for the international protection and promotion of human rights. This point does not preclude cross-cultural moral judgment and action, but it prescribes the best ways of formulating and expressing judgment and of undertaking action. As Geertz states, morality and knowledge cannot be placed beyond culture. In intercultural relations, morality and knowledge cannot be the exclusive product of some cultures but not of others. The validity of cross-cultural moral judgment increases with the degree of universality of the values upon which it is based; further, the efficacy of action increases with the degree of the actor's sensitivity to the internal logic and frame of reference of other cultures.

... The object of internal discourse and cross-cultural dialogue is to agree on a body of beliefs to guide action in support of human rights in spite of disagreement on the justification of those beliefs. Jacques Maritain, a French philosopher, explained this idea more than forty years ago:

> To understand this, it is only necessary to make the appropriate distinction between the rational justifications involved in the spiritual dynamism of philosophic doctrine or religious faith [that is to say, in culture], and the practical conclusions which, although justified in different ways by different persons, are principles of action with a common ground of similarity for everyone. I am quite certain that my way of justifying belief in the rights of man and the ideal of liberty, equality and fraternity is the only way with a firm foundation in truth. This does not prevent me from being in agreement on these practical convictions with people who are certain that their way of justifying them, entirely different from mine or opposed to mine, in its theoretical dynamism, is equally the only way founded upon truth.[17]

Total agreement on the interpretation and application of those practical conclusions may not be possible, however, because disagreement about their justification will probably be reflected in the way they are interpreted and applied. We should therefore be realistic in our expectations and pursue the maximum possible degree of agreement at whatever level it can be achieved. This approach can be illustrated by the following case study of the meaning of the human right "not to be subjected to cruel, inhuman or degrading treatment or punishment."

Cruel, inhuman, or degrading treatment or punishment
Some international human rights instruments stipulate that "no one shall be subjected to torture or to cruel, inhuman or degrading treatment or punishment."[18]

---

[16] *Ibid.* at 276.

[17] J. Maritain, Introduction to UNESCO, *Human Rights: Comments and Interpretations* (1949) London: Allen Wingate at pp. 10–11.

[18] Article 5 of the Universal Declaration of Human Rights of 1948 and Article 7 of the International Covenant on Civil and Political Rights of 1966. The latter adds that "In particular, no one shall be subjected without his free consent to medical or scientific experimentation." For the texts of these

There is obvious overlap between the two main parts of this right, that is to say, between protection against torture and protection against inhuman or degrading treatment or punishment. For example, torture has been described as constituting "an aggravated and deliberate form of cruel, inhuman or degrading treatment or punishment."[19] Nevertheless, there are differences between the two parts of the right. According to the definition of torture adopted in United Nations instruments, it "does not include pain or suffering arising only from, inherent in or incidental to lawful sanctions."[20] As explained below, this qualification is not supposed to apply to the second part of the right. In other words, lawful sanctions can constitute "cruel, inhuman or degrading treatment or punishment."

The following discussion will focus on the meaning of the second part of the right, that is to say, the meaning of the right not to be subjected to cruel, inhuman or degrading treatment or punishment. In particular, I will address the question of how to identify the criteria by which lawful sanctions can be held to violate the prohibition of cruel, inhuman or degrading treatment or punishment. The case of the Islamic punishments will be used to illustrate the application of the cross-cultural perspective to this question.

The meaning of the clause in United Nations sources

Cruel or inhuman treatment or punishment is prohibited by regional instruments, such as the European Convention for the Protection of Human Rights and Fundamental Freedoms, as well as under the international system of the United Nations. While regional jurisprudence is applicable in the regional context, and may be persuasive in some other parts of the world, it may not be useful in all parts of the world. For example, the jurisprudence developed by the European Commission and Court of Human Rights under Article 3 of the European Convention would be directly applicable in defining this clause from a European point of view, and may be persuasive in North America. It may not be useful, however, when discussing non-Western perspectives on cruel, inhuman, or degrading treatment or punishment.

[Survey of interpretations based on UN sources omitted, pp 30–2.]

---

instruments see *Basic Documents on Human Rights*, ed. Ian Brownlie, 2nd ed. (Oxford: Clarendon Press, 1981), 21 and 128, respectively.

[19] Article 1.2 of the Declaration on the Protection of All Persons From Being Subjected to Torture and Other Cruel, Inhuman or Degrading Treatment or Punishment of 1975. United Nations General Assembly Resolution 3452 (XXX), 30 U.N. GAOR, Supp. (No. 34) 91, U.N. Doc. NIOO (1975).

[20] *Ibid.*, Article 1.1 and Article I of the Convention Against Torture and Other Cruel, Inhuman or Degrading Treatment or Punishment. United Nations General Assembly Resolution 3946 (1984). This convention came into force in June 1987. For the text of the convention, see *International Commission of Jurists Review* 39 (1987): 51.

It is interesting to note that whereas the 1975 Declaration requires such pain and suffering to be consistent with the United Nations Standard Minimum Rules for the Treatment of Prisoners, the 1984 Convention omitted this requirement. This was probably done in order to encourage countries that do not comply with the Minimum Rules for the Treatment of Prisoners to ratify the Convention.

Cross-cultural perspectives on the concept

Some predominantly Muslim countries, such as Afghanistan and Egypt, have already ratified the 1984 Convention; others may wish to do so in the future. The meaning of cruel, inhuman, or degrading treatment or punishment in Islamic cultures, however, may be significantly, if not radically, different from perceptions of the meaning of this clause in other parts of the world. ...[21]

Due to the religious nature of Shari'a, Muslim jurists did not distinguish among devotional, ethical, social, and legal aspects of the law, let alone among various types of legal norms. The equivalent of penal or criminal law would therefore have to be extracted from a wide range of primary sources. For the purposes of this discussion, Islamic criminal law may be briefly explained as follows.[22] Criminal offenses are classified into three main categories: *hudud, jinayat*, and *ta'zir. Hudud* are a very limited group of offenses which are strictly defined and punished by the express terms of the Qur'an and/or Sunna. These include *sariqa*, or theft, which is punishable by the amputation of the right hand, and *zina*, or fornication, which is punishable by whipping of one hundred lashes for an unmarried offender and stoning to death for a married offender. *Jinayat* are homicide and causing bodily harm, which are punishable by *qisas*, or exact retribution (an eye for an eye) or payment of monetary compensation. The term *ta'zir* means to reform and rectify. *Ta'zir* offenses are those created and punished by the ruler in exercising his power to protect private and public interests.

It is important to emphasize that the following discussion addresses this question in a purely theoretical sense and should not be taken to condone the application of these punishments by any government in the Muslim world today. The question being raised is: Are Muslims likely to accept the repudiation of these punishments as *a matter of Islamic law* on the ground that they are cruel, inhuman, or degrading? This question should not be confused with the very important but distinct issue of whether these punishments have been or are being applied legitimately and in accordance with all the general and specific requirements of Islamic law.

Islamic law requires the state to fulfill its obligation to secure social and economic justice and to ensure decent standards of living for all its citizens *before* it can enforce these punishments. The law also provides for very narrow definitions of these offenses, makes an extensive range of defenses against the charge available to the accused person, and requires strict standards of proof. Moreover, Islamic law demands total fairness and equality in law enforcement. In my view, the prerequisite conditions for the enforcement of these punishments are

---

[21] On the sources and development of Shari'a see generally, Abdullahi A. An-Na'im, *Toward an Islamic Reformation: Civil Liberties, Human Rights and International Law* (Syracuse: Syracuse University Press, 1990), chap. 2.

[22] For fuller explanations see, generally, *ibid.*, chapter 5; Mohamed S. El Awa, *Punishment in Islamic Law* (Indianapolis: American Trust Publications, 1982); and Safia M. Safwat, "Offenses and Penalties in Islamic Law," *Islamic Quarterly*, 26 (1982): 14–9.

extremely difficult to satisfy in practice and are certainly unlikely to materialize in any Muslim country in the foreseeable future. Nevertheless, the question remains, can these punishments be abolished as a matter of Islamic law?

Shari'a criminal law has been displaced by secular criminal law in most Muslim countries. Countries like Saudi Arabia, however, have always maintained Shari'a as their official criminal law. Other countries, such as Iran, Pakistan, and the Sudan, have recently reintroduced Shari'a criminal law. There is much controversy over many aspects of the criminal law of Shari'a that raise human rights concerns, including issues of religious discrimination in the application of Shari'a criminal law to non-Muslims.[23] To the vast majority of Muslims, however, Shari'a criminal law is binding and should be enforced today. Muslim political leaders and scholars may debate whether general social, economic, and political conditions are appropriate for the immediate application of Shari'a, or whether there should be a preparatory stage before the reintroduction of Shari'a where it has been displaced by secular law. None of them would dispute, at least openly and publicly, that the application of Shari'a criminal law should be a high priority, if not an immediate reality.

Although these are important matters, they should not be confused with what is being discussed here. For the sake of argument, the issue should be isolated from other possible sources of controversy. In particular, I wish to emphasize that I believe that the Qur'anic punishments should *not* apply to non-Muslims because they are essentially religious in nature. In the following discussion, I will use the example of amputation of the right hand for theft when committed by a Muslim who does not need to steal in order to survive, and who has been properly tried and convicted by a competent court of law. This punishment is prescribed by the clear and definite text of verse 38 in chapter 5 of the Qur'an. Can this punishment, when imposed under these circumstances, be condemned as cruel, inhuman, or degrading?

The basic question here is one of interpretation and application of a universally accepted human right. In terms of the principle Maritain suggests – agreement on "practical conclusions" in spite of disagreement on their justification – Muslims would accept the human right not to be subjected to cruel, inhuman, or degrading treatment or punishment. Their Islamic culture may indicate to them a different interpretation of this human right, however.

From a secular or humanist point of view, inflicting such a severe permanent punishment for any offense, especially for theft, is obviously cruel and inhuman, and probably also degrading. This may well be the private intuitive reaction of many educated modernized Muslims. However, to the vast majority of Muslims, the matter is settled by the categorical will of God as expressed in the Qur'an and, as such, is not open to question by human beings. Even the educated modernized Muslim, who may be privately repelled by this punishment, cannot risk the consequences of openly questioning the will of God. In

---

[23] An-Na'im, *supra* note 21, at 114–18 and 131–33.

addition to the danger of losing his or her faith and the probability of severe social chastisement, a Muslim who disputes the binding authority of the Qur'an is liable to the death penalty for apostasy (heresy) under Shari'a.

Thus, in all Muslim societies, the possibility of human judgment regarding the appropriateness or cruelty of a punishment decreed by God is simply out of the question. Furthermore, this belief is supported by what Muslims accept as rational arguments.[24] From the religious point of view, human life does not end at death, but extends beyond that to the next life. In fact, religious sources strongly emphasize that the next life is the true and ultimate reality, to which this life is merely a prelude. In the next *eternal* life, every human being will stand judgment and suffer the consequences of his or her actions in this life. A religiously sanctioned punishment, however, will absolve an offender from punishment in the next life because God does not punish twice for the same offense. Accordingly, a thief who suffers the religiously sanctioned punishment of amputation of the right hand in this life will not be liable to the much harsher punishment in the next life. To people who hold this belief, however severe the Qur'anic punishment may appear to be, it is in fact extremely lenient and merciful in comparison to what the offender will suffer in the next life should the religious punishment not be enforced in this life.

Other arguments are advanced about the benefits of this punishment to both the individual offender and society. It is said that this seemingly harsh punishment is in fact necessary to reform and rehabilitate the thief, as well as to safeguard the interests of other persons and of society at large, by deterring other potential offenders.[25] The ultimately *religious* rationale of these arguments must always be emphasized, however. The punishment is believed to achieve these individual and social benefits because God said so. To the vast majority of Muslims, scientific research is welcome to confirm the empirical validity of these arguments, but it cannot be accepted as a basis for repudiating them, thereby challenging the appropriateness of the punishment. Moreover, the religious frame of reference is also integral to evaluating empirical data. Reform of the offender is not confined to his or her experience in this life, but includes the next life, too.

Neither internal Islamic reinterpretation nor cross-cultural dialogue is likely to lead to the total abolition of this punishment as a matter of Islamic law. Much can be done, however, to restrict its implementation in practice. For example, there is room for developing stronger general social and economic prerequisites and stricter procedural requirements for the enforcement of the punishment. Islamic religious texts emphasize extreme caution in inflicting any criminal punishment. The Prophet said that if there is any doubt (*shubha*), the Qur'anic

---

[24] Rationality is also relative to the belief system *or* frame of reference. What may be accepted as rational to a believer may not be accepted as such by an unbeliever, and vice versa.

[25] Mahmoud Mohamed Taha, *The Second Message of Islam*, trans. Abdullahi A. An-Na'im (Syracuse: Syracuse University Press, 1987), 74–75.

punishments should not be imposed. He also said that it is better to err on the side of refraining from imposing the punishment than to err on the side of imposing it in a doubtful case. Although these directives have already been incorporated into definitions of the offenses and the applicable rules of evidence and procedure, it is still possible to develop a broader concept of *shubha* to include, for example, psychological disorders as a defense against criminal responsibility. For instance, kleptomania may be taken as *shubha* barring punishment for theft. Economic need may also be a defense against a charge of theft.

Cross-cultural dialogue may also be helpful in this regard. In the Jewish tradition, for instance, jurists have sought to restrict the practical application of equally harsh punishment by stipulating strict procedural and other requirements.[26] This theoretical Jewish jurisprudence may be useful to Muslim jurists and leaders seeking to restrict the practical application of Qur'anic punishments. It is difficult to assess its practical viability and impact, however, because it has not been applied for nearly two thousand years. Moreover, the current atmosphere of mutual Jewish-Muslim antagonism and mistrust does not make cross-cultural dialogue likely between these two traditions. Still, this has not always been the case in the past and need not be so in the future. In fact, the jurisprudence of each tradition has borrowed heavily from the other in the past and may do so in the future once the present conflict is resolved.

I believe that in the final analysis, the interpretation and practical application of the protection against cruel, inhuman, or degrading treatment or punishment in the context of a particular society should be determined by the moral standards of that society. I also believe that there are many legitimate ways of influencing and informing the moral standards of a society. To dictate to a society is both unacceptable as a matter of principle and unlikely to succeed in practice. Cross-cultural dialogue and mutual influence, however, is acceptable in principle and continuously occurring in practice. To harness the power of cultural legitimacy in support of human rights, we need to develop techniques for internal cultural discourse and cross-cultural dialogue, and to work toward establishing general conditions conducive to constructive discourse and dialogue.

It should be recalled that this approach assumes and relies on the existence of internal struggle for cultural power within society. Certain dominant classes or groups would normally hold the cultural advantage and proclaim their view of the culture as valid, while others would challenge this view, or at least wish to be able to do so. In relation to Islamic punishments, questions about the legitimate application of these punishments – whether the state has fulfilled its obligations first and is acting in accordance with the general and specific conditions referred to earlier are matters for internal struggle. This internal struggle cannot and should not be settled by outsiders; but they may support

---

[26] *Encyclopedia Judaica* (Jerusalem: Keter 1971), vol. 5, 14-2-4-7; vol. 6, 991–93.

one side or the other, provided they do so with sufficient sensitivity and due consideration for the legitimacy of the objectives and methods of the struggle within the framework of the particular culture.

Conclusion: toward a cross-cultural approach

I have deliberately chosen the question of whether lawful sanctions can be condemned as cruel, inhuman, or degrading punishment or treatment in order to illustrate both the need for a cross-cultural approach to defining human rights standards and the difficulty of implementing this approach. The question presents human rights advocates with a serious dilemma. On the one hand, it is necessary to safeguard the personal integrity and human dignity of the individual against excessive or harsh punishments. The fundamental objective of the modern human rights movement is to protect citizens from the brutality and excesses of their own governments. On the other hand, it is extremely important to be sensitive to the dangers of cultural imperialism, whether it is a product of colonialism, a tool of international economic exploitation and political subjugation, or simply a product of extreme ethnocentricity. Since we would not accept others' imposing their moral standards on us, we should not impose our own moral standards on them. In any case, external imposition is normally counterproductive and unlikely to succeed in changing the practice in question. External imposition is not the only option available to human rights advocates, however. Greater consensus on international standards for the protection of the individual against cruel, inhuman, or degrading treatment or punishment can be achieved through internal cultural discourse and cross-cultural dialogue.

It is unrealistic to expect this approach to achieve total agreement on the interpretation and application of standards, whether of treatment or punishment or any other human right. This expectation presupposes the existence of the interpretation to be agreed upon. If one reflects on the interpretation she or he would like to make the norm, it will probably be the one set by the person's culture. Further reflection on how one would feel about the interpretation set by another culture should illustrate the untenability of this position. For example, a North American may think that a short term of imprisonment is the appropriate punishment for theft, and wish that to be the universal punishment for this offense. A Muslim, on the other hand, may feel that the amputation of the hand is appropriate under certain conditions and after satisfying strict safeguards. It would be instructive for the North American to consider how she or he would feel if the Muslim punishment were made the norm. Most Western human rights advocates are likely to have a lingering feeling that there is simply no comparison between these two punishments because the Islamic punishment is "obviously" cruel and inhuman and should never compete with imprisonment as a possible punishment for this offense. A Muslim might respond by saying that this feeling is a product of Western ethnocentricity.

I am not suggesting that we should make the Islamic or any other particular punishment the universal norm. I merely wish to point out that agreeing on a universal standard may not be as simple as we may think, or wish it to be.

In accordance with the proposed approach, the standard itself should be the product of internal discourse and cross-cultural dialogue. Moreover, genuine total agreement requires equal commitment to internal discourse and equally effective participation in cross-cultural dialogue by the adherents or members of different cultural traditions of the world. In view of significant social and political differences and disparities in levels of economic development, some cultural traditions are unlikely to engage in internal discourse as much as other cultural traditions and are unable to participate in cross-cultural dialogue as effectively as others. These processes require a certain degree of political liberty, stability, and social maturity, as well as technological capabilities that are lacking in some parts of the world.

The cross-cultural approach, however, is not an all-or-nothing proposition. While total agreement on the standard and mechanisms for its implementation is unrealistic in some cases, significant agreement can be achieved and ought to be pursued as much as possible. For example, in relation to cruel, inhuman, or degrading treatment or punishment, there is room for agreement on a wide range of substantive and procedural matters even in relation to an apparently inflexible position, such as the Islamic position on Qur'anic punishments. Provided such agreement is sought with sufficient sensitivity, the general status of human rights will be improved, and wider agreement can be achieved in relation to other human rights. We must be clear, however, on what can be achieved and how to achieve it in any given case. An appreciation of the impossibility of the total abolition of the Qur'anic punishment for theft is necessary for restricting its practice in Muslim societies as well as for establishing common standards, for instance, in relation to punishments that are, from the Islamic point of view, the product of human legislation.

3.5 Islam and the secular state*

(a) Why Muslims need a secular state

In order to be a Muslim by conviction and free choice, which is the only way one can be a Muslim, I need a secular state. By a secular state I mean one that is neutral regarding religious doctrine, one that does not claim or pretend to enforce Shari'a – the religious law of Islam – simply because compliance with Shari'a cannot be coerced by fear of state institutions or faked to appease their officials. This is what I mean by secularism [in this book], namely, a secular state that facilitates the possibility of religious piety out of honest conviction. My call

* Extracts from *Islam and the Secular State: Negotiating the Future of Shari'a* (2008) pp. 1–5((a)), 109–11((b)), 269((c)), 270((d)), 271((e)), reproduced with kind permission of Harvard University Press.

for the state, and not society, to be secular is intended to enhance and promote genuine religious observance, to affirm, nurture, and regulate the role of Islam in the public life of the community. Conversely, I will argue that the claim of a so-called Islamic state to coercively enforce Shari'a repudiates the foundational role of Islam in the socialization of children and the sanctification of social institutions and relationships. When observed voluntarily, Shari'a plays a fundamental role in shaping and developing ethical norms and values that can be reflected in general legislation and public policy through the democratic political process. But I will argue in this book that Shari'a principles cannot be enacted and enforced by the state as public law and public policy solely on the grounds that they are believed to be part of Shari'a. If such enactment and enforcement is attempted, the outcome will necessarily be the political will of the state and not the religious law of Islam. The fact that ruling elites sometimes make such claims to legitimize their control of the state in the name of Islam does not mean that such claims are true.

The fact that the state is a political and not a religious institution is the historical experience and current reality of Islamic societies. From a theoretical point of view, Ali Abd al-Raziq, for instance, conclusively demonstrated the validity of this premise from a traditional Islamic perspective more than eighty years ago[1] (Abd al-Raziq 1925). In the 1930s, Rashid Ridda strongly affirmed in *al-Manar* that Shari'a cannot be codified as state law. My purpose ... is not only to support and substantiate this view, but also to contribute to securing its practical benefits for present and future Islamic societies. In particular, dispelling the dangerous illusion of an Islamic state that can enforce Shari'a is necessary for legitimizing and implementing the principles and institutions of constitutionalism, human rights, and citizenship in Islamic societies.

Since ... Shari'a principles by their nature and function defy any possibility of enforcement by the state, claiming to enforce Shari'a principles as state law is a logical contradiction that cannot be rectified through repeated efforts under any conditions. In other words, it is not simply a matter of improving upon a bad experience in any country, there or elsewhere, but an objective that can never be realized anywhere. Yet this does not mean the exclusion of Islam from the formulation of public policy and legislation or from public life in general. On the contrary, the state should not attempt to enforce Shari'a precisely so that Muslims are able to live by their own belief in Islam as a matter of religious obligation, not as the outcome of coercion by the state. ...

An initial issue in this regard is whether the success of my proposal is contingent on substantial reform in the way Muslims understand certain aspects of Shari'a ... [T]his reform is indeed necessary, and I believe that it can best be realized through the methodology proposed by Ustadh Mahmoud

---

[1] Ali Abd al-Raziq (1925) *al-islam wa-usul al hukm, bahth fi al-Khilaifah al hukumah fi al-Islam* {Islam and the Principles of Government} (Cairo: Matbaat Misr).

Mohamed Taha[2] (Taha 1987). This does not, of course, preclude the possibility of alternative approaches that are capable of achieving the necessary degree of reform. My primary concern [here] is to promote normative standards and institutional conditions for free and orderly public debate and contestation of various approaches to personal choices and responsibility for them. In this regard, the point to emphasize is that there are competing methodologies for the development of Shari'a, which will always remain the total obligation of Muslims to observe in their daily lives …

The premise of my proposal is that Muslims everywhere, whether minorities or majorities, are bound to observe Shari'a as a matter of religious obligation, and that this can best be achieved when the state is neutral regarding all religious doctrines and does not claim to enforce Shari'a principles as state policy or legislation. That is, people cannot truly live by their convictions according to their belief in and understanding of Islam if rulers use the extensive coercive powers of the state to impose their view of Shari'a on the population at large, Muslims and non-Muslims alike. This does not mean that the state can or should be completely neutral, because it is a political institution that is supposed to be influenced by the interests and concerns of its citizens. Indeed, legislation and public policy should reflect the beliefs and values of citizens, including religious values, provided this is not done in the name of any specific religion, since that would necessarily favor the views of those who control the state and exclude the religious and other beliefs of other citizens. While this proposition may at one level appear obviously valid to many Muslims, they may still be ambivalent about its clear implications because of the illusion that an Islamic state is supposed to enforce Shari'a. I am therefore concerned with challenging the core claim of an Islamic state as a postcolonial discourse that relies on European notions of the state and positive law. But I am equally concerned with mounting this challenge in ways that are persuasive to Muslims in particular.

… From this fundamental religious perspective, the state must not be allowed to claim the authority of implementing Shari'a as such. It is true that the state has its proper functions, which may include adjudication among competing claims of religious and secular institutions, but it should be seen as a politically neutral institution performing necessarily secular functions, without claiming religious authority as such. It is also true that the religious beliefs of Muslims, whether as officials of the state or as private citizens, always influence their actions and political behavior. But these are good reasons for keeping a clear distinction between Islam and the state while regulating the connectedness of Islam and politics … Islam is the religion of human beings who believe in it, while the state signifies the continuity of institutions like the judiciary and administrative agencies. This view is fundamentally Islamic, because it insists

[2] Mahmoud Mohamed Taha (1987) *The Second Message of Islam* Syracuse: Syracuse University Press.

on the religious neutrality of the state as a necessary condition for Muslims to comply with their religious obligations. Religious compliance must be completely voluntary according to personal pious intention (*niyah*), which is necessarily invalidated by coercive enforcement of those obligations. In fact, coercive enforcement promotes hypocrisy (*nifaq*), which is categorically and repeatedly condemned by the Qur'an.

The state is a complex web of organs, institutions, and processes that are supposed to implement the policies adopted through the political process of each society. In this sense, the state should be the more settled and deliberate operational side of self-governance, while politics serves as the dynamic process of making choices among competing policy options. To fulfill that and other functions, the state must have a monopoly on the legitimate use of force: the ability to impose its will on the population at large without risking the use of counterforce by those subject to its jurisdiction. This coercive power of the state, which is now more extensive and effective than ever before in human history, will be counterproductive when exercised in an arbitrary manner or for corrupt or illegitimate ends. That is why it is critically important to keep the state as neutral as humanly possible. The establishment of this neutrality requires constant vigilance by the generality of citizens acting through a wide variety of political, legal, educational, and other strategies and mechanisms.

(b) Islam, Shari'a, and constitutionalism: non-Muslims

… The Islamic reforms I am calling for are intended to encourage and support efforts to require complete equality for women and non-Muslims from a Shari'a point of view and not simply for political expediency. Such reforms will also contribute to the process of legitimizing the values of political participation, accountability, and equality before the law, thereby enhancing the prospects for constitutionalism in Islamic societies. To avoid confusion here, my point is that while the underlying moral and social norms of the Medina society remain the ideal for which all Muslims should always strive, the actual structure and operation of that state cannot be reenacted today. Instead of continuing to pay lip service to the ideal of the Medina state and society without applying it, Muslims should reaffirm the underlying values of that ideal and the rationale for its social and political institutions through more workable systems of government, administration of justice, and international relations. The principles of constitutionalism, human rights, and citizenship are in fact more appropriate for realizing the ideal of the Prophet's community of Medina in the concrete context of present Islamic societies than unrealistic adherence to earlier models that are no longer workable.

For instance, the traditional oath of allegiance (*bay'a*) should now be seen as an authoritative basis for a mutual contract between the government and the population at large, whereby the former assumes responsibility for the protection of the rights and general well-being of the latter in exchange for their acceptance of the authority of the state and compliance with its laws and public policy.[1] However, any modern constitutional theory, whether founded on Islamic principles or not, must develop adequate mechanisms and institutions for the election and accountability of government and for the safeguarding of fundamental rights like freedoms of expression and association for that notion of mutual allegiance to be meaningful today. This can be done by developing the idea of *shura* into a binding principle of representative government rather than merely discretionary consultation. Human rights and equal citizenship principles are necessary, not only for evolving this modern concept of *shura*, but also for the proper implementation of the ensuing constitutional theory, which must be inclusive of all men and women, as well as Muslims and non-Muslims alike, as equal citizens of the state.

Islam and human rights

Speaking of Islam is really speaking about how Muslims understand and practice their religion rather than about religion in the abstract. Moreover, this discussion of the relationship between Islam and human rights does not mean that Islam, or any other religion, is the sole "cause" of or explanation for the attitudes and behavior of believers. Muslims may accept or reject the idea of human rights or any of its norms regardless of what they believe to be the orthodox view of their religion on the subject. In fact, various levels of acceptance or compliance with human rights norms are more likely to be associated with the political, economic, social, and/or cultural conditions of present Islamic societies than with Islam as such. Consequently, whatever the role of Islam may be, it cannot be understood in isolation from other factors that influence the way Muslims interpret and attempt to comply with their own tradition. It is therefore misleading to attempt to predict or explain the degree or quality of human rights compliance by Islamic societies as the logical consequence of the relationship between Islam and human rights in an abstract theoretical sense. Still, this relationship is important enough for most Muslims that their motivation to uphold human rights norms is likely to diminish if they perceive those norms to be inconsistent with Islamic precepts. Conversely, their commitment and motivation to protect those rights will increase if they believe them to be at least consistent with, if not required by, their belief in Islam.

A second general point to emphasize here is that Shari'a principles are basically consistent with most human rights norms, with the exception of some specific and very serious aspects of the rights of women and non-Muslims and the freedom of religion and belief ... While appreciating the seriousness of these issues and seeking to address them through Islamic reform,

---

[1] Ann K.S. Lambton (1985) *State and Government in Medieval Islam* Oxford: Oxford University Press at p. 18.

I am calling for mediation rather than confrontation in this regard, because I know that if I, as a Muslim, am faced with a stark choice between Islam and human rights, I will certainly opt for Islam. Instead of presenting Muslims with this choice, I am proposing that we as Muslims consider transforming our understanding of Shari'a in the present context of Islamic societies. I believe that this approach is required as a matter of principle and is desirable in pragmatic tactical terms.

I am therefore calling for framing the issue in terms of the contextual nature of human understandings and practice of Islam, on the one hand, and the universality of human rights, on the other. This approach is more realistic and constructive than simplistic assertions of compatibility or incompatibility of Islam and human rights that take both sides of this relationship in static, absolute terms. This view does not uphold human rights as the standard by which Islam itself should be judged, but only proposes that these rights constitute an appropriate framework for *human* understanding of Islam and interpretation of Shari'a … [T]he real issue is always about human understanding and practice and not about Islam in the abstract. Since traditional interpretations of Shari'a are human and not divine, they can change through the process of reinterpretation and consensus building … What I am proposing here is that human rights provide an appropriate framework for that unavoidably human process.

(c) Audiences

My primary audience is Muslims everywhere, but that is neither a monolithic, exceptional, nor static category of readers. Muslim intellectuals and professionals, who tend to be the ruling elite and opinion-makers in their societies, are largely shaped by European-style education, which enables them to appreciate philosophical concepts and terms that may not be known to those educated in the traditional Islamic schools (*madrasas*). Thus, even if this book were addressed exclusively to Muslims, that would still be a diverse and dynamic group. Ironically, Western media and some scholars tend to take an "orientalist" view of Islam and Muslims that is based on a narrow view of traditional interpretations of Shari'a and medieval scholarship. Conversely, the views of liberal, Western-educated Muslims are assumed to be unauthentic and their values unrepresentative of "real" Islam. In this way, Western media and public opinion call upon Muslims to "modernize" and adhere to universal values of constitutionalism and human rights. Yet those who do that are dismissed in Western public discourse as "westernized" and not sufficiently Muslim, a view shared by traditional conservative Muslims. Part of the argument I am making … is that Muslims can be liberal in their own right, from an Islamic perspective, without having to satisfy preconceived notions of how they ought to be "sufficiently Muslim," whether in Western or conservative Islamic discourse.

In view of this concept of the state and the critical role of civic reason, the future of Shari'a cannot be secured without due regard for the interests and concerns of those who are not Muslim; they must also be included in my intended audience, though not in the same way as Muslims. Focusing on a particular audience would mean selecting a certain methodology of argumentation and choosing terms and concepts that resonate with the intended readers. Since no audience lives in isolation from other human beings near and far, my mode of argumentation and choice of terms and concepts should also be comprehensible for non-Muslims.

(d) Inclusive public debate

Since this subject should be a matter of general concern because of its implications for human dignity and social justice at home and abroad, I am also calling on non-Muslims to participate in debating these issues in relation to public policy and state law. Muslims are also encouraged to participate in debates among other religious communities in relation to public policy and state law. Such debates regarding all relevant religious traditions should of course be conducted with civility, mutual respect, and discretion. They should also focus on matters of public policy and law and avoid questions of religious doctrine and ritual practices. These standards may often be difficult to maintain in practice, but consensus about the propriety, manner, and limits of internal debate and interreligious dialogue will evolve over time.

Part of this inclusive approach is the consideration of concepts and arguments from broader comparative perspectives, including Western political and legal theories and experiences, all as part of the civic reasoning process proposed … The point here is not only that including non-Muslims in an Islamic discourse regarding public policy is expedient or tactical, but also that this is the way it has been done throughout Islamic history and should continue to be done in the future. It is neither possible nor desirable, in my view, to identify and deploy purely "Islamic" arguments, to the exclusion of non-Islamic arguments, as if the two forms of discourse can evolve in isolation or be separated from each other. The spectacular spread of Islam, which was sustained for a thousand years, has partly been the result of its ability to adapt to local conditions and adopt preexisting sociopolitical institutions and cultural practices. The philosophical and jurisprudential foundations of early Islamic social and political institutions evolved through active debate with Jewish, Christian, Greek, Indian, Persian, and Roman traditions during the seventh through ninth centuries. Moreover, Islamic discourse continued to adopt, adapt, and negotiate with preexisting religious and cultural traditions as Islam spread into central and Southeast Asia and sub-Saharan Africa over the following centuries.

These processes continued through the encounter with European colonialism from the sixteenth century up to the present. This phase is particularly important for the argument I am making in this book, because of the continuing and multifaceted impact of European colonialism and Western hegemony generally over Islamic societies and communities.

(e) Secularism in context

Any conception of the secular state is always deeply historical and contextual everywhere. Each of the Western systems that are commonly accepted today as secular evolved its own deeply contextual definition out of its own historical experience. Upon close examination of American, British, Italian, French, Swedish, Spanish, or any other Western European experience, we find that it is unique and specific to the history and context of the country. Whatever common features can be found among these systems are the product of comparative analysis in hindsight and not the result of the uniformity of preconceived models that were deliberately applied to produce specific results. Indeed, the meaning and implications of secularism in each of those situations are contested and contingent, varying over time, sometimes in different parts of the same country. As illustrated by continuing controversy over school prayers and public displays of religious symbols in the United States and religious education in France and Germany, secularism can have different connotations in different Western societies, sometimes across parts of the same society or over time.

3.6 Economic, social and cultural rights (ESCR)*

Human rights and social policy

The essential purpose of human rights is to ensure the effective protection of certain fundamental entitlements for all human beings, everywhere, without distinction on such grounds as race, sex or religion. In other words, the rationale of the whole initiative is to ensure the protection of human rights even in the countries where they are not provided for as fundamental constitutional rights precisely in order to *safeguard them from the contingencies of the national political and administrative processes.* As global experience had repeatedly shown that states cannot be trusted to respect and protect the inherent human dignity of all those who are subject to their jurisdiction, the United Nations sought to establish a set of *universal standards* in this regard ...

---

* From "To Affirm the Full Human Rights Standing of Economic, Social and Cultural Rights" in Yash Ghai and Jill Cottrell (eds.) (2004) *Economic, Social and Cultural Rights* pp. 8–13, reproduced here with kind permission of Interights, London. See the response by Lord Lester and Colm O'Cinneide in ibid. at pp. 17–22 and the excellent overview by Jill Cottrell and Yash Ghai at pp. 58–89; see also below pp. 153–4.

... I believe that however high the level of provision for education, health care, social security, and so forth, by any government, that should not be accepted as compliance with international human rights standards if that state refuses to acknowledge the human rights status of ESCR. This distinction, I suggest, is critical for the coherence and integrity of the human rights idea for two reasons. First the issue is whether the government of the day should exercise exclusive discretion in deciding which services to provide, for whom, and on which terms, or be bound by some external criteria which apply everywhere regardless of considerations of ideology or political expediency. The *added value* of the human rights idea is to provide an internationally agreed frame of reference to the normal course of ideological, cultural or political struggles over power and resources in domestic politics and foreign policy. Second, a commitment to providing these services as a matter of international human rights obligation should extend beyond a state's commitment to the well-being of its own citizens to embrace all human beings everywhere. Since human rights are for all human beings, not only the citizens of one state or another, the measure of commitment of any state to these rights should be willingness to support their implementation everywhere and not only within its domestic jurisdiction.

However, I should emphasize here that I am not at all suggesting that human rights are the only approach to good domestic social policy or humane foreign relations. Indeed, over time it may prove to be an effective or counterproductive approach on either or both counts. Rather, my point is to clarify the meaning and implications of a human rights approach as such in order to assess its utility and efficacy.

ESCR and the universality of human rights

... It is clear that failure to fully accept ESCR as universal human rights will undermine the development of sufficient political support for the implementation of all human rights, including civil and political rights. Since resistance to ESCR is primarily coming from West European and North American countries, the active support of those countries for civil and political rights will probably be viewed in other parts of the world as simply an instrument of post-colonial hegemony and cultural imperialism. Governments that violate human rights can then use the hostility or indifference of their own populations to these rights to justify suppressing the advocates of these rights at home, in addition to dismissing international protests and pressure as neo-colonial interference in the internal affairs of sovereign states.

The fallacy of the classification of human rights

The relegation of ESCR to a lower class of human rights goes back to the division of the human rights proclaimed by the UDHR into two groups during a particularly 'hot' phase of the Cold War in the early 1950s. That clearly ideological and political classification of human rights was initially expressed in the adoption of two separate Covenants, with different formulations and implementation mechanisms for each set of rights. The dichotomy between the two sets of rights was also re-enforced by the mounting Western-Soviet rivalry in the cooptation of newly emerging states in Africa and Asia to their respective camps. Since West European and North American government and their allies emphasised civil and political rights, while the Soviet Bloc and some developing countries favoured ESCR, the division of human rights became entrenched in a global power struggle. But this classification is objectionable as a matter of principle, and difficult to maintain in practice in light of the following considerations.

There is no justification for this classification in the concept or nature of human rights as defined or specified by any of the approaches indicated earlier and briefly explained below. Indeed, it can be reasonably argued that the original vision of the UDHR provided for an integrated, interrelated scheme of rights. Consider, for instance, Article 28 of the UDHR which provides that: 'Everyone is entitled to a social and international order in which the rights and freedoms set forth in this Declaration can be fully realized'. In other words, the obligation is to create whatever social and international order that is necessary for the protection of the full range of rights provided for by the UDHR, whether at the domestic or international level.[1]

From a practical point of view, it is difficult to identify coherent and consistent criteria of classification. Indeed, the rights in both purported categories are indivisible and interdependent, collectively as well as individually, simply because they are all essential for the wellbeing and dignity of every person as a whole being. For example, freedom of expression will be the prerogative of the privileged few without a right to education that enables all people to benefit from that freedom. Conversely, a right to education is not meaningful unless a person also has the freedom to create knowledge and exchange information. Neither of these rights is practically useful for a person who lacks shelter or health care. Moreover, the ideological and political basis of the classification of equally essential and interdependent rights tends to undermine the universality of all human rights and diminish the prospects of political support for their practical implementation ...

The role of the judiciary in the implementation of ESCR

As emphasised at the beginning, certain fundamental entitlements are recognised as human rights precisely in order to protect them from the contingencies

---

[1] On the drafting of the UDHR see, for example, Morsink. J. (2000) *The Universal Declaration of Human Rights: Origins, Drafting and Intent* University of Pennsylvania Press, Philadelphia, pp. 222–38.

of the normal political and administrative processes of any country. While it is generally accepted that this function requires some degree or form of judicial enforcement for civil and political rights, there has so far been little effort to explore similar possibilities for ESCR, except in India and South Africa. Moreover, it is sometimes claimed that judicial enforcement is neither appropriate nor feasible for ESCR, because their implementation requires allocation of resources among competing objectives of social policy, and other forms of affirmative action, that should be left to the discretion of politically accountable public officials. For example, it is said that the judges are unqualified by their training and requirements of political neutrality from and within the judicial process render it inherently inappropriate for evaluating and determining issues of social and economic policy raised by a right to housing or education. However, the fact that such objections are not raised against the judicial enforcement of civil and political rights which also involve vital questions of social policy, and risks of political controversy, indicates to me that the issue is more ideological or cultural than being inherent to ESCR as such.[2]

The reason for insisting on a judicial role is simply the need to ensure that the state lives up to its affirmative obligations to provide for ESCR beyond what the political and administrative organs of the state are prepared to concede on their own accord.[3] There is as much need for appropriate and credible supervision of the positive provision for ESCR by the state as there is for ensuring that it does not encroach on civil and political rights. As a matter of constitutional and human rights doctrine, that supervisory role must be entrusted to the judiciary, especially where the state itself is a party to a dispute about the legal entitlements of its citizens. Moreover, since judicial enforcement has not been seriously attempted for ESCR, all apprehensions about judges and the judicial process in this regard are merely speculative. By the same token, one can assert that judicial enforcement is unlikely to slide into detailed determination of policy and practice precisely because judges are aware of the limitations of their office and nature of the judicial process. Given the record of judicial enforcement of civil and political rights that can raise similar concerns, it is reasonable to expect the courts to define and observe appropriate limits for the judicial process for ESCR. In any case, the risk of judicial usurpation of the role of elected officials should be checked through practical adjudication, instead of denying a whole group of rights any possibility of judicial enforcement because of that risk.[4]

In a partial concession to the need for some supervisory role for the judiciary regarding ESCR, it has been suggested this should be limited to ensuring that there is no discrimination on such grounds as race, sex, or religion in the

[2] Donnelly J. (1993) *International Human Rights*. Westview Press. Boulder, pp. 24–8.
[3] *The Domestic Application of the Covenant* UN Committee on Economic, Social and Cultural Rights General Comment 9. UN Doc. E/C 12/7998/24, 3 December 1998, para. 10.
[4] Hunt. P. (1996) *Reclaiming Social Rights: International and Comparative Perspectives* Aldershot, Dartmouth, pp. 24–31.

protection of these rights. I find limiting the role of the judiciary in this way for ESCR is unacceptable, because it means one cannot object on discrimination grounds as long as the actions or omissions of the state apply equally to all. Failure to provide for education or health care by the state for the rich and poor alike cannot be contested as impermissible discrimination, while the equal denial of freedom of expression to both groups equally is deemed a human rights violation. Of course, I am not in the least suggesting that there is no violation of civil and political right to freedom of expression unless it happens in a discriminatory manner. On the contrary, my point is that the absurdity of such a proposition should be equally acknowledged for ESCR. A denial of the right to shelter, education or health care is as much a violation of human rights as an encroachment on freedoms of belief, expression or association, regardless of its being discriminatory or not in a particular case.

This objection is not adequately answered by calling for an extended definition of the principle of non-discrimination to include 'discrimination in effect or outcome'. Without judicial supervision regarding the active provision of essential social, economic and cultural services in the first place, the state can avoid all responsibility for discrimination in effect or outcome by simply doing nothing. In the final analysis, an ESCR to shelter is not a human right at all if its provision is entirely left to the political and administrative will of the state, without any possibility of independent judicial supervision and guidance beyond the prohibition of discrimination. The special protection as a human right would then be confined to non-discrimination, instead of ensuring the actual provision of shelter.

It is true that there are legitimate concerns about serious political backlash against excessive judicial activism or usurpation of the legitimate role of elected officials. But that is true for civil and political rights as it is for ESCR. Moreover, the appropriate limits of judicial intervention were neither self-evident for civil and political rights from the beginning, nor are they settled now. This point can be appreciated from the existence of profound differences among and within liberal West European and North American societies over 'hate speech' as a matter of freedom of expression, or requirements of due process and fair trial in criminal prosecutions. The only difference between the substantive adjudication of civil and political rights and ESCR is that the former relies on centuries of theoretical and practical development under national constitutional and legal systems, while the process is still to begin for ESCR.

3.7 Suggestions for further reading[1]

The text of Mahmoud Mohamed Taha's *The Second Message of Islam* is available in translation with an Introduction by An-Na'im (1987). An Na'im's *Toward an Islamic Reformation* (1996) interprets and develops Taha's ideas

---

[1] For full references, see the Bibliography (below pp. 222 ff.).

over a range of legal fields. *African Constitutionalism and the Contingent Role of Islam* (2006) and *Islam and the Secular State* (2008) contain An-Na'im's fullest statement of his position on constitutionalism, political theory, and Islam. In addition, he has edited several collections of essays on a range of topics. For citations to his most recent writings see his website at Emory Law School, Atlanta (http://people.law.emory.edu/~abduh46). Lindholm and Vogt (eds.) (1993) contains good discussions of An-Naim's work up to 1992.

4

Yash Ghai

4.1 Introduction[1]

William Twining

Yash Pal Ghai, a Kenyan citizen, was born in Nairobi in 1938. He went to school there and then studied law in Oxford and Harvard and was called to the English Bar. He started teaching law as a lecturer in Dar-es-Salaam in 1963, eventually becoming Professor and Dean, before leaving in 1971. Since then he has held academic posts in Yale, Warwick, and Hong Kong. In addition to numerous visiting appointments, he was Research Director of the International Legal

---

[1] This is a revised and abbreviated version of Twining (2006) pp. 237–57.

Center in New York 1972–73 and a Research Fellow at Uppsala University from 1973–78. He has written or edited nearly 20 books, mainly about public law and constitutionalism, covering several states and regions, but particularly Commonwealth countries.

Ghai is highly respected as a scholar, but he is even better known as a legal adviser to governments and agencies, especially in Asia, the South Pacific and East Africa. He has been highly influential on post-independence constitutional development in the South Pacific, serving as constitutional adviser in Papua New Guinea, Vanuatu, Fiji, Western Samoa, and the Solomon Islands, among others.[2] He has also been involved in a variety of peace-keeping and trouble-shooting activities in Bougainville, Sri Lanka, Afghanistan, East Timor, and Nepal. More recently he served as a constitutional adviser in Iraq and Nepal and is currently facilitating negotiations between the Indian Government and the Nagas. He has been prominent in debates about public law in Hong Kong and China and is an adviser to the Tibetan Government in Exile in its negotiations with China on autonomy for Tibet. In 2005 he was appointed the Special Representative of the UN Secretary-General on human rights in Cambodia. Over the years he has received numerous honours, including election as a Corresponding Fellow of the British Academy in 2005.

From November 2000 to July 2004 he was full-time Chair of the Constitution of Kenya Review Commission, on leave from Hong Kong. Despite enormous difficulties, the Commission produced a draft Constitution in September 2002, not long before the ouster of President Moi and the ruling party, KANU, in an election that was accepted by foreign observers as being generally "free and fair". The Kenya National Constitututional Conference (serving as a const-ituent assembly), which he chaired, adopted the draft with some changes. Unfortunately, once in power President Kibaki and his close associates were less keen on reform than they had been when in opposition and sabotaged the Conference's draft. Instead a draft, which stripped the Conference draft of many key provisions, was offered to, and rejected by, the people in a referen-dum. At the time of writing no new constitution has been enacted.[3] The killings and displacement of over half a million people that followed the elections of December 2007 were widely attributed by Kenyans and external mediators to the failure to implement the Conference constitution.

Ghai has unrivalled experience of constitution-making in post-colonial states. Besides his unquestioned academic and practical expertise, he has succeeded in winning the trust of many rival political leaders of different persuasions, often in tense situations, not least because of the obvious sincerity of his commitment to opposing all forms of colonialism and racism. He has shown great courage in standing up to domineering Heads of Government,

---

[2] For a more complete listing see Ghai (2005) n. 1.
[3] Jill Cottrell and Yash Ghai reflect on the constitutive process in Kenya in Cottrell and Ghai (2007).

such as President Moi of Kenya and Prime Minister Hun Sen of Cambodia. His courage and negotiating skills are legendary.

Almost all of the constitutions that Yash Ghai has helped to design and introduce have included a Bill of Rights.[4] They have generally fitted broadly liberal ideals of parliamentary democracy, judicial independence, and the Rule of Law. He has been an outspoken critic of governmental repression, especially detention without trial and torture; but there has been a discernible ambivalence in his attitude to human rights. For example, he was editor and principal draftsman of an important report by the Commonwealth Human Rights Initiative, entitled *Put Our World to Rights*,[5] published in 1991. Yet in 1987 he was co-editor (with Robin Luckham and Francis Snyder) of *The Political Economy of Law: A Third World Reader* which presented a distinctly Marxian perspective and which contains no mention of rights, human rights, or constitutional rights in the index, except a few references to habeas corpus.

After the "collapse of communism", symbolized by the fall of the Berlin Wall, some former Marxist intellectuals adopted the discourse of human rights.[6] However, Ghai's ambivalence has deeper roots. Perhaps the key is to be found in his own account of his intellectual development. In a refreshingly frank memoir, he tells how he moved from orthodox legal positivism (Oxford and the English Bar), through a phase of liberal reformism (Harvard and the early years in Dar-es-Salaam) to accepting the basics of Marxist critiques of neo-colonialism and of Julius Nyerere's African Socialism from about 1967.[7] He acknowledges that his acceptance of Marxism was not whole-hearted. He recognized the value of Marxian structural analysis of political economy. But this was tempered by three concerns: first, as an East African Asian he was especially sensitive to racist attitudes that he discerned among locals as well as expatriates: "What passed in general for radicalism in those days included a large amount of racism and xenophobia."[8] Secondly, he had a "predilection for free debate", which was beginning to be stifled by a local form of political correctness; and, thirdly, while his colleagues were academically stimulating,

---

[4] The most influential model has been the Nigerian Bill of Rights (1959/60), which in turn was heavily influenced by the European Convention on Human Rights. The Independence Constitution of Nigeria represented a change of attitude by the Colonial Office in London, who until then had been lukewarm about Bills of Rights. Thereafter the Nigerian Bill of Rights became a model for many Commonwealth countries in the period of decolonisation. The story is told in A.W.B. Simpson, *Human Rights and the End of Empire* (Oxford: Oxford University Press, 2001) at 862–873. However, the constitutions with which Ghai has been associated generally involved extensive participatory constitutive processes and are to some extent "home grown".

[5] Ghai was the main author of a report by Commonwealth Human Rights Initiative, *Put Our World to Rights* (1991).

[6] E.g. Shivji (1989).

[7] This essay appears in a volume commemorating the twenty-fifth anniversary of the Law Faculty of Dar-es-Salaam, edited by Issa Shivji (1986). The book is revealingly entitled *The Limits of Legal Radicalism*.

[8] Ibid. p. 27.

most lacked any sense of the importance of legal technicality and practical sense. They taught their students to despise the law, but not how to use it:

> My experience seemed to point to the problems when fidelity to the law weakens – the arrogance of power, the corruption of public life, the insecurity of the disadvantaged. I was not unaware, of course, of other purposes of the law which served the interests of the rich and the powerful. But the fact was that it did increasingly less and less so; a whole body of statutory law since TANU [the ruling party] came to power had begun to tip the scales the other way. I retained my ambivalence about the legal system, and was not attracted to the attitudes of many private practitioners I met (or the interests they served). At the same time I knew the evasion of the law or the dilution of its safeguards harmed many of the people the radical lawyers were championing.[9]

Ghai's experiences in Dar-es-Salaam were formative in important respects. In nearly all of his work since then three tensions are apparent: a strong commitment to certain basic values, tempered by a pragmatic willingness to settle for what is politically feasible in the circumstances; a genuine interest in theory, especially political economy, and a determination to be effective in the role of a good hard-nosed practical lawyer;[10] and a materialist, Marxian perspective on political economy sometimes in tension with a sincere belief in liberal values embodied in the Rule of Law, an independent judiciary, and human rights. For the last thirty years he has also had to balance the demands of teaching, research, and writing with practical involvement in high-level decision-making in a continually expanding range of countries. As a consultant he has also had to reconcile his belief in the importance of local context – historical, political, and economic – with a general approach to constitution-alism and constitution-making. He is a rare example of a foreign consultant who genuinely rejects the idea that "one size fits all" and he has very extensive practical experience of the tensions between universalism and relativism on the ground.[11]

In the early years of his career, Ghai wrote about many issues mainly from a public law perspective. He joined in East African debates about the arguments for and against Bills of Rights[12] and he addressed particular topics, such as

---

[9] Ibid. p. 29–30.   [10] Ibid. p. 31.

[11] Ghai's "A Journey Around Constitutions" (2005) ends with a lament (at p. 831): "Comparative constitutional law has been mired in formalism and pseudo-universalism and the wonderful multiplicity of the constitution has been lost."

[12] Ghai and McAuslan (1970), Ch XI and XIII. At Independence Kenya opted for a weak Bill of Rights, while Tanganyika (later Tanzania) decided against one at this stage of development and nation-building. See Julius Nyerere, *Freedom and Unity* (selected speeches and writings) (1966) passim, esp. Ch. 62 (1964). Ghai and McAuslan argued that even a limited Bill of Rights is one way of making a government publicly accountable, but after the disillusioning experience of the Kenya Bill of Rights in the immediate post-Independence period, they reluctantly concluded that "an ineffective Bill is worse than no Bill at all, as it raises false hopes … [t]he total effect of the Bill of Rights in practice is occasionally to require Government to do indirectly what it cannot do directly – a strange mutation of its normal role." Ghai and McAuslan (1970) at pp. 455–56. For a subsequent assessment of the Kenyan Bill of Rights, see Ghai (1999b). This

habeas corpus, racial discrimination and the position of ethnic minorities.[13] However, it was not until about 1990 that he focused his attention regularly on human rights as such. This is perhaps due to "the increased salience" that human rights discourse achieved during this period.[14] Even then, he has consistently viewed Bills of Rights and the international human rights regime as one kind of means among many that may serve to protect the interests of the poor and the vulnerable as well as satisfying majority and minority interests.[15] His approach has generally been more pragmatic than idealistic and it is only quite recently that he has devoted much space to writing about human rights theory. More than the other three jurists considered in this book, Ghai's main focus has been on domestic bills of rights and constitution-making.

After involvement in an extraordinarily wide range of local, often highly contentious, political processes, towards the end of his career Yash Ghai reflected more generally about constitutionalism, human rights, and democracy.[16] This chapter draws mainly on two recent papers. In "Universalism and Relativism: Human Rights as a Framework for Negotiating Interethnic Claims", Ghai argued that despite, or perhaps because of, its philosophical obscurity, in practice human rights discourse provides a useful and flexible framework for negotiating constitutional settlements that balance competing interests in multi-ethnic societies. The first extract in this paper outlines his quite sceptical perspective on debates between universalism and relativism. The second extract draws some general lessons from case studies of constitution-making in India, South Africa, Canada, and Fiji. In 2008, Ghai published a paper entitled "Understanding Human Rights in Asia". This is reproduced in full here because it contains a succinct statement of his views on a wide range of issues and, although it is specifically about Asia in all its diversity, it has general implications for the world as a whole. The paper explores three main themes: the existence of some clear patterns despite the historical, cultural and political diversity of Asian countries; the paradox that all Asian states are signatories to the main international human rights conventions and have their own domestic bills of rights, yet the foreground is dominated by massive violations of human

---

theme is echoed in his more recent writings, for example Ghai (2007). On the post-Independence history of human rights in Tanzania, see Widner (2001).

[13] See especially, Ghai (1967), Y. Ghai and D.P. Ghai (1971), Ghai and McAuslan (1970).

[14] Ghai (2000b).

[15] For example, in discussing issues and prospects for constitution-making in post-war Iraq, "full respect for the principles of universal human rights" is only one of nine principles to be accommodated in a settlement likely to be acceptable to the Shia and other groups. Ghai, Lattimer and Said (2003).

[16] In his fascinating, largely autobiographical, "A Journey Around Constitutions" (2005) Ghai emphasised the multiplicity and the fragility of modern constitutions, which nevertheless can be powerful instruments of reconstruction and change. Having initially been highly sceptical about the campaign leading to the Declaration of the Right to Development, Ghai found in the document the potential for transformation of the colonial and post-colonial state, with development in the broadest sense being built into the structure of every department of government through a development-oriented constitution ("Redesigning the State for Right Development" (2006)).

rights in most Asian countries, not least by the very same states; and, thirdly, that, notwithstanding recent history, the best hope for stability, genuine development and poverty reduction lies in politically legitimated constitutional structures grounded in the central values of human rights.

One of Ghai's central themes is that a strong regime of human rights significantly increases the power and responsibilities of an independent judiciary. In a debate about the role of litigation and adjudication in regard to economic, social and cultural rights (ESCR), Cottrell and Ghai argued that the judiciary has a potential, but limited role, in developing and implementing such rights, but that legal process is only one means among many for the full realisation of the potential of human rights.[17] Regretfully it has only been possible to include a brief extract from a very rich paper, along with other short quotations that provide links with topics that are developed in other relevant writings.

READINGS

4.2 Universalism and relativism: human rights as a framework for negotiating interethnic claims*

Introduction

The controversy surrounding the universalism or relativism of human rights has intensified in recent years, and has been brought to bear on the credentials of the Universal Declaration of Human Rights ("UDHR").[1] The controversy has relevance not only in the context of East-West debates, but also, and more immediately and concretely, in the political and cultural organization of most states which are now multi-ethnic and multicultural. The international community, particularly the Organization for Security and Co-operation in Europe ("OSCE"),[2] has attempted to make respect for human rights, especially of cultural minorities, a condition for the recognition of states and the framework for settling conflicts in divided societies.

There are various reasons for the resurgence of the controversy. An obvious one is the salience that the rights discourse has achieved and the reaction to it. Moreover, until now the non-Western world did not feel able to challenge the

---

[17] On his exchange of views with An-Na'im about ESCR see above pp. 98–102.

* This section contains two long extracts from an essay on "Universalism and Relativism: Human Rights as a Framework for Negotiating Interethnic Claims", which was first published in 21 *Cardozo Law Review* 1095–140 (2000b). The passages (from pp. 1095–102 and 1135–40) are reproduced here with kind permission of the copyright holders. For comments by Upendra Baxi, Suzanne Stone, and Michel Rosenfeld see the same volume at 1183–242.

[1] See Universal Declaration of Human Rights, G.A. Res. 217A, U.N. GAOR, 3d Sess., U.N. Doc. A/810 (1948).

[2] See "The Human Dimension of the Helsinki Process: The Vienna Follow-up Meeting and its Aftermath" (A. Bloed & P. van Dijk eds., 1991); see also Charter for European Security, November 19, 1999, Organization for Security and Cooperation in Europe www.osce.org.

West. The rapid economic development of Southeast and East Asian states gave those states the confidence to challenge what they considered the intellectual hegemony of the West. Their assertion of "Asian values" was partly a response to what was perceived to be the imposition on them of Western values in the form of human rights. Therefore, we have to recognize a significant element of "nationalism" rather than some simple notion of culture in the debate on relativism. This factor becomes even more important as more states assume the responsibility to foster their "indigenous" culture. Furthermore, "Asian values" were asserted for domestic reasons as an attempt to legitimize authoritarianism.[3]

Another challenge to universalism has come from schools of Islamic thought, particularly in the Middle East, which are also resentful of Western pressures.[4] The globalization of economies has also brought cultures into greater contact, and made most states multi-ethnic, with contradictory consequences. On one hand, there is greater knowledge of other cultures that produces a sympathetic understanding of diversity and emphasis on human solidarity. On the other hand, globalization itself has produced a sense of alienation and powerlessness in the face of new global forces, in which one's identity depends even more fundamentally on one's culture, while that culture may be perceived to be under threat from external forces. Amidst predictions of the clash of cultures, there is the danger that the controversy will become damaging, as it has already proved sterile and unproductive.

The concept of the universality of human rights is based on the notion that: (a) there is a universal human nature; (b) this human nature is knowable; (c) it is knowable by reason; and (d) human nature is essentially different from other reality.[5] This centrality of the human being elevates the autonomy of the individual to the highest value; rights become essentially a means of realizing that autonomy. Each individual is, in a certain sense, absolute. He or she is irreducible to another and separated in his or her autonomy from society. In the formative years for the recognition of human rights in the West, rights were seen as catering to the selfish instincts of man – the bourgeois man of Hobbes and Locke,[6] although Kantian revision introduced the notion of self-esteem which in our own times has been considered the basis for identity.

The relativist challenge to universalism is based on challenging some of these assumptions. Opponents of "universalism" admit that rights are drawn from human nature, but assert that human nature is not an abstraction, because humans are defined by their relation to others and as part of a society of

---

[3] See Yash Ghai, "Human Rights and Governance: The Asia Debate", The Asia Foundation's Center for Asian Pacific Affairs, Occasional Paper No. 4, Nov. 1994; Yash Ghai, "Human Rights and Asian Values", 9 Pub. L. Rev. 168–82 (1998).

[4] See Ann Mayer *Islam and Human Rights: Tradition and Politics* (1991).

[5] See Raimundo Panikkar, "Is the Notion of Human Rights a Western Concept?", 120 *Diogenes* 75 (1982).

[6] See C.B. Macpherson, *Democratic Theory: Essays in Retrieval* 224–50 (1973).

like-minded people.[7] A human person is not separate from, or above, society. Since societies vary from culture to culture, evaluations are relative to the cultural background out of which they arise; a society or culture cannot be criticized on the basis of its external value.

It is often assumed in this debate that "universalists" are westerners and "relativists" are easterners. It is also assumed that the UDHR represents Western concepts of the individual and his or her rights. However, many easterners argue that their cultural and religious texts contain ideas of justice, equality, and fairness, which are the foundations of rights. They compare rights in the UDHR with the values of their own cultures and religion, and thereby support the notion of universalism.[8]

Relativist positions are not based only on culture, although this is the most common source of relativism. Until recently, the view of the People's Republic of China was that rights and rights consciousness were based on the material conditions in society. Rights which are appropriate to, and feasible in, a rich and developed country are not suitable for, or possible in, a poorer country – a kind of materialistic relativism.[9]

The positions of cultural relativists vary widely. The most extreme position is that the validity of human rights depends entirely on the "culture" of the community. It is therefore not possible to criticize the conduct of a state on grounds of some supposed universal norms (although it can, of course, be criticized internally for failing to live up to that culture's standards). Another version of an absolute "relativist" position holds that there are indeed cultural differences which bear on the concept of rights, but that only the Western concept of human rights is acceptable as a basis for universal norms.[10] A similar kind of approach seems to be adopted by some Asian politicians who, resentful of the criticism by the West of their human rights record, now argue that their societies are superior to the West, as they are based on harmony rather than conflict.[11] Duties are a better way to ensure the objectives sought by rights; they are less adversarial and help in the cultivation of virtue. Human rights are not desirable, as they elevate the individual above the community, and can damage the fabric and cohesion of society. The moderate cultural relativist position is that some human rights standards are universal and must be respected by all. There is an overlapping of values which can be used to establish a common core of human rights.[12]

---

[7] See generally Will Kymlicka, *Liberalism, Community and Culture* (1989); Charles Taylor, *Multiculturalism and 'The Politics of Recognition'* 25–74 (Amy Guttman ed., 1992).

[8] See generally *Asian Values: An Encounter with Diversity* (Josiane Cauquelin et al. eds., 1998).

[9] See Information Office of the State Council, *Human Rights in China* (1991).

[10] See generally Jack Donnelly, *Universal Human Rights in Theory and Practice* (1989).

[11] See Fareed Zakaria, "Culture is Destiny: A Conversation with Lee Kuan Yew", 73 Foreign Aff. 109 (1994).

[12] See Charles Taylor, "Conditions of an Unenforced Consensus on Human Rights", in *The East Asian Challenge for Rights* 124–46 (Joanne A. Bauer & Daniel A. Bell eds., 1999).

Some commentators argue for cultural pluralism, believing that it is possible to reconcile conscience with love of tradition.[13] They believe that there are some necessary international standards for human rights, but cultures will have various ways of understanding them. If there is to be any legitimacy to these standards among the people of the culture, it will have to come from within that culture by reinterpreting texts. Advocates of intercultural discourse are connected with the preceding view. They argue that all cultures have valuable norms and insights. By acknowledging this, and by seeking intercultural understanding, we can enrich the concept of rights and strive towards a new form of universalism.[14] Just as the mixing of cultures has enriched cultures, so variations in contexts and concepts of rights can be enriching.

Traditional discussions of the controversy on universalism and relativism have been conducted in ideological terms, with relatively little attention paid to the actual practices of states. Some resolution of this controversy is necessary for further progress in developing policies to implement human rights. More recent studies have moved away from the older polarities towards a creative potential on the part of intercultural discourses for enriching the concept and substance of rights. In this article, I criticize many of the assumptions underlying the controversy, and argue for a more pragmatic and historical, and less ideological, approach. There is no simple way to argue about universalism or relativism in light of the expansion of the concepts and contents of rights, which came as a response to the multiplicity of values and traditions in a rapidly changing global culture.

In seeking to go beyond the debates on universalism and relativism, I do not engage them directly. Instead, operating at a more empirical level, I discuss how a multicultural society organizes the protection of human rights by examining debates about the provisions on and (to a lesser extent) the practice of rights in four countries – India, Canada, South Africa, and Fiji. These countries not only represent different cultural and religious traditions, but also share the common experience of struggling to manage conflicts arising from their ethnic and religious diversity. The conclusion that I draw from their experiences is that, in the discourse on rights, concerns with culture are less important than the balance of power and the competition for resources. Rights are rarely absolute; there are various mechanisms for balancing different interests that inhere in or surround the right. Balance must also be struck between different types of rights. Some forms of special treatment are not incompatible with the right to

---

[13] See generally Abdullahi Ahmed An-Na'im, *Toward an Islamic Reformation: Civil Liberties, Human Rights, and International Law* (1990); *Human Rights in Cross-Cultural Perspectives: A Quest for Consensus* (Abdullahi Ahmed An-Na'im ed., 1992); Abdullahi Ahmed An-Na'im, "Problems of Universal Cultural Legitimacy for Human Rights", in *Human Rights in Africa: Cross-Cultural Perspectives* 331–68 (Abdullahi Ahmed An-Na'im & Francis M. Deng eds., 1990); Panikkar, supra note 5.

[14] See generally Boaventura De Sousa Santos, (1995), *Towards a New Common Sense: Law, Science and Politics in the Paradigmatic Transition*.

equality. All of these factors allow considerable flexibility in using rights as an organizing matrix. The framework of rights has been used with considerable success in mediating competing ethnic and cultural claims. As the cultural problems of more and more states take on a common form, a new version of universal human rights is emerging.

(a) Relativism: a critical assessment

The danger in the debate outlined above lies in drawing false polarities. The debate misses many dimensions of rights. It makes a number of assumptions with little, if any, empirical support. There are many contradictions, too. The most strident critics of universalism are themselves ardent proselytizers. Those who decry external criticism are vehement in their own denunciations of foreign cultures or political systems. I shall make several points in a brief and dogmatic manner; they provide the groundwork for my national case studies. The following propositions relate to the nature of rights, to the nature of culture, and to the relationship between the two concepts:

(1) Rights are not necessarily emanations or reflections of culture. In many societies there is much oppression in the name of culture and tradition. "Rights" are valuable because they are ahead of "culture." Rights talk has produced powerful ideas which interrogate culture: equality, feminism, social justice. Most cultures have some notion of rights. In some they are latent – they can germinate when conditions change.

(2) Even more fundamentally, the concept of culture is problematic. Culture is protean: it is usually connected with religion, language, history, folklore, values, dress, cuisine, and, more broadly, the way people live. Which of these is privileged at a particular moment, as the crucial manifestation of "culture," is more a matter of political choice than inherent value to the identity of a community. States have always claimed the right to elaborate the culture of their communities; the current debate is essentially between states advancing different views of culture for reasons only tangentially connected with culture.

(3) No community has a static culture, especially today when each community is confronted with a multiplicity of images, and exposure to others' ways of life. Rights consciousness itself affects culture; knowledge of other cultures or moral ideas may make an individual aware of his or her inferior status in society.

(4) Cultures change and intermix – there are multiple cross-cutting cleavages which blur cultural differences between nations, although there are times when, under manipulation by some, one characteristic seems to dominate all others.

(5) There is no homogeneity of culture in a state. Considerable state effort is expended in creating a common culture, even (or perhaps especially) in

states whose leaders pose as champions of relativism. There is, for example, the culture of: the military; bureaucrats; academics; professionals; diplomats; trade unionists; and business people. Each has different interests in "rights." Individual or group perception of rights depends on one's economic or social class in society. It is more important to pay attention to the scope and politics of "rights" than to preconceptions of their cultural lineages.

(6) The material bases of "rights" are stronger than cultural bases. The concept of rights has changed over time. Historically rights have been both revolutionary and conservative. Different political systems use different ideologies of rights. Rights serve different purposes in different societies, making the cultural relativism argument exceedingly complex. It is also possible to periodize phases in the rights movement which owe more to global material factors than to the force of culture.

(7) Rights are primarily a matter that arises between state and citizens. They originate in response to the development of market economies and the centralization of states. They are less cultural than "political," are considered necessary whenever political power separates itself from the community, and therefore are particularly necessary in many Asian and African countries where states, however weak internationally, tend to dominate their civil societies.

(8) It follows that the threat to culture from rights may be exaggerated. Culture, as defined in the debate, is primarily a matter of interpersonal or intrafamily relations, and thus no great concern of rights.[15]

(9) There is little doubt that forcing diverse communities to live together has sharpened the debate about relativism, especially in the post-colonial period. The key moral question of our time is the basis on which diverse peoples can coexist and interact. More specifically, the question is whether in this multicultural world a particular view or belief can be regarded as the overriding international consensus on rights and values. I believe that a regime of rights, because of its inherent diversity, is a suitable foundation for intercultural dialogues and consensus.

(10) There are many kinds of rights now. Much of the debate on relativism takes place in the context of civil and political rights, which are supposed to have their origins in Western philosophy. This view disregards the fact that rights are no longer tied to one dominant tradition. Rights are justified on differing bases – from "natural law," or nature of the human person, to more material explanations. The concept of rights is much more diverse today, in response to different economic or social traditions

---

[15] This is increasingly so with the adoption of the Convention on the Elimination of All Forms of Discrimination Against Women, Jan. 22, 1980, 19 I.L.M. 33, and the Convention on the Rights of the Child, Nov. 20, 1989, 28 I.L.M. 1448, which cut across traditional distinctions in regimes of rights between public and private, and between civil/political and economic/social.

and to emerging needs. In particular, there is wide acceptance of social, economic, and cultural rights. There is great concern (at least at the level of rhetoric) with the disadvantages or oppression of particular classes of persons: women, children, and indigenous peoples. This has, to some extent, shifted the focus away from individuals and has facilitated the recognition of group rights and remedies. It has also focused attention on the material conditions and civil society as causes of oppression, balancing the obsession with the wickedness of the state.

(11) These enriching developments in the menu of rights have prompted the need for tradeoffs between different categories of rights. The diversity also facilitates the "contextualization" of rights and allows a balance between different values and goals.

(12) The notion of rights as used by anthropologists or philosophers is different from that employed by lawyers. Anthropologists consider rights more absolute, interpersonal, and more comprehensive in their range. Lawyers are less committed to absolutes and often seek to strike balances. They operate under some form of the doctrine of margin of appreciation,[16] permitting qualifications of rights. The grounds for qualifications are drawn from notions of proper conduct embedded in culture. The doctrine leads to the new orthodox view that to accept universality does not mean that each culture has to understand a right in precisely the same way or accept the whole range of rights.

(13) For multicultural states, human rights as a negotiated understanding of the acceptable framework for coexistence and the respect for each culture are more important than for monocultural or mono-ethnic societies, where other forms of solidarity and identity can be invoked to minimize or cope with conflicts. In other words, it is precisely where the concept and conceptions of rights are most difficult that they are most needed. The task is difficult, but possible, even if it may not be always completely successful. And most states today in fact are multicultural, whether as a result of immigration or because their peoples are finding new identities.

(b) Generalizations from national studies*

In all of these countries, there were serious ethnic conflicts or competing claims. It might have been possible to deal with them through negotiations and compromises. However, at least in South Africa and Fiji, where the conflict

---

[16] See Howard Charles Yourow, "The Margin of Appreciation Doctrine in the Dynamics of the European Human Rights Jurisprudence", 3 Conn. J. Int'l L. 111 (1987) (using the phrase used by the European Court of Human Rights).

* From 21 *Cardozo Law Review* 1135–40 (2000). The detailed case studies on India, Canada, South Africa, and Fiji have been omitted for reasons of space, but the generalizations derived from them are largely self-explanatory. For shorter country studies of human rights regimes in India, China, and Iraq see below pp. 126–31 (ed.).

was intense, and a clear framework for the settlement of competing claims was hard to establish, the process would have been protracted, and even then might not have succeeded.

In all cases, the relevance of human rights to the construction of the state was acknowledged. In South Africa and Fiji, a prior agreement on this question was a prerequisite to the start of negotiations on other matters. It was in Fiji that there was perhaps the greatest initial resistance (by the indigenous Fijians) to accepting rights as the framework. The use of the framework of rights facilitated the application of norms that enjoyed international, and some domestic, legitimacy and were sufficiently malleable to provide broad satisfactory outcomes.

The contents and orientation of rights were drawn from external sources: in India's case, from foreign national precedents,[17] but in other instances from international instruments. A comparison of precedents used in India (1947) and Fiji (1995) provides insight into periodization of rights that speaks to the concerns of universality. At the time of the Indian independence, there was no internationally accepted body of norms or procedures. Nor was there a consensus that constitutions had to include a bill of rights. By the 1990s there was both a substantial body of internationally negotiated norms and a consensus that they had to be implemented in national constitutional systems. Likewise, between the Canadian Bill of Rights (1960)[18] and the Charter (1982),[19] a certain distance had been traveled in the use of international norms. In this way international law and procedures of human rights have the effect of binding states into a common regime, and building a presumption of "universality" into the negotiating process.

"Culture" has nowhere been a salient element determining attitudes to rights. It has been important in Fiji, Canada, and South Africa, but it has been important in different ways. The Francophones do not object to the philosophical basis of rights (indeed, they could hardly object to an instrument which draws its inspiration from the French revolution), but see the "universalizing" tendency of rights as a threat to the survival of French culture and language. In that sense it can be seen as a defensive reaction. In Fiji, on the other hand, rights were presented as antithetical to underlying values of indigenous social and political organizations. "Culture" itself, as already indicated, was very broadly defined. It was used in an aggressive, rather than a defensive, way – as justifying claims to Fijian "paramountcy." Then paramountcy implied a wide degree of political and economy supremacy which had little to do with culture as such. Using human rights as a framework helped to pare down, but not eliminate,

---

[17] The subcommittee report on which the human rights provisions are based gives a remarkably wide range of sources, mainly national constitutions. See B.N. Rau's "Notes on Draft Report dated April 8, 1947", reprinted in 2 *The Framing of India's Constitution: Select Documents* (B. Shiva Rao ed., 1967).

[18] Canadian Bill of Rights, 1960.

[19] Can. Const. (Constitution Act, 1982) pt. I (Canadian Charter of Rights and Freedoms), 25.

paramountcy. Demands by South African traditional leaders and the Inkatha Freedom Party were based on culture; the ability of the latter to derail the transition to democracy gave its demands an importance that otherwise seemed to have had little support. It was perhaps in the stance of the Canadian aboriginals that "culture" was most crucial. It was central to their demands for autonomy, the settlement of outstanding claims, and the preservation of their internal social organization. It was also the hardest case for accommodating cultural claims within the general framework of the Charter. The accommodation was secured through wide exclusions from the Charter, rather than through balancing competing interests, as in other instances discussed in this paper.

With the exception of the Canadian first nations, the proponents of the cultural approach to rights were not necessarily concerned about the general welfare of their community's cultural traditions. They were more concerned with the power they obtain from espousing those traditions. It is widely recognized that Quebec's separatist politics were mobilized by young Francophone professionals who found it difficult to compete with the more established English speaking professionals. The manipulation of "tradition" by Inkatha is well documented. Fijian military personnel and politicians who justified the coup were accused of similar manipulations by a variety of respectable commentators.

Difficult questions arise if the culture of a group can only be maintained at the expense of the rights of another community, or via the agency of the state, as in the case of Fijian claims of paramountcy. A cultural relativism argument in a homogenous community, where the issue is purely between local values and international standards, is less problematic than in a multicultural state, where it can be divisive and lead to the subordination of one community by another. Thus, the debate about relativism in Tonga or Samoa (both homogenous Polynesian societies) is of a different dimension than in Fiji. The aboriginal claims in Canada are easier to negotiate because, for the greater part, aboriginal peoples live in reservations where contact with other communities is minimal.[20]

In my view, the more interesting issues arose when the question of the relationship of rights to culture was debated within the cultural community itself; for example, when women opposed the claims of the "traditionalists," as with the first nations in Canada, the Muslims in India with regard to the application of the sharia, and the traditional leaders in South Africa. Hindus in India were divided over reforms of Hindu law, which followed from the mandate to codify and unify personal laws. More generally, significant numbers within the cultural community were anxious to build a more inclusive community instead of isolating their own community from the mainstream developments. Such divisions not only

---

[20] This may explain why the accommodation of Metis people, who are more spread and less well anchored in one culture, has proved more problematic.

provided opportunities for using rights to interrogate culture, but also offered interesting insights into the nature of rights.

In no case are rights seen merely as protections against the state. They are instruments for the distribution of resources, a basis for identity, a tool of hegemony, and they offer a social vision of society. Rights are not necessarily deeply held values, but rather are a mode of discourse for advancing and justifying claims. Thus, important sectors of the white community in South Africa opt for group rights when it comes to autonomy, but settle for individual rights when it comes to economic rights.

Groups present their claims in different paradigms of rights: individual versus group; equality versus preference; and uniformity versus group identity. In Fiji, for example, the conflict between the two communities is played out in the competing currencies of human rights.

These case studies also dispel the myth that those who advocate for universalism are westerners, and those who oppose it are easterners. It was the British who resisted a bill of rights in India; it was the whites who set up one of the most repressive regimes of this century in South Africa. Both of them believed in relativism of rights – one for whites and another for coloreds. The most powerful resistance to the Charter has come from the French Canadians. Indians wanted a universal regime, but had to make concessions to accommodate the claims of the historically disadvantaged minorities. The majority of the blacks in South Africa showed the greatest commitment to a universal regime. In Fiji, it was the dominant majority within the Methodist Church who most strenuously resisted the regime of rights.

Constitutional settlements in multi-ethnic societies require the balancing of interests. This balancing is particularly important if there are prior, existing disparities of economic, social, or political resources, and particularly if these disparities are the result of state policies. Achieving this balance has various implications for the regime of rights. First, it requires the recognition of corporate identities as bearers of rights (this issue, however, remains deeply controversial, as does the scope of the recognition). It is in that sense that one can speak of collective rights. But we also find individual rights which are connected to being a member of a group. Most rights of affirmative action in India and, to a lesser extent, Fiji may fall into this category. Second, there cannot be, in relation to most rights, a notion of the absolutism of rights. Ethnic accommodations necessitate qualifications on, or reconceptualization of, rights, as with the right to equality. This exercise of qualification or reconceptualization forces constitution-makers to try to understand and define the core of the rights concerned, in order to establish the qualifications that may be made consistent with maintaining that right. Third, the appropriate formulation and protection of social, economic, and cultural rights, especially the "positive duties" of the state, is often fundamental to a settlement, both as an acknowledgement of the importance of culture and as a redress of ethnic inequalities. This is perhaps less so in Canada, where the Charter is more oriented towards civil and political rights; but there, too, problems associated with the first nations are dealt with through redistributions. Thus, for this reason (and other reasons of "ethnic" management), the necessity for an activist state arises. Fourth, since interethnic relations are so crucial to an enduring settlement, and past history may have been marked by discrimination or exploitation, a substantial part of the regime of rights has to be made binding on private parties. Thus, we see that a liberal regime of rights is modified significantly when adapted to the exigencies of a multi-ethnic state, without losing a fundamental commitment to rights and freedoms.

These aims of rights in a multi-ethnic state are reflected in the juridical methods for balancing: reliance on the limitation clauses; directions as to the methods of, and resources for, interpretation; and the balancing of one right against another,[21] of which the most difficult is the balancing of "negative" with "positive" rights (e.g., the protection of property versus affirmative action or other forms of social justice). Sometimes these dichotomies are resolved by new conceptualization, e.g., "equality" defined in substantive terms, as in India and South Africa. The Indian technique of juxtaposing Fundamental Rights with Directive Principles has not been followed elsewhere, perhaps because of the difficulties that the technique presented there.

A particular consequence of using the framework and language of rights, and the juridical techniques mentioned above, is the increase in the power and responsibility of the judiciary for the settlement of claims and disputes. It then falls ultimately to the courts to do the balancing of interests and rights, which is essential in applying the human rights framework. They may represent a different understanding of the permissible limits of the balance, and may come in conflict with determinations by the legislature or the executive branch. This was the Indian experience, in which the courts took a different view from that of the other branches as to primacy of property rights over social rights. On the other hand, vesting the final authority in courts means that close attention is paid to the framework of rights, and that the balancing between the core of the right and its modification is done in a reasoned and principled way. Furthermore, the prestige of the courts also helps to bring the dispute to some resolution, although the Indian experience in the *Shah Bano* case suggests that judicial decisions can themselves be a source of conflict.*

On the broader question of universalism and relativism, it is difficult to generalize. It cannot be said that bills of rights have a universalizing and homogenizing tendency, because by recognizing languages and religions, and

---

[21] See Marc Galanter, *Competing Equalities: Law and the Backward Classes in India* (1984) (calling this balancing "competing equalities").

* In the *Shah Bano case* (1985) 2 Sup. Ct. Cases 556 the Supreme Court held that a claim for maintenance by a Muslim divorced woman against her former husband was to be determined under the general national law, which provided a higher amount than she would get under the *Shari'a*. The government gave way to pressure from the Muslim community and legislatively overruled the decision.

by affirmative policies, a bill of rights may in fact solidify separate identities. Nevertheless, a measure of universalism of rights may be necessary to transcend sectional claims to maintain national cohesion. Simple polarities such as universalism/particularism, secular/religious, or tradition/modernity do not explain the complexity; a large measure of flexibility is necessary to accommodate competing interests. Consequently, most bills of rights are Janus-faced (looking towards both liberalism and collective identities). What is involved in these arrangements is not an outright rejection of either universalism or relativism, but rather an acknowledgment of the importance of each, and a search for a suitable balance by employing, for the most part, the language and parameters of rights.

4.3. Understanding human rights in Asia*

Context

In so far as the prevalence and enjoyment of rights are based on history, traditions, religion, culture, social structure, the state of political and economic development, organization of the economy, and ideology, the vastness and complexity of Asia make it hard to generalise about human rights in that continent. Asia, containing half of the world's population, is home to all the world's major religions: Islam (e.g. in Saudi Arabia, Pakistan, Bangladesh, Indonesia, Iraq, and Afghanistan), Hinduism (India and Nepal), Buddhism (Bhutan, Burma, Thailand, Vietnam, Cambodia, Japan, China, and Nepal), Christianity (the Philippines, India, and South Korea), and Confucianism (China, Korea, and Vietnam). Many states have state religions (e.g. Indonesia, Iraq, Pakistan, Afghanistan, as Islamic; Thailand and Cambodia, as Buddhist, and until recently Nepal as Hindu). What may be more important is not religion as such but the politicization of religion and religious conflict, of which South Asia is a sad example (although prescriptions in some religions or beliefs may seem to be more negative than others to or resist human rights – here one may compare the more textual tradition of Islam to the more fluid Confucianism in the Far East).

Another important factor is the colonial background of a number of Asian countries; former British colonies (e.g. India, Maldives, Hong Kong, Pakistan, Sri Lanka, and Malaysia) share the common law and to some extent the constitutional tradition of England which may cut across, for example, the background in the dominant religion (and the same can be said of former French possessions).

---

* This is a slightly revised version of a paper that is also published in Caterina Krause and Martin Scheinin (eds.) *International Protection of Human Rights: A Textbook* (Turku: Institute for Human Rights, Åbo Akademi University (2008)) and is published here with the agreement of the copyright holders.

In most states there is tendency towards the use of the market mode of economy, with China in a somewhat ambiguous position, for now it is neither a free market nor a planned economy – perhaps it is best described as an administered economy, relying considerably on market mechanisms. There are big differences in the levels of economic and political development and the exposure to education and modern ideas; the majority of the population still live in rural areas, embedded more in the community than the state, in subsistence living than exchange.

These diversities are not only to be found across states but also within states. A particular challenge to human rights lies in the diversity and sometimes the fragmentation of the political and social community, the co-existence and sometimes the competition between different values and life styles within each state. In situations where the state is still the principal means to accumulation of influence and wealth, ethnic diversities often become salient and politicized, raising complex problems of state and nation building, with very specific consequences for human rights.

The preceding statements may seem inconsistent with the universality of human rights – for surely, are they not independent of time, place, economic or social development, religion or culture? Certainly a number of Asian governments and leaders do not think so. They think that human rights are dependent on culture and development, and some of them have posed an alternative to the theory or premise of human rights in the form of Asian Values. At one time much attention was paid to Asian Values as a counter argument to the hegemony of rights discourse and practice. The most common way to challenge the validity or at least the universality of rights is the invocation of cultural relativism – and no continent has done this as vigorously as Asia. According to this line of attack, notions of rights or particular kinds of rights are dependent on and a reflection of culture. Since cultures vary so greatly, it is claimed, each group must be allowed its own understanding of rights, and no one may criticize the standards of a group by reference to external norms. It is then argued that the international regime of rights draws upon Western philosophy or ideas, and therefore they are alien to non-Western societies.

This is by no means the unanimous view in Asia. A number of governments are deeply committed to human rights (India and Japan among them); some are ambivalent (e.g. the Maldives and Malaysia) and some are opposed to or severely restrict rights (China, North Korea, Saudi Arabia, Myanmar, and Cambodia).[1] Within each state there are differences in the perception of, and support for, human rights: much may depend on the class or social position from which rights are perceived (ministers, government officials, traders or peasants, trade unionists or employers, minorities or majorities, NGOs or state

---

[1] Throughout the chapter I identify a number of countries which are illustrative of the statement preceding the list. By this practice I do not imply that there are no other countries with similar situations, nor indeed that the listed countries are the most egregious.

agencies are all likely to have different perspectives and positions). However, these positions are not static. Sometimes the reaction to authoritarianism is a serious commitment to rights, with the flowering of the human rights movement and the refurbishing of the constitution (Korea, Taiwan, the Philippines, and Indonesia). Sometimes there is decline from a previous condition of scrupulous respect for rights to massive state lawlessness and oppression (Sri Lanka). These examples suggest that the influences of culture, religion, and tradition may be less important than state craft and the politics of control and accumulation (the defining characteristic of some Islamic states, particularly in the Middle East, is the dynastic regime and the preservation of the interests of the ruling families, as opposed to more democratic Muslim states).

Against the background of international developments in human rights and the changing role of international law and institutions, I try to locate the Asian debate in the context of the social, political, and economic situation in specific Asian countries. Whatever the importance of the international human rights regime, the prospects for the exercise of rights for individuals and communities depend fundamentally on national systems, of ideology and practice, and laws and institutions.[2] In what has become a controversial area, I want to briefly outline my approach. I believe that rights are historically determined and are generally the result of social struggles. They are significantly influenced by material and economic conditions of human existence. It is for that reason unjustified to talk of uniform attitudes and practice of rights in such a diverse region as Asia. Rights became important both as political principles and instruments with the emergence of capitalist markets and the strong states associated with the development of national markets. Markets and states subordinated communities under which duties and responsibilities were deemed more important than entitlements.[3] Rights regulate the relationship of individuals and corporations to the state. Despite the lip service paid to the community and the family by certain Asian governments, the reality is that the state has effectively displaced the community and increasingly the family as the framework within which an individual or group's life chances and expectations are decided.[4] The

---

[2] The distinguished Indian scholar, Upendra Baxi writes, "An understanding of constitutionalism at work from the perspective of internationally proclaimed human rights is never quite the same as the constitutionally based understandings of human rights put to work by judges and lawyers, social movements, and the political processes in each national context" ("Production of Human Rights and Production of Human Rightlessness in India" in Randal Peerenboom, Carole Petersen and Albert Chen (eds.) *Human Rights in Asia* (London: Routledge, 2006) p. 384.

[3] This is a principal theme of Norberto Bobbio, *The Age of Rights* (Cambridge: Polity Press, 1996). In a somewhat similar vein, tracing the growth of the idea of human rights, Albert Chen, who has written extensively on human rights in China, says, "Human rights are thus not part of pre-modern Western civilization, but rather are a modern invention" ("Conclusions: Comparative Reflections on Human Rights in Asia" in Randall Peerenboom, Carole Petersen and Albert Chen (eds.), *Human Rights in Asia* (London: Routledge, 2006)).

[4] For an *elaboration* of my argument, see my paper "Human Rights, Social Justice and Globalisation" in Joanne Bauer and Daniel Bell (eds.), *The East Asian Challenge to Human Rights* (Cambridge: Cambridge University Press, 1998). It is interesting that Singapore, which claims to

survival of the community itself now depends on rights of association and assembly, less so on concepts of duties and responsibilities.

I am also wary of approaches to rights that seek, as the claim about Asian Values does, to lock us into polarities, Western versus Eastern, European versus Asians, Christian versus Confucian. I believe that a person's attitude to rights and duties is determined by various factors, principally location in class and social structures. We have now reached a broad international consensus on the importance and substance of rights. Within what has become an ever expanding menu of rights, different social and economic groups emphasize those rights that favour their positions. It is thus hard to say that there are characteristic "national" attitudes or perceptions of rights. Trade unionists in Asia share with their counterparts in Europe the support for rights to strike, of collective bargaining, standards for industrial safety and so on, just as there is much that unites the business communities, or academics, or judges, or the police, and so on, of Asia and Europe. The project of human rights is difficult in all cultures and political systems, for neither in the abstract or in practice are all its norms acceptable to all the people, and are frequently regarded as inconvenient by governments. This is why we should regard the universal respect for rights as the collective responsibility of us all.

Rights themselves become the terrain of struggles, different groups offering alternative conceptions of rights. Rights of self-determination compete with claims of sovereignty (as in the claims of the autonomy of indigenous or ethnic groups); the rights of individuals clash with customs or morality of society; the right of property competes with the demands of equity or democratic labour practices; and so on.[5] The conflict has been aggravated with the rapid pace of globalization (particularly those aspects of the process which are connected to the spread of the market systems throughout the world and the removal of national restrictions on factors of production and trade) served by a particular species of rights, pre-dominantly property and its protection (this point is elaborated later). The IMF and the World Bank have transformed rights into "governance", emphasizing property and the sanctity of commercial transactions, the eradication of barriers for the operation of market freedoms, and the exclusion of social rights, and thereby diminished rights. Under similar compulsions, others have engaged in the denigration of particular rights, such as labour rights in much of South East and East Asia.[6]

---

be the most Confuc[ian] state in Asia, introduced *legislation* some years ago to require children to look after their aged parents.

[5] These themes are explored in S. Bowles and H. Gintis, *Democracy and Capitalism: Property, Community and the Contradictions of Modern Social Thought* (Basic Books, 1996); L. Gostin (ed.), *Civil Liberties in Conflict* (London: Routledge, 1988); H. Hannum, *Autonomy, Sovereignty and Self-Determination* (Philadelphia: University of Pennsylvania Press, 1990).

[6] See Ghai, in Bauer and Bell (eds.), op. cit. For labour rights in particular, see L. Compa and S. Diamond (eds.), *Human Rights, Labor Rights and International Trade* (Philadelphia: University of Pennsylvania Press, 1996); B. Langille, *Eight Ways to Think About Labour Standards and Globalization* (Geneva: Graduate Institute of International Studies, c.1997); and Anthony Woddis, *Globalisation, Human Rights and Labour Law in the Pacific Asia* (Cambridge: Cambridge University Press, 1998).

Asia's engagement with the international human rights system

At one level these cultural and national differences have not mattered. There are powerful global forces at work which reduce cultural and intellectual differences across the world, bring uniform forms of technology and management, and produce national elites which have more in common with each other than with lower orders in their countries. The rights discourse is important for political and social mobilisation throughout much of Asia. There is much discussion of the context for and strategies for human rights. There is very considerable support for rights among parliamentarians, judges, academics, trade unionists, women's groups and other non-governmental organizations. Based on, sometimes quite comprehensive bills of rights, there is considerable litigation on human rights issues (in which Western and international precedents are regularly cited – in fact courts have become the most important institutions for incorporation of international ideas and standards of human rights in a large number of Asian states). Some leading judgments on the scope of rights and the obligations of governments to protect them have come from Asian, and particularly Indian and Hong Kong judges.[7] There has been special emphasis on social and economic rights which have been invoked through public interest litigation pioneered by the Indian Supreme Court and now adopted in many states in and outside Asia.[8]

---

[7] In 1975 Prime Minister Indira Gandhi declared a state of emergency under which many rights were suspended and the federal government assumed the powers of states. The Supreme Court failed to protect human rights during this period and lost considerable legitimacy. After the restoration of democracy, however, in a move to restore its prestige, it developed a most progressive jurisprudence on rights and social justice. For example, the Court has ruled as unconstitutional: (a) pre-censorship (*Brij Bhushan v. State of Delhi* (AIR 1950 SC 129)); (b) the banning of a film for fear of hostile audience reaction (*Rangrajan v. Jigjivan Ram* 1989 2 SCC 780); and (c) it has given a broad meaning to the right to the protection of life, including "the protection of the health and strength of the workers men and women, and of the tender age of children against abuse, opportunities and facilities for children to develop in a healthy manner and in conditions of freedom and dignity, educational facilities, just and humane conditions of work and maternity relief" (*Bandhua Mukti Morcha v. Union of India* (1984) 3 SCC 161). See U. Baxi, "Taking Suffering Seriously" in R. Dhavan (ed.), *Judges and the Judicial Power* (Bombay: Tripathi, 1985) and J. Cottrell, "Third Generation and Social Action Litigation" in S. Adelman and A. Paliwala (eds.), *Law and Crisis in the Third World* (London: Hans Zell, 1993).

[8] Radhika Commaraswamy says: "If one studies the type of cases which have come up before the Indian Supreme Court under provisions for right to life, one notices that almost all of them involve issues of economic and social justice, bonded labour, minimum wage, conditions of living in state institutions, etc. The facts presented by an Indian reality have forced Indian lawyers and the Indian Supreme Court to take the initiative and create new vistas with regard to human rights in Third World societies. As a result of these developments, the Indian Supreme Court has relaxed the rule of standing to allow human rights activists to come before the courts with the use of an open letter. They have set up independent commissions with independent fact-finders, especially in cases where there was need to look into the social and economic issues. None of these procedures was available in Western jurisprudence. They have been created by Indian conditions and Indian needs. Therefore the transportation of the human rights idea to India as part of the Federal Indian constitution has not only given these ideas a new cultural context, but the cultural context itself has enhanced and developed the concept of human rights", "Comments" in A. Eide

Most states have independent human rights commissions (based on the Paris Principles[9]). Asia is drawn deeply into the international regime of human rights. Most states have participated in the drafting of international human rights treaties, have ratified them and take part in the machinery for reporting and supervising their implementation. National courts routinely use judgments of regional and international courts for the interpretation of human rights. The international community has intervened in several Asian countries for gross violations of rights; and leaders of the Khmer Rouge government in Cambodia are now being tried by a semi-international court applying the law on crimes against humanity. The UN has appointed special representatives in a number of Asian countries for human rights (Cambodia, Burma, North Korea) and a number of Asians have been appointed as rapporteurs.[10] Asian human rights NGOs are playing an active role for the promotion of human rights in Asia as well as globally.

There is no regional system of human rights protection in Asia. Perhaps this is because Asia is too vast, with too many differences in culture, religion, and history. There are no regional organizations which bring all governments together. Inter-state systems for the protection of rights would be more feasible at sub-regional levels where there are certain bonds of history and values (such as South Asia, the Middle East, and the Far East). South East Asian States (ASEAN) do have their own economic and trade organization, and although there has been some discussion about developing a human rights system under it, there has not been much enthusiasm. Civil society has expressed scepticism about the value of establishing a regional system at present, when there are several authoritarian regimes, although in recent years dialogues between civil society organizers and the ASEAN have taken place for the establishment of a regional system. Meanwhile Asian NGOs are able to work together on a pan-Asian basis.

But perhaps these factors do not provide sufficient explanation for the absence of a regional system. Regional systems tend to be much more searching and intrusive than the international system, often with binding rulings of the regional tribunal. Asian states are simply not willing for any outside body to examine the domestic condition of human rights (given the massive violation of rights and the challenge to, and the fragility of, states). There is a tacit understanding among states that each state would be left alone so far as its record of

---

and B. Hagtvet (eds.), *Human Rights in Perspective: A Global Assessment* (Oxford: Blackwell, 1992) at pp. 108–9.

[9] Paris Principles were adopted by the General Assembly in 1993, to provide the basis for the mandate and competence of national human rights institutions or commissions, their composition, responsibilities, activities and modes of operation. The Principles seek to ensure both the competence and independence of the commissions. Their roles include investigation of human rights violations, promotion of awareness of rights, advice to government and responsibility for ensuring conformity with international human rights treaties and norms.

[10] Joshua Castellino and Levira Dominguez Redondo, *Minority Rights in Asia: A Comparative Legal Analysis* (Oxford: Oxford University Press, 2006) pp. 23–33.

human rights is concerned, particularly relating to the maintenance of public order – even the ASEAN states have refused to criticize its member Myanmar, notorious for the suppression of human rights.

Bills of Rights in Asia

Constitutions of all Asian countries have bills of rights. These, for the most part drawn up locally, may give a better idea of the true attitudes towards rights than international covenants and conventions, although in many respects they are similar to bills of rights in other regions (in terms of the scope of rights, formulation of limitations, enforceability, and remedies). Some reflect the colonial origins of the country, in terms of the drafting style, or the importance of legal institutions. Others are more influenced by ideological considerations (liberal or communist). Some bills of rights in Muslim countries are oriented towards the supremacy of Islamic values and rules as they impact on rights. This means that they reflect considerable variations as between one Asian country and another. I briefly examine three bills of rights which provide interesting contrasts – India, China, and Iraq.

India

The Indian bill of rights, one of the oldest in Asia, was drafted before even the Universal Declaration of Human Rights (though inspired by the same values). Indians saw the bill of rights as the foundations of great political, social, and economic transformation of India. The constitutional arrangements under which Britain had ruled India did not include a bill of rights (which reflected both colonial practices as well as traditional British hostility to, or at least scepticism about, bills of rights). The initiative for a bill of rights came entirely from Indian politicians. Indians first expressed an interest in a bill of rights due to their resentment at the privileged position of the British; the bill would provide parity for Indians with the British. But Indians had to confront various dilemmas before agreeing on the form of the bill of rights. A bill of rights had to unify the country and promote a common identity at the same time as it had to deal with: (a) cultural diversity; (b) minorities; (c) poverty; (d) social hierarchies and societal oppression. Far from regarding these factors as obstacles to a bill of rights, rights were deemed essential to resolve them. It was only when the Indian Constituent Assembly was established that Indian leaders had an opportunity to implement their ideas.

In 1928 the Indian National Congress had constituted a committee representative of a wide cross section of opinion and interests to prepare a declaration of rights as part of constitutional review.[11] It is interesting that the committee based rights on the principle that all the powers of the state are

---

[11] Granville Austin, *The Indian Constitution: Cornerstone of a Nation* (Clarendon Press, Oxford, 1966) pp. 52–58.

"derived from the people". The committee produced a list of rights which was strong on civil and political rights, with non-discrimination a persistent theme. It also proposed free primary education, and imposed on Parliament the obligation to make "suitable laws for the maintenance of health and fitness for work of all citizens, securing a living wage for every worker, the protection of motherhood, welfare of children, and the economic consequences of old age, infirmity and unemployment". Indian leaders were very conscious of the poverty of the masses; they had to reconcile rights directed towards maintaining the status quo, particularly property rights, with those directed towards social change and social justice. Congress considered that "in order to end the exploitation of the masses, political freedom must include the real economic freedom of the starving millions". They were conscious of the oppression that inhered in social and economic structures (such as untouchability or caste); and were committed to empowering the disadvantaged groups. This suggested some restrictions on liberal rights of property or equality. It also suggested an activist state, engaged in the distribution of resources and the direction of the economy.

They were anxious to protect minorities (but after the partition of the sub-continent, they wanted to avoid forms of entrenchment which might promote fresh demands for separatism). They wanted to move away from what they regarded the divisive way the British had ruled India, abandoning the confer-ment of corporate identities to religious or cultural groups, shifting towards a more liberal framework.

They were, more generally, conscious of the cultural diversity of India and the need to fit rights within this diversity. At the same time they were pre-occupied by the imperative of "nation building", cultivation of a common identity and common loyalties, especially as they were drawing the constitution at a time when the country was being torn asunder, with horrendous problems of security, lawlessness, and communal carnage.

To an extent these opposing objectives were balanced by adopting the device of an enforceable Bill of Rights for, but not exclusively, civil and political rights, and a non-justiciable charter of Directive Principles for measures of social and economic equality. Where the necessary social and economic reforms could only be achieved by qualifying civil or political rights, such as those of equality and property, this was clearly stated in the Bill of Rights and authority or obligation for remedial action laid down.

China

Unlike the Indian approach that rights were derived from people's sovereignty, the Chinese authorities regard rights as defined and conferred by the state, drawing from Marxist interpretation of history. The Marxist view, opposed to the natural theory of rights, regards rights as part of the ideological super-structure of the state, to justify and legitimize the particular. Marx's own critique was based on and directed at bourgeois rights, particularly in respect of the relationship to the market economy. Rights were thus the products of society and state. Marxists constructed their rights on the needs of a state-owned and planned economy – and the political dominance of the Leninist state. The bill of rights discussed here appears in the 1982 Constitution, a constitution adopted in the wake of the atrocities and disruptions of the Cultural Revolution, and before the more fundamental economic reforms of Deng Xiao Ping (so the version considered here did not provide for property rights – an omission made good since then).

Unlike the Indian bill of rights, the Chinese is not addressed to the complexity of its society (Chapter III, Section 6 of the Constitution deals with the "nationality question" and the principles of "autonomy" to be guaranteed to national minorities). A significant number of rights are given: equality before the law (and equal rights for men and women), right to vote, freedom of expression, the press, assembly, procession and demonstration, religion, liberty, protection of dignity and reputation, privacy and inviolability of the home, and rights of the family. As one would expect, there are number of social and economic rights (employment, training, pensions, education, and support for the disabled).

However, the rights are in the nature of declarations. The constitution itself is not directly enforceable but requires further legislation to give effect to its provisions, including those on human rights. Thus a right cannot be enforced until a law so provides (although there is a well-publicized case where the Supreme Court seems to hold a constitutional right directly enforceable).[12] Nor, unlike the Indian Constitution, does it provide a procedure for their enforcement. In most cases, legislation defines rights quite narrowly (e.g. regulations on religion basically amount to a denial of religious freedom).[13]

There is a nationalist tinge to the bill of rights. Most rights are confined to Chinese citizens. Religious bodies and religious affairs are not "subject to any foreign domination" (art. 36(4)). Citizens must "safeguard the security, honour, and interests of the motherland" (art. 54). Another article says that "it is the sacred obligation of every citizen to defend the motherland and resist aggression", and "military service" is described as "honourable duty" (art. 55). There is heavy emphasis on the duties of citizens (they have to pay taxes, work (which is described as "glorious"), safeguard the unity of the country and the unity of all its nationalities, they must abide by the laws and the Constitution, protect public property and observe labour discipline and public order and "respect social ethics"). In exercising their rights, citizens "may not infringe upon the interests of the state, society or of the collective, or upon the lawful freedoms and rights of other citizens" (art. 51).

---

[12] Chinese case.

[13] Pitman Potter, "Belief in Control: Regulation of Religion in China" 174 *China Quarterly* (2003) pp. 317–337.

The Constitution provides for various limitations on rights (by using expressions like "according to law", only "normal" religious activities are protected, which also must not "disrupt public order, impair the health of citizens or interfere with the educational system of the state", etc.). The precise formulation seems unimportant as rights are not directly enforceable. Rights and freedoms in the Chinese Constitution are nominal, that is to say, that they have little effect in practice.[14] The exercise of rights depends on the good will of the state (which means that of the ruling Communist Party). Rights do not affect policies or public discourses (although in recent years, particularly with the massive appropriations of land owned by the peasants, both the discourse and litigation on human rights have become prominent).[15]

Iraq

Constitutions of most Islamic states contain bills of rights. The rights which are guaranteed cover most rights that are protected under international treaties. Difficulties arise only in relation to a small number of issues (although their implications can be significant, depending on interpretations). The Koran itself does not say much about the relationship of the individual or community to the state – and it says relatively little about the organization of the state.[16] *Sharia*, which covers other sources of Islam law also, is much older than the modern conception of human rights, and there are indeed conflicts between some of its principles and those of human rights, centred around to a considerable extent on the notion of equality, and relations within the family. The *Sharia* assumes unequal rights between men and women, and between believers and non-believers. A Muslim man is free to marry a non-Muslim woman (provided she belongs to one of the religions of the book), but a Muslim woman cannot marry outside Islam. Some punishments prescribed in the Koran are inconsistent with what would be acceptable under human rights norms. The *Sharia* punishments of death by stoning for adultery or pre-marital sex and of amputation of hands and feet for the offences of theft and robbery are often considered incompatible with human rights, as constituting torture or cruel, inhuman, or degrading punishment. The final critical issue relates to the liberty to choose one's religion or to convert another. Although the Koran rules out compulsion in matters of religion, it is considered apostasy for a Muslim to abandon Islam, and attempt to convert a Muslim to another religion is prohibited.

[14] The contrast between the living reality of constitutional rights in India and the nominalism in China is illustrated by the thousands of cases that the Indian Supreme Court had dealt with compared to the almost total absence of human rights litigation in China.

[15] Eva Pils, "Land Disputes, Rights Assertion and Social Unrest: a Case from Sichuan", 19 *Columbia Journal of Asian Law* (2006) 365–292; (Reprinted as *New York University School of Law Global Law Working Paper Series* 07/05).

[16] Bernard G. Weiss, *The Spirit of Islamic Law* (Athens, Georgia: University of Georgia Press, 2006), chap. 8.

Different Islamic countries have dealt with these issues differently.[17] The *Sharia* may be declared supreme law, but the matters covered by it are often restricted to family matters.[18] Some have traditional clauses about religious freedom and say nothing about conversion. Some qualify equality provision by reference to the *Sharia*. These issues were closely debated when Iraq drafted its constitution in 2005.[19] Apart from divisions within different Islamic sects (the Kurds and Sunnis being inclined towards the secular more than the Shias), the US government put great pressure on the drafters to ensure that the Constitution was as secular and democratic as possible. The compromise was reflected in various provisions, the most important being Article 2. The first clause of the Article is as follows:

Article 2:
Islam is the official religion of the State and it is a foundation source of legislation:

A. No law that contradicts the established provisions of Islam may be established.
B. No law that contradicts the principles of democracy may be established.
C. No law that contradicts the rights and basic freedoms stipulated in this constitution may be established.

This formulation attempted to balance Islam with the other more universally inclined sets of principles. Also the use of the expression "established provisions of Islam" was intended to limit the rules that could not be violated (there are in fact relatively few rules which can be said to be accepted by all).

The second clause of Article 2 was also intended to provide a sort of balance, between different religions with a special place given to Islam. It reads as follows:

This Constitution guarantees the Islamic identity of the majority of the Iraqi people and guarantees the full religious rights of all individuals to freedom of religious belief and practice such as Christians, Yazedis, and Mandi Sabeans.

A concession to the more militant Islamists was given in Article 3 as follows:

Iraq is a country of many nationalities, religions and sects, and is a part of the Islamic world and the Arab people therein are a part of the Arab Nation.

Islamic law is not homogenous in all its beliefs and practices, which were for the most part developed by different schools of jurisprudence. Differences applied in relation to matters of family law. In the 1920s legislation in Iraq provided for a codified law on personal status, which aimed at uniform rules. These were seen as more liberal than the *Sharia* and were resented by the Shias above all.

---

[17] See www.uscrif.gov/countries/global/comparative_constitutions/03082005/Study0305.pdf.

[18] The Malaysian constitution, for instance, restricts the application of Islamic law to enumerated areas, including succession, marriage, divorce, adoption, gifts and trusts, charities, mosques and places of worship, establishment and procedure in *Sharia* courts, and the determination of matters of Islamic law and doctrine. See Malaysian Constitution, Ninth Schedule, List II.

[19] Ashley S. Deeks and Mathew D. Burton, "Iraq's Constitution: Drafting History" 40 *Cornell International Law Journal* 1 (2007).

The compromise was to recognize the different schools but in a way that left the choice to individuals, and to provide for flexibility in the law governing the matter, as shown in Article 41, "Iraqis are free in their commitment to their personal status according to their religions, sects, beliefs, or choices, and this shall be regulated by law".

Finally, agreement was reached that scholars in Islamic law would be included in the Supreme Court so that the *Sharia* would be properly administered. Article 92(2) says that "The Federal Supreme Court shall be made up of experts in Islamic jurisprudence".

Deeks and Burton say that "the negotiations on these issues were among the most contentious of the entire process, less because of their substantive complexity and more because of what references to Islam in the constitution connote – in the views of some – for rights and protections therein, as well as for future laws enacted under the constitution".[20] These provisions on the whole provided a relatively open system, which would allow for the elaboration of human rights and ways of balancing these with Islamic principles. They show the flexibilities with which human rights and Islam can be harmonized.

General reflection

There is of course limited value in textual analysis of the kind I have attempted. One reason is the notorious distance between rhetoric and reality, especially regarding human rights. How far rights are respected, what kind of remedies are available and used, and how the bill of rights can cope with mass violations of rights that are so endemic in Asia, are empirical questions, fit for sociological research. Another reason is that, even within the confines of the constitution, it is not sufficient to parse the text. Unless the institutions of the state are oriented towards the promotion of rights (are "rights friendly"), chances are that the state would neither desist from its own violations of rights nor protect citizens from the violation by others. Courts are so frequently bought or subordinated to the executive that the constitution is constantly subverted. The legislature and the executive themselves have to be democratic, alert to national needs, and accountable to the public before there would be respect for rights.[21] The strength of the Indian bill of rights comes only partially from its text, for it depends on a competent and honest judiciary (which the country has had for most of its history), a legislature responsive to public pressure and able to hold the government to account, and an alert and engaged civil society– unfortunately all these factors are missing in China – and only slowly developing in Iraq.

---

[20] At p. 6, ibid.

[21] I have examined the role of the constitutional allocations of responsibilities and the structures of the state as critical to the promotion of rights in the chapter "Redesigning the State for 'Right Development'" in Bård-Anders Andreassen and Stephen Marks (eds) *Development as a Human Right: Legal, Political and Economic Dimensions* (Harvard University Press: Cambridge, Mass.) 2006.

Pattern of human rights violations in Asia

Many millions of Asians are not able to enjoy rights and freedoms, if by that we mean a life lived in dignity, peace, and comfort. The regime of rights and freedoms covers critical aspects of our lives and existence. Civil and political rights give us possibilities of developing our spiritual and intellectual capacities, expressing our opinions, preferences, and dissents, associate with like-minded persons, worship with co-believers, influence public opinion and policies, and participate in affairs of the state. Cultural rights enable us to define and preserve our identity, give an orientation to cope with ourselves and others, while rights of the family protect an important sphere of our private lives and our intimate relationships. Social and economic rights aim to assure us adequate housing in a good and sanitary environment, sufficient food for healthy sustenance, and access to medical services. They are intended to equip us with the means of earning our livelihood, through education and equal access to social services and amenities of the state, and employment opportunities. For workers economic rights ensure at least a living wage and decent conditions of work, and the right to join a trade union to protect and promote their entitlements, and to express their solidarity. In institutional terms, there must be a competent and impartial system of judiciary to protect human and other rights. Above all the state must ensure personal, emotional, and moral security for everyone and protect against its violation by private actors.

I have described in some detail what I understand are the postulates of a regime of rights in order to demonstrate there are few effective human rights regimes in Asia. [Hundreds of thousands] of people are killed every year in the most brutal manner; many blown to pieces by suicide bombs, largely innocent victims of sectarian violence (Iraq, Sri Lanka, Pakistan, Indonesia, India). There are numerous extrajudicial killings and thousands of persons are abducted and disappear.

Many millions have been displaced from their homes, as part of ethnic cleansing, or civil war, living in camps with few amenities, with women in constant threat of molestation or rape, and children denied opportunities for education or acquisition of skills (in 2006 alone 213,000 were displaced in Sri Lanka). Millions live in slums, where the most basic rights are denied, leading a life of great deprivation, without privacy, sanitation, water, electricity or other basic amenities. Life is a daily struggle, against extraordinary odds, rapacious landlords working in cahoots with corrupt policemen, equally rapacious money lenders, without secure employment or other means of livelihood. Women and children suffer most in these situations. They easily become the victims of trafficking and sexual violence – and other forms of exploitation. They are malnourished, have no prospects of education, are not able to develop their potential – condemned to a life of poverty. Millions of others are forced to take refuge in foreign lands, cut off from their cultural roots, perhaps never to return. Families, and friends, are separated.

Child labour is rampant in many places (most notoriously in Myanmar) and millions of children have no opportunities for education. Many individuals and communities are not allowed to profess or practise their religious beliefs (Pakistan, China, Iraq, Vietnam). Members of several faiths or spiritual beliefs are persecuted, not able to worship in communion with others or in public – or at all. Sectarian fights claim many thousands every year. Many more are not allowed to express themselves freely in arts or politics (in states too numerous to cite). In some countries, people are locked up for their political beliefs or for resistance to unjust laws or policies – and have no prospects of an independent trial (Cambodia). The new anti-terrorism laws operate on profiling so that members of certain communities become the target of security forces, and the courts connive at the removal of long-cherished safeguards of due process. Enormous powers of investigation and detention are vested in state authorities, inconsistent with principles and procedures of due process – without any meaningful scrutiny or accountability. Torture or other forms of inhuman treatment are commonplace in many countries.

There are enormous disparities of wealth and opportunities. Globalization has produced many Asian millionaires in the last two decades or so, even as it has deepened the poverty of millions. Human solidarity is the casualty of economies driven by the profit motive – and greed. In many countries corruption is rampant – and leads to the violation of rights and entitlements, and the general breaches of law or codes of conduct. Significant proportions of the population live below the poverty line. There is acute poverty – and indebtedness – in rural areas; in India this has led to so many suicides by farmers that the situation has become something like a national crisis. There is forced labour (most notoriously in Myanmar). The number of migrant workers increases by the day, often illegal, and thus, without the protection of the laws, easy victims.

Political rights are fragile in many states, and only a few enjoy stable democracy (among which the largest state in the world, China, cannot be included). Many opponents of the regime are forced into exile (particularly in Myanmar, China, and Cambodia). Others are silenced. Political parties are banned. Radio stations are shut. Violence and the absence of the rule of law become functional to the operation of state, society, and economy (outstandingly in Cambodia[22]). Friends of the regime enjoy huge impunities, while opponents become victims of the judicial process. There is no equality before the law. And judiciaries in many countries are corrupt and beholden to the government. State and society alike have become increasingly militarized. Criminal and politically driven militias rule slums and parts of the countryside. For large sections of the population, the state is unable or unwilling to provide the minimum of human security.

---

[22] Report of the SRSG for human rights in Cambodia (2008), A/HRC/7/42; and Global Witness, *Cambodia's Family Trees: Illegal Logging and the Stripping of Public Assets by Cambodia's Elite* (London, 2007).

This depiction of the state of human rights in Asia may seem grossly exaggerated. But I have drawn the above picture from annual reports of international agencies and international and local NGOs, scholarly literature, and personal observation in numerous countries. The principal causes of this pattern of violations are obvious: ethnic conflicts (Pakistan, Sri Lanka, India, Iraq, China, Thailand), terrorism as well as the fight against it (India, Indonesia, Pakistan, the Philippines) and the consequent instability of the government, persecution of religious or ethnic minorities, intolerance of religion or particular sects (China, Pakistan, Vietnam), fundamentalism (Pakistan, Iran, India), authoritarian regimes intolerant of any opposition (China, Myanmar), social oppression due to caste or other social structures (India, Nepal, Japan), poverty (China, India, the Philippines, Nepal), globalization whose benefits are unevenly distributed, as between sectors of society and as between rural and urban populace (China, India), and between national and migrant labour, particularly women (Malaysia, Singapore, and Hong Kong).

The patterns outlined above indicate that massive violations of human rights take place as a result of state action or non-action. Many deaths occur of persons in police or prison custody, for example. So do disappearances. But much oppression also takes place in civil society and cultural domains. Particularly notorious is the practice of "honour killings"; when a girl or woman is deemed to have broken some rule in the moral code (like marrying without parental permission, or outside the caste or religion) she may be killed by members of her family – with total impunity (Pakistan, Afghanistan, North India).[23] The injustices that take place are through discrimination against and denigration of low caste groups in most of South Asia, but particularly India and Nepal, are truly appalling – and violate the most fundamental human rights norms – the equality and dignity of all.

The general lack of respect for human rights among governments and turning a blind eye to violations are demonstrated by the fact when the Asian states were chosen for the new UN Human Rights Council (which was intended to strengthen international machinery), the list included some states with notoriously appalling human rights records, like Sri Lanka and Bangladesh. It is also clear that the scope and dimensions of human rights violations in Asia are quite different from violations of rights in Europe. Not only is the discourse of rights different, but the impact of the respect for or the disregard of rights is massive. Perhaps for this reason there is less emphasis on jurisprudential aspects of human rights than in the West (which occupy most textbooks on human rights) and more on social action. The specificities of human rights in Asia can be explored through the following mega-themes.

---

[23] Lynn Welchman and Sara Hossain (eds.), *Honour: Crimes, Paradigms, and Violence Against Women* (London: Zed Press, 2005).

Rights and culture

Discussions on the connection between human rights and culture have had much greater salience in Asia than in other regions. There may be several reasons for this. One is the greater persistence of Asian cultures, and the less devastating effect of colonialism than in Africa and Latin America. Most of the world's great religions emerged in Asia, and still have a strong hold on the imagination and customs of the people. The persistence of these religions and the relative survival of customs and rituals embedded in communities draw attention to the importance of culture and its role in social cohesion. Economic growth, and pockets of prosperity, in Asia has also led the elites to challenge aspects of Westernization which may be perceived as threatening to their dominance of state and society – of which human rights is one. Traditional cultures are perceived to be superior to external values, which have sustained societies for so long and which respond to the genius of these societies.

Consequently, the most common way to challenge the validity or at least the universality of rights is the invocation of cultural relativism. The earliest attack, based on diversity of cultures, to the UN's project on universality of human rights in the late 1940s, came not from Asia (which at the time was emphasizing democratic rights in the struggle of many people for freedom from colonial rule), but from the Association of American Anthropologists. Its members challenged the individual orientation of human rights, saying that in a world order (of which the Universal Declaration of Human Rights would be a part), "respect for the cultures of differing human groups is equally important."[24] Their principal position was that cultures were important, moral judgments are formed by association with the community and its culture. Consequently human rights declarations must take full account of "the individual as a member of the social group of which he is a part, whose sanctioned modes of life shape his behaviour, and with whose fate his own is thus inextricably bound". They argued that definitions of freedom and concepts of the nature of human rights were narrowly drawn, ignoring the cultures of non-European peoples as well as hard core similarities between cultures.

There was a period in the last quarter of the twentieth century when the leaders of certain Asian states (particularly ASEAN states, led by Singapore and Malaysia) started to attack the notion of the universality of human rights, for these sorts of reasons. Against the human rights notions of the West (which they said had led to moral decay, individual selfishness, litigiousness, and problems of social order) they began to posit the virtues of Asian Values. They argued that Asian societies have maintained social stability, economic progress, and a sense of moral purpose because, given their different culture, they place a higher value on duties and subordinate the interests of the

---

[24] Executive Board, American Anthropological Association 1947 "Statement on Human Rights" in *American Anthropologist* Vol. 49 No. 4 October–December 1947 reproduced in Philip Alston (ed.) *Human Rights Law* (Aldershot, Hants.: Dartmouth Publishing Co., 1996).

individual to the higher good of the community. A special value is placed on the integrity of family relationships, which facilitates public order and induces a sense of responsibility in its members for the welfare of others. Underlying these values and practices are the imperatives of harmony and consensus, and of obedience to authority.

Some (like Lee Kuan Yew of Singapore) attributed these qualities to Confucianism, others to vague notions of Asian culture.[25] The West was accused of imposing its values and practices on Asia, in order to subvert the political and economic success of Asia. It is not entirely clear why the ASEAN countries (who were more closely tied, politically and economically to the West than most other Asian countries) pursued this line. It was widely suspected that it was directed at internal liberal, political opposition to the regime. It was also directed at local NGOs who severely criticized the policies and practices of these states for violations of human rights. Perhaps it was also intended to assert the sovereignty of states, fearing that notions of international responsibility for universal human rights might erode that sovereignty and allow external intervention. Less is made of Asian Values these days; the West seemed to have survived remarkably well, economically and politically, despite human rights, and the ideology of globalization has provided a new framework which, for this group, seemed to harmonize the interests of the East and the West.

There is considerable variation in Asian attitudes to the relationship between culture and human rights. Much depends on the position that an individual or group occupies in class or economic positions. Those who do well in traditional social orders or the contemporary state tend not to favour rights (for rights would erode their privileges or require accountability). But many realize that the most acute forms of discrimination, unfairness and oppression take place in "culture", and that human rights, especially with its emphasis on equality, are necessary for fundamental social and economic reforms (reversing the Lee Kuan Yew priority between rights and culture). It was evident to Indians a long time ago, well before independence, when human rights were regarded even more important than democracy for the modernization of society. Notwithstanding that India was a deeply religious society, with many beliefs between whom there was tension, the Indian Constituent Assembly decided that the Bill of Rights was to be the principal agency of social reform. The bill is strongly oriented towards universalism and social reform. Most rights are

---

[25] The principal writings by the proponents of "Asian Values" are an interview by Lee Kuan Yew by the editor of Foreign Affairs, Fareed Zakaria, "'Culture is Destiny': A Conversation with Lee Kuan Yew" (1994) 73 *Foreign Affairs* 109–126 and B. Kausikan, "Asia's Different Standard" in (1993) 92 *Foreign Policy* 24–41. A riposte to Lee was delivered promptly by Kim Dae-jung, then usually referred to as a Korean dissident, who later became president of South Korea, "Is Culture Destiny?" in (1994) *Foreign Affairs* 189–194. For a discussion of the debate and a critique of Asian Values, see Yash Ghai, *Human Rights and Governance: The Asia Debate* (The Asia Foundation's Center for Asian Pacific Affairs, No. 4, 1994). This paper has been reprinted in various anthologies, including Philip Alston (ed.) *Human Rights Law* (Aldershot, Hants.: Dartmouth Publishing Co., 1996).

drawn from Western precedents. Rights are used as a critique of culture, especially Hindu culture. "Untouchability" is abolished and its practice prohibited (art. 17). Traffic in human beings and *begar* (a form of servitude) and similar practices of forced labour are also abolished (art. 23). The freedom of conscience and religion was drawn carefully to ensure that practices like *purdah* or *sati* (widow burning) were not indirectly entrenched (art. 25(2) says that the freedom of conscience shall not prevent the state from regulating or restricting any economic, financial, political or other secular activity associated with religious practice, or to provide for social welfare and reform or the throwing open of Hindu religious institutions of a public character to all classes and sections of Hindus). Reform of Hindu practices is also aimed at by provisions which prohibit discrimination in access to the use of wells, tanks, bathing ghats, and roads and places of public resort maintained wholly or partly out of public funds or dedicated to the use of the general public – with the abolition of discrimination against lower castes the primary objective. The imperative of social reform is evident also in Directive Principles, particularly in article 38(1) which requires the state to "strive to promote the welfare of the people by securing and protecting as effectively as it may a social order in which justice, social, economic and political, shall inform all the institutions of the national life". India placed limitations on the protection of property to reduce the obstacles it would face in the abolition of *zamindari* (a feudal-like form of landholding).

Many other Asian countries have used rights to bring about social reform (including Korea and Taiwan), particularly to promote the situation of women and children. Numerous NGOs exist to promote specific social reforms or the improvement of the situation of particular groups (such as women, children, indigenous peoples, the disabled). Human rights instruments and organizations provide for many of them critical means of networking continent and worldwide. Asian human rights NGOs are among the strongest in the world, and have a forum which links them together for effective co-ordination. The values and the legal structures of human rights are increasingly and often exclusively, the means to mobilize social protests and demands. Human rights are used to critique social relationships and institutions. The empowerment that consciousness of rights has brought to women, peasants, workers, disabled, is among the strongest threats to discriminatory and oppressive cultural beliefs and practices (although the traditional forms of deference and obedience still have a powerful hold in many places).

[On culture and relativism see above pp. 113–15.]

Rights, states and diversity

Understandings of human rights have been shaped by the conceptions of the state. The lineages of human rights in Asia are not to be found in ancient beliefs or texts (despite earnest attempts to trace them, or at least their legitimacy, to the Koran, Vedic scriptures or Confucian classics). The ancient Asian states did not have significant need of "rights" as protection against political authority. These polities cherished cultural diversity. It was no function of the state to impose moral or religious order, much less to impose conformity. The public sphere was narrow and the private extensive, allowing ample space for diverse cultural and religious traditions. Nor did the centre aim towards a tight or detailed regulation of society, but was content with a large measure of decentralization, frequently based on cultural communities. It accepted pre-existing bodies of customs and laws. There were multiple layers of authority and borders were porous, adding to the flexibility of the polity.[26]

Human rights developed in the West simultaneously with the emergence of the modern state, with its enormous monopolies of power, the centralization of authority, and the imposition of legal and administrative uniformities. Rights were adopted as mechanisms of protection against this concentration of power. The specific form that rights took was also to defeat the authority of feudalism and enhance the interests of the new rising class, the bourgeoisie. Conceived within the framework of the "nation state" (the convergence of the territory of state with nation, whose members are united by ties of history and culture), the principal basis of rights and obligations was citizenship. All citizens are equal before the law and enjoy the same rights. The sovereignty of the people is expressed through the state, which provides a common regime of laws, the machinery for justice, democratic rights of franchise and candidacy in elections, protects other rights of individuals, and ensures law and order through its monopoly of the use of force. Linguistic, religious, and cultural affiliations, and membership of a community, of the citizen are irrelevant to his or her relationship to the state. In so far as there are differences of culture (which in a nation state are assumed not to be serious) they are expressed in the private sphere or civil society. Civil and political rights characterize this state, to hold it accountable to the dominant forces in civil society – but on whom depend the question of social justice.

The genesis of human rights in Asia is this legacy of the state, reproduced through colonialism or imitation. Human rights in Europe focussed largely on the relationship between the state and citizens, both protecting and empowering citizens. The state generally reflected civil society values and was held responsible to the people. In Africa and Asia, the modern state, a product of Western expansion, was somewhat abstracted from, and an imposition on, civil society. Few Asian states could be described as nation states, whatever their aspirations. Nor is the state merely the reflection of civil society. It is a powerful means of accumulation, which can exercise considerable autonomy of social

---

[26] Similar accounts of the diversity and flexibility of pre-modern or pre-colonial polities have been presented by other authors (for example, Sudipta Kaviraj, "The Modern State in India" and Bhiku Parekh, "Cultural Diversity and the Modern State" in Doornbos and Kaviraj, Sudipta (eds.) *Dynamics of State Formation* (New Delhi: Sage Publishers, 1997); and Stanley Tambiah, *Buddhism Betrayed? Religion, Politics, and Violence in Sri Lanka* (Chicago: University of Chicago Press, 1992).

forces. The post-colonial state was soon faced with serious challenges. The notion of equal, undifferentiated rights did not quite fit a state where the basic identity was not the national, but communal, religious or ethnic. No country today has cultural, religious, linguistic or even historical homogeneity. A nation state based approach in effect privileges the culture or language of the majority and marginalizes that of other communities even where the state professes neutrality. The attack is sometimes conducted in terms of identity, which has become a fashionable term. Minorities in so-called "nation states" do not get proper recognition of their culture or history or other basis of identity, and this is demeaning to them. While this attack is based on the psychological harm a community suffers, the marginalization of minorities takes other forms as well: exclusion from or under-representation in the institutions of the state, limited opportunities in the economy, social discrimination, lack of access to the legal system, and the denial of justice in many sectors of life.

A considerable part of the attack is expressed in the terms of human rights. Minorities and other disadvantaged communities emphasise the rights of participation (which are not possible unless they have separate representation in state institutions) or access to the basic necessities of life or special measures to overcome their historic or cultural discrimination and injustices. They claim that their right to culture is threatened by educational systems in which their children have to learn in a foreign language, and the conduct of state business in another language further marginalizes their own language at the same time as their economic, political, and social prospects are jeopardized (due to insufficient familiarity with the official language). All these, they claim, are violations of the fundamental right of equality.

Disadvantaged communities sometimes invoke the right of self-determination to advance their claims. In its origin "self-determination" was conceived of as entitling a cultural or national community to a state of its own; successive disintegration of empires was based on this principle, largely in Europe. The UN Charter gave special attention to territories still under colonial rule and highlighted the need to bring them to an independent status, determining this an act of self-determination (under which of course a colony could vote to stay allied to the imperial power or enter into a special relationship). These origins suggested that self-determination was justification for secession, in appropriate circumstances (although outside the colonial context, there was considerable controversy as to what were "appropriate circumstances"). Unlike the approach taken in Europe during the dissolution of empires like the Austro–Hungarian or the Ottomon, when new states emerged largely on the basis of linguistic nationalism, a curiously paradoxical approach was taken in respect of Asia and Africa.[27] While the UN pushed for decolonization, it also set its face against

[27] T.M. Franck, "Postmodern Tribalism and the Right to Secession" in Catherine Brolman, René Lefeber and Marjoleine Zieck (eds.) *Peoples and Minorities in International Law* (Dordrecht: Martinus Nijhoff, 1993).

disturbing boundaries established during imperialism. So many new states emerged with highly diverse peoples (and some communities barely integrated with the rest during colonialism (as in the north east of India and the present ethnic minorities in Myanmar)). Many of whom have not acknowledged the authority of the independent states over them.[28]

The adoption in the two major human rights covenants of the right to self-determination provided a new focus for "self-determination": as the principle of the democratic organization of the state. It means that every citizen and community should have full rights of participation in the decisions on the structure and operation of the state. "Self-determination" could take several forms: special modes of representation, or federalism or autonomy. "Self-determination" in its extreme manifestation of secession (sometimes called the "external aspects of self-determination") would come into operation only if there was a massive denial of human rights to a community. Meanwhile the indigenous peoples claimed, and secured, the right of self-determination in the limited form of autonomy and land rights, as necessary to preserve their life style. Although the accepted orthodoxy now is this restricted understanding of self-determination (endorsed by the UN Human Rights Committee), self-determination evokes powerful emotions of a community wronged and entitled to its own sovereignty. In the political discourse over numerous troubled spots in Asia, self-determination is proclaimed as the moral and legal authority for a disenchanted community to secede. But when both sides are pragmatic, self-determination has provided or can provide the basis of autonomy (India, Indonesia, the Philippines). Autonomy was accepted in India at an early stage of its independence, to accommodate linguistic minorities, and most recently tribal communities in North East India (India like many other Asian states does not like to refer to such communities as indigenous peoples). An aspect of tribal autonomy is the disapplication of considerable national or state laws in favour of customary laws or local legislation.

---

[28] The outstanding exception was British India which was split into two, with the establishment of Pakistan. The claims of a sizeable portion of the Muslim community was based on the European theory of the "nation state". The leading ideologue of the secessionist movement, the poet Muhammed Iqbal, said that the proposition that religion is a private matter is "not surprising on the lips of a European", because Christianity is a "monastic order, renouncing the world of matter and fixing its gaze entirely on the world of spirit". In his view the experience of the Prophet as revealed in the Quran is of a wholly different nature, "creative of a social order". "The religious ideal of Islam is, therefore, organically related to the social order it has created. The rejection of one will eventually involve the rejection of the other. Therefore the construction of a polity on national lines, if it means the displacement of the Islamic principle of solidarity, is simply unthinkable to a Muslim". He rejected Renan's view that nation is not tied to race or religion or geography: "a great aggregation of men, sane of mind and warm of heart, creates a moral consciousness which is called a nation", due to the persistence in India of caste divisions and rivalries (Presidential address to the All India Muslim League, December 1930, reprinted in Sir Maurice Gwyer and A. Appadurai (eds.) *Speeches and Documents on the Indian Constitution 1921–47*, Vol. II (London; Oxford University Press, 1957). Ethnic carnage and the transfer of a population of millions of people no doubt contributed to the international position against revision of colonial boundaries of new states.

In large part because partition or secession was denied under the principle of self-government, ethnicity has become a powerful political force. That force has challenged the paradigm of the regime of rights that rights belong to individuals. If the quarter century after the end of the Second World War saw the rise of the ideology of individual oriented human rights, the last quarter of that century saw a major challenge, in the name of the community, to that approach. If in the first period, self-determination was the foundation of state sovereignty, in the second period it was mobilized to challenge that sovereignty. Ethnicity has not yet vanquished earlier understandings of human rights (and indeed feeds on it) but it has posed a greater challenge to it than autocrats ever did – precisely because it presents the challenge in the language of human rights.

There seem various contradictions between human rights and ethnicity. Human rights seek to be colour blind, aloof from religious or other affiliations; ethnicity makes these affiliations basic to identity and human existence. Human rights empower the individual; ethnicity the group. Human rights are the framework for relations between citizens *inter se* and between citizens and the state; ethnicity compels attention to and regulation of inter-ethnic relations, and the relations of the group to the state. Human rights aim to be inclusive, ethnicity exclusive. Ethnicity has posed problems for human rights in a way that nationalism did not, for the principal reason that nationalism did not seek accommodation of rights within an existing state, but its own state; ethnicity seeks accommodation within an existing state. It internalizes to the state problems that would otherwise dissipate on the formation of a new state; it brings problems of cultural relativism not as concerns between distant societies, but as basic to the very definition and existence of a state, and of the co-existence of groups which under the theory of nationalism are incompatible. Ethnicity seeks to reconfigure the state, the principal framework for the formulation and enforcement of rights, with fundamental implications for how the scope and nature of rights are perceived.

Ethnicity dulls the consciousness of rights (although ethnicity can also be emancipatory, as a basis for resistance to oppression and a primary source of identity, pride and solidarity). While human rights seek to bring groups within a broader unity, emphasizing our common humanity, ethnicity fragments. Violations of rights of members of other groups excite little disquiet; indeed considerable gratification, as the foundation for its own prosperity (e.g. Malays did not criticize the prime minister Muhathir's disregard of human rights whose victims were principally citizens of Chinese and Indian origin and it was only when a fellow Malay, Anwar Ibrahim, was persecuted that Malays took to the streets). There is intolerance of the rights of others to the freedom of expression if that expression is interpreted as a slight on one's religion or culture (which is surely a function of that freedom). India, with a reasonably good record of the freedom of expression banned Salmam Rushdie's book, *The Satanic Verses*, to placate its Muslim citizens (and perhaps also Islamic states). Even more serious is the suspension of rights that accompany ethnic conflicts: freedom of speech; due process; habeas corpus; rights of personal liberty or movement; personal or group security; leading to the militarization of state and society. When ethnicity is translated in the language of rights, it takes the form of group rights which often undermine the essential principles of human rights such as equality, autonomy, and due process, both of outsiders and members of the group. In other words, the conflict between human rights and cultural relativism cannot be treated simply as a philosophical or political discourse, but as a conflict which must be resolved concretely if some degree of order, stability, and mutual respect is to be achieved.

The challenge to individual, citizen-oriented rights is cast in terms of group or collective rights: rights to autonomy, language, religion, special measures ("affirmative action" or "quotas"), regimes of personal laws, separate electoral laws, representation in the government, and proportionality in public services. In these instances citizenship rights of equality would have to be sacrificed to the claims of particular communities, leading to differentiated citizenship.[29] While there is increasing recognition of collective rights, the matter remains deeply contested and controversial, not only at the philosophical level, but also at the material level, for it concerns the distribution of resources and benefits. Some say that if there are too many group rights, the national interest suffers and the national unity is threatened. Others say that unless group rights to benefit minorities are provided, they will protest and try to secede. Yet others say that individual and collective rights have to be fairly balanced so that both national and group identities are recognized, for it is only in this way that national unity can be preserved or enhanced. Constitutional settlements in multi-ethnic societies require the balancing of interests – which is particularly important if there are prior, existing disparities of economic, social or political resources, and particularly if these disparities are the result of state policies.

Achieving this balancing has various implications for the regime of rights. It involves the recognition of corporate identities as bearer of rights (which issue, however, remains deeply controversial, as does the scope of the recognition). To preserve their culture, some communities claim wide exemptions from the application of the bill of rights. This has a dual effect on possibilities of rights.

---

[29] There is now a vast and growing literature on the subject. A great deal of it is inspired by Arend Lijphart who developed the concept of consociation under which ethnic communities are recognized as political communities and participate in state institutions as corporate groups. The idea of consociation is much older than Lijphart's writing – the debate on constitutional reform in India from the early twentieth century contains a bewildering variety of consociation devices. The other strand of literature adopts an "integrative" approach with the emphasis on individual rights, but devices to encourage ethnic communities to co-operate, of which Donald Horowitz is a principal proponent. Here again Indians presaged this approach, in the policy statements of the Indian Congress during the freedom struggle. A modest attempt to describe these approaches and suggest a middle ground is my chapter "Constitutional Asymmetries: Communal Representation, Federalism, and Cultural Autonomy" in Andrew Reynolds (ed.), *The Architecture of Democracy: Constitutional Design, Conflict Management, and Democracy* (Oxford: Oxford University Press, 2002).

One is internal to the community which seeks exemptions: cultural values may in many respects be hostile to rights and modern democratic thought, and this places groups within the community at risk, such as women and lower castes. Discrimination within the community has become a matter of intense controversy in India and Israel, where the Islamic and Jewish personal laws disadvantage women. The discrimination is resented both within the community as well as by groups outside the community. The consequences spill over into the political domain, raising questions of national integration. In Israel, for example, 14 religious communities are recognized, each with its own system of courts. For Muslims, the presence of sharia courts has reinforced their sense of community and its values. But it has disadvantaged women (as also in India) and has isolated Arabs from the mainstream of Israeli politics. For the Jews, the rabbinical courts have been deeply divisive, symbolizing the fundamental schism between orthodox and secular Jews. In both instances the courts give the clergy, committed to the preservation of orthodoxy, a specially privileged position. The law is slow to change in these circumstances, and lags well behind social attitudes and social realities.[30]

Special regimes of laws can also disadvantage members of other communities. Affirmative action in Malaysia and India for "indigenous" Malays or Dalits or tribals in India have caused much resentment among other communities as this limits their access to education, business opportunities, and employment in the public sector. At the same time it reinforces ethnic and caste communities, particularly among the disadvantaged communities who would have an interest in national and social integration as an escape – for it is only through preserving those classifications that the preferential scheme can be sustained. And yet it is by redressing past or present injustices that a sense of national unity can be fostered.[31]

The lesson perhaps is that there cannot be, in relation to most rights, a notion of absolutism; there must be an acceptance of qualifications on rights. This exercise of qualifying rights forces constitution-makers to try to understand and define the core of the rights concerned, so that qualifications are consistent with maintaining that right. The appropriate formulation and protection of social, economic, and cultural rights, emphasizing the "positive duties" of the state, is often fundamental to a settlement, both to acknowledge the importance of culture and of redress of ethnic inequalities. Thus for this (and other reasons

---

[30] For contrasting views on the effect of personal laws in Israel, see Martin Edelman, *Courts, Politics and Culture in Israel* (Charlottesville: University of Virginia, 1994) and G. J. Jacobsohn, *Apple of Gold: Constitutionalism in Israel and the US* (Princeton: Princeton University Press, 1993).

[31] Various attempts have been made to reconcile these conflicts of interests within a framework of rights (including, at least in the case of personal laws, possibilities of "exit" for a person or group unhappy with the rule of the community – but this is seldom satisfactory, for it posits a sharp separation of identities). One such interesting effort (not entirely convincing to me) is Will Kymlicka "The Good, the Bad and the Intolerable – Minority Group Rights" in *Dissent* Summer 1996.

of "ethnic" management) there arises the necessity for an activist state. Since inter-ethnic relations are so crucial to an enduring settlement and past history may have been marked by discrimination or exploitation, a substantial part of the regime of rights has to be made binding on private parties.

An indication of the Indian solution to problems of diversity has already been given in this chapter. It is clear from that that simple polarities, universalism v particularism, secular v religious, tradition v modernity, do not easily work; a large measure of ambiguity is necessary for the accommodations that must be made. Consequently most Bills of Rights are Janus-faced (looking in the direction of both liberalism and collective identities). What is involved in these arrangements is not an outright rejection of either universalism or relativism; but an acknowledgment of the importance of each, and a search for a suitable balance, using for the most part the language and parameters of rights.[32] (In Fiji, for example, political parties sought to base their constitutional settlement on the balance between indigenous rights favoured by the Fijian community and individual rights favoured by the Indo-Fijians.[33])

Poverty, human rights and globalization

Inevitably, given that a large proportion of the Asian people live in appalling poverty, there is considerable interest in the relationship of rights to poverty. It is widely accepted that poverty denies the most fundamental of human rights, including life. Poverty is not merely the lack of income. Poverty is about exclusion, physical and economic insecurity, fear of the future, a constant sense of vulnerability. It is the lack of qualities that facilitate a good life, defined in terms of access to the conditions that support a reasonable physical existence and enable individuals and communities to realize their spiritual and cultural potential – opportunities for reflection, artistic creativity, development of and discourse on morality, and contribution to and participation in the political, social, and economic life of the community.*

In an influential article, the Indian political scientist, Rajni Kothari attributes many ethnic and human rights problems in South Asia to globalization, defined in terms of political, economic, and technological forms established by the West.[34] Relations between linguistic, religious, and caste communities began to be mediated through the state and the market at the same time as the social and cultural bonds of the community were weakened. The pace of globalization, in

---

[32] I have discussed this issue in respect of India, Canada, Fiji, and South Africa in "Universalism and Relativism: Human Rights as a Framework for Negotiating Interethnic Claims" 21:4 *Cardozo Law Review* (2000) 1095–1140.

[33] Yash Ghai and Jill Cottrell, "A Tale of Three Constitutions: Ethnicity and Politics in Fiji", 5:4 *International Journal of Constitutional Law* (2007) 639–669.

* See further below pp. 154–5 (ed.).

[34] The article is reprinted in Rajni Kothari, *Rethinking Development: In Search of Humane Alternatives* (Delhi: Ajanta Publications, 1988) as "Ethnicity".

its economic aspects, has accelerated since Kothari's article was published. There is much debate in Asia on the effect of globalization on human rights, and in particular whether it has accentuated the poverty of the poor. A few states such as Singapore, Korea, and Malaysia had at an early stage embraced globalization as such. But in many states, particularly in South Asia, foreign capital was regarded with some suspicion, as another form of exploitation. The resistance to full incorporation into the international economic system was seen not only as a defence of national sovereignty but also as protection of local economy and the interests dependent on it. Some countries refused to subscribe to international intellectual property rights; wanted to control the export–import regime, and even reserved some industries for state ownership.

In recent years the huge tide of globalization swept all this away. China and India, which until recently resisted the ideological and material forms of Western capitalism, have now embraced them with great enthusiasm (both countries had resisted the international regime of intellectual property law with its tentacles in Western capitalism until the rise of the World Trade Organization – which with international financial institutions now guards global capitalism – and its associated regime of TRIPS, which made adherence to that property law a condition of WTO membership). As a result their economy has grown rapidly, but at considerable social cost. Disparities of income and opportunities have widened greatly. Millions find it more difficult to access social services.[35] Corruption has increased with new opportunities for illicit collaboration between Asian politicians and bureaucrats with international capital – and with it has come the denial of many rights of ordinary people and workers (including the rule of law). The dominance of the economic ideology of globalization has diminished values of equality, solidarity, and social justice. Globalization has arisen on the bases of a series of asymmetries – which are at the root of growing poverty and inequalities. To be fair, these asymmetries were always implicit in the international economic system but globalization has brought a qualitative change with negative consequences for the enjoyment of human rights.

The first asymmetry concerns the relationship between the state and the market. Privatization and liberalization have produced a more "autonomous" market system by decreasing the scope of the powers of the state. Many of the conditionalities imposed on states in the name of structural adjustment policies

---

[35] Albert Chen writes of China: "Although past achievements in social and economic rights have been considerable, given the initial starting point of extreme poverty, marketisation has in recent years resulted in the weakening of state welfare provisions and a greater pressure on families and social groups to take care of themselves, as well as increasing social and economic inequalities among the people' p. 503. op. cit. (footnote 2). In India the dominance of the ideology of globalization has also infected the Supreme Court which appears to have lost its enthusiasm for the protection of the downtrodden, see for example, Surya Deva, "Globalisation and its Impact on the Realisation of Human Rights" in C. Raj Kumar and K. Chockalingam (eds.), *Human Rights, Justice, and Constitutional Empowerment* (New Delhi: Oxford University Press, 2007).

were aimed at "globalizing" national economies through opening them to foreign investment and trade. The moving frontier of the market has opened communities hitherto living in autonomous circumstances with control over their natural resources to the predatory practices of corporations. The conditions of global competitiveness give great leverage to corporations over public policies and practices. Because corporations can move around the globe freely, states compete for investments by, for example, lowering taxes, removing regulations over business, lowering environmental standards, and restraining workers' organizations. The consequent loss of revenue to the state means that it is less able to implement social, economic, and cultural rights at the same time as workers and other communities cannot protect their rights. And there is little check now on the natural tendencies of the market to create or reinforce inequalities.

The excesses and failures of the market led in the twentieth century to a class compact that culminated in social democratic orders in the West. The essence of this compact was a politically and democratically regulated market, in which rights and protections of labour, including minimum wages and safe working conditions, were recognized, basic services and social security were to be provided by the state, and the externalities of corporations were to be regulated. Globalization has upset this balance between the market and social democracy, leaving the market as the primary regulator of political, economic, and social relationships. Consequently the negative consequences of markets can no longer be moderated, and most states are threatened with social disintegration. Globalization has produced a new configuration of relationships and powers, between transnational corporations and governments of their states, between investors and the elites of host states, between corporations and professional associations like those of accountants, engineers, and lawyers, between them all and international financial and trade organizations and international media.

Democracy has also been weakened by the shift of power from the state to corporations, and other global institutions. Increasingly, national policies and laws are determined by these global forces. States are forced into the role of agencies of international capital, and to act against the wishes of their own citizens. There is no democracy when a state becomes answerable to external forces instead of citizens.

The right to self-determination is also diminished when a state joins a regional economic association, which is a product of globalization. In regional associations, capital generally wields more power than other social groups, resulting in democracy "deficit". Forces and institutions which replace state institutions as governing forces are themselves not democratic, being run by bureaucrats on behalf of powerful corporations. Corporations, wielding enormous power, are not subject to the regime of human rights, although they claim the benefits of human rights. The asymmetry between the rapidly emerging world market and the lack of a global democratic order reinforces the power of capital. In these circumstances civil and political rights lose their significance.

A fundamental asymmetry in globalization is between capital and labour. Capital is now free to move across national frontiers; the daily flow of dollars and other major currencies runs into billions. There is no similar mobility for labour. Another asymmetry is between corporations and societies – workers, consumers, and other communities. For many countries, contemporary globalization began with the establishment of "free" economic zones, where many state laws were suspended or modified, including trade union and minimum wages regulations. This puts the workers at an immediate disadvantage vis-à-vis corporations, as they were unable to organize the traditional mode of worker protection. These conditions have now been generalized, no longer confined to enclaves – due to a fundamental asymmetry between capital and labour. Likewise, capital is entitled to national treatment wherever it chooses to go, but not migrant workers, who are subject to considerable legal and practical discrimination in the host countries. Corporations therefore hold labour at ransom, threatening to disinvest if legitimate workers' demands are not moderated either by themselves or the state. Capitalists are much better able to organize and co-ordinate policies and strategies globally than labour – through chambers of commerce, cartels, interlocking relationships, and influence over governments and international financial and trade organizations. The consequence is that labour cannot negotiate with capital in the structuring of industrial relations. Worker rights to association, fair wages, pensions, and safe working conditions have declined sharply as a consequence even as the scale of migration has increased greatly.

Corporations and policies associated with commoditization and marketization are having a profound effect on communities. The growth of wage employment disturbs the rhythm and balance of traditional communities. The appropriation of their resources destroys the basis of their way of life and communal solidarity. Numerous individuals and communities live in fear of eviction from their historical homelands, by corrupt politicians or bureaucrats or their cronies, developers, and corporations, and get little compensation for the loss of their land. In many parts of Asia, indigenous peoples have suffered the loss of their land, in violation of local laws and international conventions, their vulnerabilities exploited and their cultures denigrated or destroyed (as in Cambodia). Mega-projects result in the displacement of communities, exposing them to vulnerabilities over which they have no control; the poor suffer most from the degradation resulting from these projects. Increasingly, communal resources are passing out of the control of communities, converted from commons to individual property, as many tribal and indigenous peoples have discovered.

Freed from national regulation, the global market subordinates societies; the result is greater social polarization, alienation and the disintegration of social bonds, which are weakening the social consensus on growth objectives within the global economy; with the growth of long-term unemployment and precarious forms of work, channels of upward mobility are gradually being closed off, with serious consequences for both the stability and the dynamic evolution of society. There are widespread fears that international economic integration will contribute to domestic social disintegration.

The consequences of these asymmetries for human rights are that the principal framework for human rights, that is the state, is considerably weakened. The state is unable to provide adequate protections for rights, especially social and economic rights. The enormous power and reach of global corporations means that they are the primary determinative of the prospects of the enjoyment or otherwise of rights. Attempts to bring the discipline of human rights on corporations through self-regulating mechanisms have been largely ineffective. The worship of the market has privileged rights of property and the concept of property itself has expanded greatly, particularly "intellectual" property rights. The dominance of property rights has weakened the position of states and labour, and seriously downgraded social and economic rights. Also weakened is the effectiveness of democratic rights in the face of the power of capital. These asymmetries have in this way upset the conception and scheme of human rights.

Conclusion

Human rights did not originate in Asia. They came, indirectly, through colonialism or other forms of influence from the West; they indeed became the ideology and the tool to regain freedom. At that time Asian leaders did not say that human rights were a Western artefact, not suitable for Asia. The absence of the notion of human rights did not mean that the powers of the rulers were arbitrary. The two major influences on governments in south and east Asia – Confucius and Hindu ideas – emphasized the duties of the rulers. But the duties were not converted into the rights of the ruled – nor was there any machinery to enforce the duties. The conversion of duties into rights came only with the establishment of modern states. Both in Confucianism and Hinduism, the ruler's duties came in societies with complex and hierarchical social structures which distributed resources and privileges unevenly, in which the subordinated groups had come to accept, to a considerable extent, their inferior status as part of the natural order of society.[36] Governments did not for the most part welcome rights and the downtrodden, further impoverished by politics and economy, were too afraid to invoke them. Some of the most terrible violations of rights take place when the marginalized communities are trying to assert their rights (particularly Dalits in India, and workers everywhere). Human rights in Asia continue to suffer from this dual disability.

---

[36] Yash Ghai, "Rights, Duties and Responsibilities" in J. Cauquelin, P. Lim, and B. Mayer-König (eds.) *Asian Values: An Encounter with Diversity* (Richmond, Surrey: Curzon Press, 1998) 20–42.

One reason governments did not welcome human rights was that rights seemed to complicate the task of nation building, in states which represented a wide diversity of religions, languages, and historical traditions and histories. Human rights appeared in Europe when the broad framework of the state and its authority was well established (for the most part, in France of course a revolution was needed for the recognition of rights). As this chapter has tried to demonstrate, discourses and claims around rights have become central to Asian polities, with a certain degree of external scrutiny and concern as well as internal mobilization – and governments see the politics of human rights just as another complication, and derogation of their authority.

For similar reasons, human rights and its discourse seem to be more important in Asia and Africa than in Europe. Over centuries' development, society in Europe has become consonant with human rights norms, even as the scope of human rights was widened. Except periodically (as with the terrible violations during the break up of the former Yugoslav federation), affairs of state and society operate in conformity with rights. Human rights litigation is important (and has been increasing at a considerable rate in recent decades) but the function is fine tuning. In Asia, human rights are at the centre of fundamental debates about the structures of state and society, a great deal of whose values and practices may be inconsistent with human rights. Critical issues are connected with oppression in civil society, the authoritarianism of the state, ethnic conflicts, poverty, and marginalization, so that while litigation is not unimportant, the more effective means of change is mass action. Human rights have provided a powerful basis for social mobilization. Litigation has taken the form of public interest litigation, which itself is more of a political than legal instrument, directed at the welfare of communities or other associations. For both these reasons, INGOs and local NGOs have played a critical role in the mobilization of human rights.

The Asian situation demonstrates that the exercise of many human rights is not possible in a state of poverty. The poor are all too susceptible to exploitation, and (despite the "weapons of the weak" available to them) can easily become servile. The poor try to muster as much dignity as possible in the circumstances of their deprivation and exploitation, but their self-respect is violated daily. Some Asian governments have used this type of argument to say that human rights must not be allowed to come in the way of economic development, so that a minimum level of the basic needs can be met. This approach has been roundly, and correctly, condemned. These governments have shown no more respect for social and economic rights than for civil and political. Their approach was long used as justification to suppress political and social opposition to their regimes. The logic of incompatibility of rights and poverty is a greater concern for social justice, and a remodelling of resources. Because human rights issues are so closely intertwined with social justice, there is considerable pressure for the implementation of social and economic rights. Increasingly constitutions address these issues through directive principles of state policy or directly in bills of rights. The collective nature of conflict and redress has also sharpened distinctions between individual rights and group rights. In an attempt to balance these, it has been necessary to abandon the notions of "absolutes" in respect of human rights.

Tensions between human rights and cultural practices are sharper in Asia than elsewhere because ideas of advanced modernity compete with deeply embedded cultural practices (of which Nepal, now undergoing many transitions simultaneously, is a good example). Because communities still provide a framework for many pursuits and relationships, the affinity with and the integrity of the community is critical (and can lead to a certain measure of intolerance of others – in the case of religious communities, this finds expression in growing legislation against attempts at conversion). But here Asia may have lessons for Europe as it wrestles with problems of "multi-ethnicity". In the early months of 2008, the Archbishop of Canterbury (the head of the Anglican Church) has proposed the application of Islamic law and tribunals for its enforcement in family matters for Muslims (to a chorus of protests from the establishment); the Runnymede Trust has issued a handbook on the integration of racial communities; and the Attorney General has issued a paper on citizenship based on "British" values. The issue of the headgear of female Muslim students in public school, although seemingly a trivial matter, was seen by many as striking at the long tradition of secularism, a defining characteristic of the French state. Perhaps globalization will provide a framework for a comparative study of human rights across states, regions, and culture.

4.4. Quotations

(a) The Asian values debate*

Asian perceptions of human rights have been much discussed, particularly outside Asia, stimulated by the challenge to the international regime of rights by a few Asian governments in the name of Asian values. Placing the debate in the context of international developments since the Universal Declaration of Human Rights 50 years ago, [the author] argues that international discussions of human rights in Asia are sterile and misleading, obsessed as they are with Asian values. On the other hand, the debate within Asia is much richer, reflecting a variety of views, depending to a significant extent on the class, economic or political location of the proponents. Most governments have a statist view of rights, concerned to prevent the use of rights discourse to

---

* Ghai wrote extensively about the "Asian Values debate". This quotation is taken from the abstract of his article "Human Rights and Asian Values" (1998a) 9 *Public Law Review* 168. Ghai's position is quite close to that of Amartya Sen, who in a well-known article wrote: "The authoritarian readings of Asian values that are increasingly championed in some quarters do not survive scrutiny. And the grand dichotomy between Asian values and European values adds little to our understanding, and much to confounding of the normative basis of freedom and democracy." (Sen (1997) at p. 40).

mobilize disadvantaged or marginal groups, such as workers, peasants, or ethnic groups, or stifle criticisms and interventions from the international community.[1] However, few of them [i.e. governments] subscribe to the crude versions of Asian values, which are often taken abroad as representing some kind of Asian consensus. [The author] contrasts the views of governments with those of the non-governmental organizations (NGOs) who have provided a more coherent framework for the analysis of rights in the Asian context. They see rights as promoting international solidarity rather than divisions. Domestically, they see rights as means of empowerment and central to the establishment of fair and just political, economic and social orders.

(b) Confucianism*

I do not wish to oppose a broader notion of duty in the sense of responsibilities or civic virtue. There is clearly much that is attractive in persons who are mindful of the concerns of others, who wish to contribute to the welfare of the community, who place society above their own personal interests. No civilized society is possible without such persons. There is also much that is attractive in societies that seek a balance between rights and responsibilities and emphasize harmony. Nor do I wish to underestimate the potential of duty as a safeguard against abuse of power and office. I am much attracted to the notion of the withdrawal of the Mandate of Heaven from rulers who transgress upon duties of rulers (although I am aware that this was largely impotent as a device of responsiveness or accountability or discipline of rulers).

(c) Hong Kong's Basic Law**

It is easy for the Central Authorities, if they were so minded, to bypass or undermine the Basic Law, and they would presumably always find people who are willing to collaborate with them in this enterprise. However, China stands to gain more from a faithful adherence to the Basic Law, to keep promises of autonomy, to permit people of all persuasions to participate in public affairs, to respect rights and freedoms, and to let an independent judiciary enforce the Basic Laws and other laws. This is a more effective way to win the loyalty of Hong Kong people. An adherence to legal norms and consultative and

---

[1] Ghai points to the highly selective presentation of Asian values by some protagonists, glossing over the hierarchical structures of relationships, subordination of women, the exploitation of children and workers, nepotism and corruption based on family ties, and the oppression of minorities. ("Human Rights and Asian Values" (1998a) at p. 177).

* In one article Ghai was less dismissive of the idea of "Asian Values", acknowledging that on one interpretation of Confucianism in which "[t]he key values are loyalty, obedience, filial piety, respect, and protection", the basic ideas can be attractive in some societies ("Rights, Duties and Responsibilities" (1998b) at pp. 37–8).

** Yash Ghai (1999a) *Hong Kong's New Constitutional Order* (2nd edn.) Hong Kong University Press, at 500.

democratic procedures would ultimately benefit the Central Authorities as they grapple with the difficult task of managing affairs on the mainland as economic reforms and the movement for democracy generate new tensions.

(d) The nature of economic, social, and cultural rights*

These rights are often drafted in language that gives considerable discretion to state authorities about standards and timing of the enforcement of the rights (exceptions are the right to free and compulsory primary education and the principle of non-discrimination). The variability of standards arises from the requirement, or, as it has been interpreted, the permission, in the International Covenant of Economic, Social and Cultural Rights (the Covenant) and many domestic instruments, that the rights are to be implemented by the state by devoting to them "the maximum of available resources" (and by not specifying how the availability of these resources is to be determined). Would, for example, a state which spends millions of dollars for a presidential jet when the country is well connected to international routes be in violation of this provision if the money could otherwise have been used for education – and would it make a difference if primary education was already free but progress towards free education at higher levels was stalled? The UN Committee on Economic, Social and Cultural Rights (the Committee) said in its General Comment 3 [para.10] (1990) that:

> In order for a state party to be able to attribute its failure to meet at least its minimum core obligations to a lack of available resources, it must demonstrate that every effort has been made to use all resources that are at its disposition in an effort to satisfy, as a matter of priority, these minimum obligations.
>
> Central to this comment is the notion of priority. It is [our argument] that the general regime of rights is intended to, and can provide, the framework for state policies and priorities.

A further element of variability and discretion arises from the notion of "progressive realisation"…

(e) The justiciability of economic, social, and cultural rights**

Courts can play an important role in "mainstreaming" ESCR by (a) elaborating the contents of rights; (b) indicating the responsibilities of the state;

---

*   From Ghai and Cottrell (2004) "The Role of Courts in the Protection of Economic, Cultural and Social Rights" in Yash Ghai and Jill Cottrell (eds.) *Economic, Social and Cultural Rights in Practice: The Role of Judges in Implementing Economic, Social and Cultural Rights* (London: Interights) at pp. 61ff. This short book explores in detail and depth issues of justiciability and implementation of ESCR and is strongly recommended.

** Ibid. at pp. 86–8. Ghai was sometimes criticized for taking a cautious view of the role of the judiciary in respect of ESCR. In fact he rejected sharp distinctions between negative and positive rights and between CPR and ESCR and, as this passage shows, acknowledged an important role

(c) identifying ways in which the rights have been violated by the state;
(d) suggesting the frameworks within which policy has to be made (to some extent the South African courts have done this, by pointing to the need to make policies about the enforcement of rights, and the Indian courts by highlighting the failure of government to fulfil [Directive Principles of State Policy] so many years after independence). There is a fine balance here, for there is always a risk that courts may cross the line between indicating failures of policy and priorities and indicating so clearly what these priorities ought to be that they are actually making policy. ...

The role of the courts is not static. It may expand as standards and benchmarks are established, as the Constitutional Court in *Grootboom* recognized. That court emphasized the need for reasonable measures for the implementation of the legislative provisions, and gave some indication of what would be reasonable legislation and "other measures". On the other hand, it said:

> In determining whether a set of measures is reasonable, it will be necessary to consider housing problems in their social, economic and historical context and to consider the capacity of institutions responsible for implementing the programme. The programme must be balanced and flexible and make appropriate provision for attention to housing crises and to short, medium and long term needs. A programme that excludes a significant segment of society cannot be said to be reasonable. Conditions do not remain static and therefore the programme will require continuous review.[1]

In other words, the right involved the creation of a system of a certain kind ("coherent, coordinated programme designed to meet" constitutional obligations) rather than the creation of fully individual protection (suggesting a major difference between ESCR and civil and political rights).

Ultimately there must be a role for the courts. But it is a rather different role than for civil and political rights. The courts refined and elaborated those rights, though they were conceived by political theorists. The courts will, or should, play a much less prominent role in the continuing process of elaborating ESCR. Arbour J. (dissenting) drew a clear distinction between the appropriate and inappropriate roles of the courts in the *Gosselin* case when she said:

> While it may be true that courts are ill-equipped to decide policy matters concerning resource allocation – questions of how much the state should spend, and in what manner – this does not support the conclusion that justiciability is a threshold issue barring the consideration of the substantive claim in this case. As indicated above, this case raises altogether a different question:

for the judiciary as one of the institutions responsible for their development. He was, however critical, of An-Na'im's more forceful rejection of any such distinctions and he cited the case of *Upendra Baxi v. State of Uttar Pradesh* (1986) 4 SCC 106 as an example of the courts getting involved in an unsuitable activity (here the court supervised a home for women for five years). Ghai and Cottrell (2004) give an excellent conspectus of the debate, but in the end the differences appear to be more of emphasis than substance.
[1] *Government of the Republic of South Africa v Grootboom and Ors* [2000] 11 BCLR 1169.

namely, whether the state is under a positive obligation to provide basic means of subsistence to those who cannot provide for themselves. In contrast to the sorts of policy matters expressed in the justiciability concern, this is a question about what kinds of claims individuals can assert against the state. The role of courts as interpreters of the Charter and guardians of its fundamental freedoms against legislative or administrative infringements by the state requires them to adjudicate such rights-based claims. One can in principle answer the question of whether a Charter right exists – in this case, to a level of welfare sufficient to meet one's basic needs – without addressing how much expenditure by the state is necessary in order to secure that right. It is only the latter question that is, properly speaking, non-justiciable.[2]

As the process of elaboration of ESCR proceeds outside the courts, the main contribution of the latter will be in developing core or minimum entitlements.

Justiciability may sometimes have a price. In a number of ways, involving judges may have an impact on the role of the courts, and even on attitudes to human rights. Human rights have, or should have, a major role to play in strengthening the accountability of government to the people … Justiciability is not enough. The classical role of justiciability is that of last resort – one goes to court when all else fails. But the problem with ESCR has been that in far too many countries all else has not been tried. What is needed is for the concepts and tools to be refined, and the institutions to be developed. When this has been done, adjudication as a last resort will no longer seem as ridiculous as it now does to some, and will also, paradoxically, be less necessary.

(f) Poverty and human rights*

Poverty is not, as some imagine, an original state, nor are the poor the victims of their own faults and weaknesses. Nor is it due to shortcomings in personality or morality, or failures in family or upbringing. Poverty is created by societies and governments … Poverty is about exclusion, physical and economic insecurity, fear of the future, a constant sense of vulnerability … This definition of poverty is sustained by the concept of human rights, which, with its overriding theme of human dignity, alerts us to the multiple dimensions of the human person. Indeed to secure an insight into the nature of poverty we should examine the ways in which poverty negates the realisation or enjoyment of human rights. The essential purpose of human rights, a life in dignity, is rendered impossible by poverty. The daily struggles of the poor constantly humiliate them and register for them their helplessness in the face of state and economy. There is no real possibility of enjoying rights, whether civil and political or social, economic and cultural, without resources such as education, physical security, health, employment, property, participation, and due process – all of which

---

[2] *Gosselin v Québec (Attorney-General)* (2002-12-19) SCC at p. 332.

* From, Yash Ghai, "Human Rights in a State of Poverty" (the inaugural Kenya Human Rights Commission National Human Rights Lecture December 2006).

poverty negates. In poverty there can be no control over one's life chances or even everyday life.

Poverty is a mockery of the concept of the "autonomous individual" which lies at the heart of the dominant tradition of human rights. Existence in hovels without the basic amenities of life allows no time or ability for self-reflection, essential for identity, self-realisation, or making moral judgments. The massive dependence that arises from poverty generates habits of subservience and docility, reinforcing a hierarchy in social and economic relations that denies, as do other aspects of poverty, the underlying premise of the equality and dignity of all persons. Poverty also forces persons into slavery and bondage, and stories of parents selling children into slavery out of desperation are now commonplace in states like India, Bangladesh, and Nigeria – and many other parts of the world. A poor man cannot support his family and tends to draw away from it, burdening the wife with additional responsibilities to sustain the family; poverty creates or reinforces divisions within the family, in which the male members get priority over scarce family resources. In this and other ways, poverty subverts decent and fulfilling family life, at the same time as the Universal Declaration of Human Rights calls the family the natural and fundamental group unit of society which is entitled to protection by society and the state.

(g) Post-modernism, globalization, and the nation state[*]

It is … not surprising that the most interesting constitutional innovations of our time derive from the imperative to accommodate diversities and plurality of identities, captured in the cliché "unity in diversity".[1] The collapse of the theory of the nation-state, which this post-modern pre-occupation leads to, tends to produce a complex, many-layered polity, with centrifugal effects on the sites of power. At the same time the economic globalization sucks state power upwards into confederal and perhaps eventually into federal regional structures – and international economic organisations. Not surprisingly, the question: whither the state? is on the lips of many. That surely is a fascinating question for scholars and practitioners of constitutions and politics. It compels a re-examination of the functions of the state when, amidst numerous global and local arms bazaars, it can no longer claim a monopoly of power – and no longer adequately perform the most basic of state functions, providing security for citizens. The principal parameters of the economic order extend well beyond state boundaries. State ideologies are vigorously, and sometimes violently, contested by particularistic

---

[*] From Yash Ghai, "A Journey Around Constitutions" (2005) 122 *South African Law Journal* 804, at 807.

[1] Neglected is perhaps the even more important concept of "diversity in unity", for unless there is unity among diverse groups, there is no diversity.

claims and interests, for which it is now possible to find support in international norms. Individual rights have to be balanced with group rights.

4.5 Suggestions for further reading[1]

In addition to the works extracted in this chapter, Yash Ghai has published extensively on human rights themes, especially in relation to multi-ethnic societies. He was the principal author of a comprehensive report for the Commonwealth Human Rights Initiative, *Put Our World to Rights* (1991), but this does not fully reveal the distinctiveness of his point of view. In addition to works explicitly on human rights, Ghai has written extensively on constitutionalism, constitution-making, and public law in several countries. His *Hong Kong's New Constitutional Order* (2nd edn., 1999a) is especially influential. "Redesigning the State for Right Development" (2006), "Constitution-Making and Democratization in Kenya (2000–2005)" (with Jill Cottrell (2007) 14 *Democratization* 1) and his semi-autobiographical "A Journey Around Constitutions" (2005) are recent writings of particular interest.

---

[1] For full references, see the Bibliography (below pp. 222ff.).

5

Upendra Baxi

5.1 Introduction[1]

William Twining

[T]he tasks of human rights, in terms of making the state ethical, governance just, and power accountable, are tasks that ought to continue to define the agendum of activism.[2]

---

[1] This is an abbreviated and updated version of Twining (2006) pp. 258–74. I am grateful to Upendra Baxi and Pratiksha Baxi for providing me with some of the background information. The Alternative Law Forum (Lawrence Liang and Arvind Narrain) and the Centre for the Study of Society and Culture (Sitharamam Kakarala and Shurti Chigateri) at Bangalore recently organized extensive conversations with Baxi as an archive for oral history.

[2] Upendra Baxi *The Future of Human Rights* (2002) at p. xii (hereafter FHR). References in this introduction are to the first edition, as it is more accessible and closer to the paper "Voices of Suffering" (1998) that is reproduced in full below. Equivalent passages in the second edition (sometimes differently worded) are referred to as FHR II, e.g. for this quotation FHR II at p. xxi. The second edition involved a considerable re-writing of the early chapters of the first edition, with an increase in clarity, but not, in my view, any substantial shift in views. It also addresses themes about proposed UN norms on the responsibilities of multinational corporations and other business entities, development, terrorism, the notion of "human", and the implications of bio-technology that are further developed in *Human Rights in a Posthuman World* (2007a) (hereafter *Posthuman*). Some of these themes are flagged in the short extracts in sections 5.3 and 5.4. below.

Human rights futures, dependent as they are upon imparting an authentic voice to human suffering, must engage in a discourse of suffering that moves the world.[3]

Upendra Baxi was born in Rajkot, Gujarat in 1938. His father was a senior civil servant and a noted scholar of Sanskrit. Upendra was brought up in a large household. He remembers his childhood environment as a mix of perpetual pregnancies, relentless micro-politics, and a complete lack of privacy. His view of the extended communal family has remained decidedly unromantic and he reacted against this aspect of Hindu culture. He went to university, did well, and soon embarked on a career as an academic, public intellectual and legal activist.

After graduating in law from the University of Bombay (LLM, 1963), he studied at Berkeley (LLM (1966), JSD (1972)) and taught at the University of Sydney (1968–73), where he worked closely with Julius Stone, the well-known legal theorist and public international lawyer.[4] From 1973 until 1996 he was Professor of Law at the University of Delhi. During this period he also served as Vice-Chancellor of South Gujarat (1982–85), Director of Research at the Indian Law Institute (1985–88), and Vice-Chancellor of the University of Delhi (1990–94). From 1996 to 2008 he was Professor of Law and Development at the University of Warwick. He has also held visiting appointments in several American law schools. He has now "retired" to New Delhi.

Baxi has been a prolific writer. In addition to producing over twenty books and many scholarly articles, he has been a frequent broadcaster and contributor to the Indian Press. His early work was largely concerned with public law and law and society in India and he consciously addressed mainly Indian audiences. As an activist he has been very influential both in India and South Asia. He contributed much to legal education; he was a leading commentator on and critic of the Indian Supreme Court and a pioneer in the development of social action litigation and "the epistolary jurisdiction" that gave disadvantaged people direct access to appellate courts. He was also extensively involved in legal action and law reform concerning violence against women,[5] opposition to major dam projects,[6] and litigation and agitation on behalf of the victims of the Bhopal catastrophe.[7] Over time Baxi's interests and audiences expanded geographically, but he has maintained his concern and involvement with Indian affairs. His more recent interests have included comparative constitutional law, the legal implications of science and technology, the aftermath of 9/11, law and development, and above all the strategic uses of law for ameliorating the situation of the worst off.[8]

---

[3] See below pp. 203–4.

[4] Baxi paid tribute to Julius Stone in "From Human Rights to Human Flourishings: Julius Stone, Amartya Sen and Beyond?" (Julius Stone Lecture, University of Sydney, 2001; forthcoming 2009).

[5] Baxi (2003b).   [6] Baxi (2001a).   [7] Baxi (2000b).

[8] Baxi has written a great deal about the uses and limitations of law in furthering the interests of the worst off; but his views on human rights extend beyond law to include ideas, discourse, and praxis.

Baxi describes his perspective on human rights as that of a comparative sociologist of law. Julius Stone, his main academic mentor, was a student of Roscoe Pound. Baxi embraced the sociological perspective, but as a follower of Gandhi and Marx (later Gramsci), and an active participant in protests at Berkeley in 1964–67,[9] he gave the ideas of Pound and Stone a distinctly radical twist. Stone called him a "Marxist natural lawyer";[10] others have pointed to his lengthy engagement with post-modernism. But such labels do not fit him. Marxism proved too rigid and doctrinaire,[11] and post-modernism too irresponsible to be of much use to a practical political agenda.[12] Neither quite fits his not uncritical sympathy for the ideas of Amartya Sen and Martha Nussbaum.[13] Above all Baxi's concern has been for those whom, following Gramsci, he calls "subaltern peoples". Perhaps more than any other scholarly writer on human rights he consistently adopts the point of view of the poor and the oppressed.

Since the early 1990s most of Baxi's work has concerned human rights. Much of it is critical of discourses of human rights, the complexities and compromises involved, and the misuses to which the discourses have been put. The tone is passionate, polemical, and radical, but the style is learned, allusive, and quite abstract.[14] While his arguments are complex, dialectical, and often ironic, one clear message rings out: taking human rights seriously must involve taking human suffering seriously.

---

[9] "It was 'heaven to be alive' those days! To go to the Greek Amphitheater adjoining the International Student House and to hear Joan Baez stringing protest melodies. To read the classic text, *Soul on Ice*, the first to utter the now heavily jargonized phrase: 'When confronted with a logical impossibility, you have the choice to be part of the problem or part of the solution'. Before Berkeley, I never marched with the processions carrying placards.

'Radicalization' occurred on a wholly different learning curve as well when I attended … Professor David Daube's seminars on the notion of impossibility in Roman and Greek law! Professor Daube's charismatic problematic of the course was the situation when a horse was sworn is as a Roman Senator! … David taught me memorably – long before the Derridean/postmodernist vogue – the ways in which the law makes the impossible possible." (Communication to the editor).

[10] Baxi (2001b). Ch. 2 of *Posthuman* contains a forceful, but quite sympathetic, critique of Amartya Sen's theory of human rights (Sen (2004)).

[11] While there is a distinct Marxian strain in Baxi's thought, especially through Gramsci, he has been as critical of Soviet ideology and praxis as of free market capitalism: "Both the triumphal eras of bourgeois human rights formations and of revolutionary socialism of Marxian imagination marshaled this narrative hegemony for remarkably sustained practices of the politics of cruelty." (FHR pp. xiv, cf. 35, 137–38; FHR II at pp. xxiii, 50). Anyway, Baxi is far too eclectic intellectually to be categorized as a Marxist.

[12] FHR pp. 97–100; FHR II at pp. 193–6.   [13] Baxi (2001b) Stone Lecture.

[14] Baxi moves smoothly from his Indian intellectual heritage (Gandhi, Ambedkar, the Supreme Court of India) to Western (especially Anglo-American) jurisprudence (he has written about Bentham, Kelsen, Rawls, Dworkin, and Stone), through Marxian theory (Marx, Gramsci, Benjamin) and Natural law (Aquinas, Gewirth), drawing on contemporary sociology (e.g. Beck, Bourdieu, and Castells) and Continental European philosophy (Foucault, Derrida, Laclau, Levinas), engaging with but distancing himself from post-modernism (especially Rorty) and critical legal studies, and dealing more sympathetically with Nussbaum and Sen.

At first sight, Baxi seems deeply ambivalent about rights: he is a fervent supporter of universal human rights, yet he is sharply critical of much of the talk and practice associated with it and he emphasizes many of the obstacles and threats to the realization of their potential.[15] Although he writes about human rights futures, Baxi is more concerned with struggle than with prediction.

Francis Deng, Abdullahi An-Na'im, and Yash Ghai use the international human rights regime as their starting point. As lawyers, they are aware that this regime is changing, dynamic, complex, and open to competing interpretations. However, they treat it, and especially the Universal Declaration of Human Rights, as being sufficiently stable and clear to provide standards for appraising and giving direction to other normative orders.[16] Like them, Upendra Baxi opposes all forms of imperialism, colonialism, racism, and patriarchy. He steers a subtle path between universalism and relativism. He agrees that humankind as a whole should be the subject of our moral concern. He treats the Universal Declaration as one high point of the development of the current human rights regime. But he sees that regime as being inherently fragile and problematic. And his general tone and positions are more radical than the other three.

Like Ghai, Baxi's initial attitude to human rights is pragmatic: we need to work within human rights discourse not because it clearly embodies universal moral principles,[17] but because in the second half of the twentieth century it became the dominant mode of moral discourse in international relations, edging out other moral tropes such as distributive justice or

---

[15] Rather than accept this as ambivalence, he recalls Gramsci's distinction between pessimism of the intellect and optimism of the will. In writing about attempts to develop "enlightened" policies for the construction of major dams, rather than ceasing their construction as inevitably involving major human rights violations, Baxi comments: "Human rights violations urge us, however, to profess pessimism of will and the optimism of intellect. We need to hunt and haunt all erudite discourses that seek to over-rationalize development. We need to defend and protect people suffering everywhere who refuse to accept that the power of a few should become the destiny of millions." Baxi (2001b) at p. 1529.

[16] Baxi criticizes Ghai for taking the international regime of human rights as his starting point for comparing four constitutional narratives, without mentioning that the Indian Constitution preceded and went further than the Universal Declaration and without emphasizing sufficiently the extent to which human rights are the product of struggles rather than benign "top down" problem solving. Baxi (2000a) at pp. 1184–92, 1203–5 (commenting on Ghai (2000b), extracted at ch. 4.2 above). On other comments on Ghai, see n. 19 below.

[17] Baxi makes interesting points about the intellectual history of who counts as "human" (FHR, pp. 28–30; FHR II), the Hegelian idea of concrete universality (what it is to be fully human) (FHR, pp. 92–7; FHR II at pp. 167–9), and the implications of biotechnology for ideas of "human dignity" (FHR, pp. 161–3; FHR II at pp. 269–72) (see further below pp. 204–7). These themes are developed more fully in FHR II and *Posthuman*. Baxi distances himself from strong relativist positions, while acknowledging that post-modernists and anti-foundationalists have usefully problematized ideas of universality (e.g. FHR, pp. 97–118; FHR II at pp. 175–99), cf. Ghai, above pp. 113–15. He concludes: "The universality of human rights symbolizes *the universality of the collective human aspiration to make power increasingly accountable, governance progressively just, and the state incrementally more ethical.*" (FHR, p. 105, original italics; cf. FHR II at p. 185, wording modified).

solidarity.[18] Just because they have become so dominant the discourses of human rights have been used to support a wide variety of often incompatible interests and this in turn has led to complexity, compromise, contradiction, and obfuscation in both the discourse and the practices of human rights. More than Ghai, Baxi consistently adopts the standpoint of the worst off.[19]

Baxi characterizes human rights discourse as ebullient, even carnivalistic. These adjectives might be applied to his own writings on human rights. Since 1990 he has published at least four books and many articles on the subject. He has written specifically on population control, bio-technology, international business ethics, environmental issues, globalization, terrorism (and responses to terrorism), and good governance, all in relation to human rights. Nevertheless, the core of his thinking is quite stable. Perhaps it can be rendered in four parts: first, the starting point is a concern for and a quite complex idea of human suffering as it is actually experienced anywhere, but especially in the Global South; second, a comprehensive assessment, often sharply critical, of the past history and current state of human rights discourse, theory and praxis, including what he calls the politics *of* human rights; third, an aspirational vision of a just world in which all human beings know and genuinely "own" human rights as resources which can empower vulnerable communities and individuals to interpret their own situations, to resist human rights violations, and to participate in genuine dialogues about alternate and competing visions for a better future in a world; that world will continue to be pluralistic, ever changing, and possessed of finite resources to meet infinite human wants; and, finally, pragmatic suggestions about possible strategies and tactics in the perpetual struggle to move realistically towards realizing this vision (the politics *for* human rights). In short, his objective is to mount a sustained and complex critique of much of the discourse and many of the practices that surround human rights at the start of the twenty-first century and to present a vision, rooted in experiences of suffering, that can serve as a secular equivalent of liberation theology.[20] For Baxi

---

[18] Like this editor, Baxi does not think that human rights discourse can adequately capture the concerns of distributive justice; unlike me he is surprisingly kind to John Rawls' much-criticized *The Law of Peoples* (1999) (cf. Twining, following Thomas Pogge, in *Globalisation and Legal Theory* (2000) at pp. 69–75 and *General Jurisprudence: Understanding Law from a Global Persective* (2009) Ch. 5).

[19] Baxi claims that *The Future of Human Rights* advances a distinctive "subaltern" activist perspective on human rights futures (FHR at p. xiii; FHR II at p. xxii). In a comment on Ghai (2000b) in the *Cardozo Law Review*, Baxi criticizes Ghai from a "subaltern perspective on constitutionalism" (Baxi (2000a) at 1191) for too readily treating international standards as the starting points for modern constitutionalism (see above n. 16), for masking the suffering involved in human rights struggles, for "a wholly utilitarian construction of rights", and for accepting too readily the views of political elites at the expense of ordinary people. Some of this criticism is, in my view, unduly harsh. The sharp tone may have spilled over from Baxi's criticism of Kenneth Karst (2000) in the same symposium for painting an idealized picture of American constitutional history without even mentioning slavery. This may give an exaggerated impression of the differences between Baxi and Ghai.

[20] E.g. Baxi and Ikeman (2006) Introduction.

such a vision – "critical human rights realism" – should become part of the symbolic capital of the poor and the dispossessed to be used as a resource in their struggles for a decent life.

The Future of Human Rights contains the most comprehensive statement of Baxi's views on human rights.[21] The aim is to decipher "the future of protean forms of social action assembled, by convention, under a portal named 'human rights'. This work problematizes the very notion of 'human rights', the standard narratives of their origins, the ensemble of ideologies animating their modes of production, and the wayward circumstances of their enunciation".[22] His central theme is that human rights discourse only has value if it fulfils the axiom "that the historic mission of contemporary human rights is to give voice to human suffering, to make it visible and to ameliorate it".

The article on "Voices of Suffering", which is reproduced in full below was first published in 1998. It contains a succinct summary of all of the main themes in the first edition of *The Future of Human Rights* (2002). The second edition (2006) refined the formulation of ideas set out in "Voices of Suffering" and contains a new chapter on "Market Fundamentalism: Business Ethics at the Altar of Human Rights". The other brief extracts reproduced here illustrate and provide links to some of Upendra Baxi's main writings published in the following decade on development, "terror", ideas of the posthuman, and his satirical rendering of the "human rights" of global capital. Some of these are collected in *Human Rights in a Post-human World*, which can be read as a sequel to and elaboration of particular themes in *The Future of Human Rights*.

READINGS

5.2 Voices of suffering and the future of human rights*

Introduction

An age of human rights?

Much of the Twentieth Century, especially its later half, will be recalled as an "Age of Human Rights." No preceding century of human history[1] has been

---

[21] These ideas are developed at greater length, often more concretely, in lectures, speeches, articles, and pamphlets scattered around websites, learned journals, and activist magazines that are spread widely both geographically and intellectually. Some take the form of detailed commentaries on particular reports or draft texts. Among the most substantial of these are "'A Work in Progress?': The United Nations Report to the United Nations Human Rights Committee" (1996), "'Global Neighbourhood' and the 'Universal Otherhood': Notes on the Report of the Commission on Global Governance" 2 *Alternatives* 525–49 (1996b) (Review essay on the Brandt Report, (1995)). See also FHR II, Ch. 9. See Suggestions for further reading below at p. 210.

[22] FHR at p. v; FHR II at p. xiii.

* First published in 8 *Transnational Law and Contemporary Problems* 125–169 (1998) and reproduced here by kind permission of the copyright holder. This paper is a succinct statement of the main themes and formulations of the first edition of *The Future of Human Rights* (2002).

[1] I use the term "human" as an act of communicational courtesy. Human is marked by the presence of *man*; so is person. My preferred non-sexist version is, therefore, a combination of the

privileged to witness a profusion of human rights enunciations on a global scale. Never before have the languages of human rights sought to supplant all other ethical languages. No preceding century has witnessed the proliferation of human rights norms and standards as a core aspect of what may be called "the politics of intergovernmental desire." Never before has this been a discourse so varied and diverse that it becomes necessary to publish and update regularly, through the unique discursive instrumentality of the United Nations system, in ever exploding volumes of fine print, the various texts of instruments relating to human rights.[2] The Secretary-General of the United Nations was perhaps right to observe (in his inaugural remarks at the 1993 Vienna Conference on Human Rights) that human rights constitute a "common language of humanity."[3] Indeed, it would be true to say that, in some ways, a human rights sociolect has emerged, in this era of the end of ideology, as the only universal ideology in the making, enabling both the legitimation of power and the *praxis* of emancipatory politics.[4]

At the same time, the Twentieth Century has been tormented by its own innovations in the politics of cruelty. The echoes of Holocaust and Hiroshima-Nagasaki suffering vibrate in the Universal Declaration of Human Rights[5] as well as in the millennial dream of turning swords into ploughshares. But the politics of cruelty continue even as sonorous declarations on human rights proliferate. A distinctively European contribution to recent history, the politics of organized intolerance and ethnic cleansing, has been universalized in the "killing fields" of post-colonial experience. The early, middle, and late phases of the Cold War[6] orchestrated prodigious human suffering as well as an exponential growth of human rights enunciations. And if Cold War practices were

first letters of both words: *huper.* I await the day when the word "huper" will replace the word "human."

[2] *See* The United Nations, *Human Rights: A Compilation of International Instruments* (1997).

[3] Boutros Boutros-Ghali, *Human Rights: The Common Language of Humanity*, in United Nations: World Conference on Human Rights, The Vienna Declaration and Programme of Action (1993).

[4] For the notion of ideology as a set of languages characterized by reflexivity – or as "sociolect," see Alvin Gouldner, *The Dialectic of Ideology and Technology: The Origins, Grammar and Future of Ideology* 61–65 (Oxford University Press 1982); J.B. Thompson, *Studies in the Theory of Ideology* (1984). A more recent variant is the use of the phrase "dialects of human rights." *See* Mary Ann Glendon, *Rights Talk: The Impoverishment of Political Discourse* (1991). *See also* David Jacobson, *Rights Across Borders, Immigration and the Decline of Citizenship* 2–3 (1996) (the state, Jacobson rightly stresses, is becoming less constituted by sovereign agency and more by "a larger international and constitutional order based on human rights." Human rights provide a "vehicle and object of this revolution."); Upendra Baxi, 'Human Rights Education: The Promise of the Twenty-first Century?', in *Human Rights Education* 142 (George J. Andreopulos & Richard Pierre Claude eds., 1997) (for a full version, see www.pdhre.org (visited Oct. 30, 1998)).

[5] G.A. Res. 217A, U.N. GAOR, 3d Sess., pt. 1, at 71, U.N. Doc. A/810 (1948), reprinted in 3 *International Law & World Order: Basic Documents* III.A.1 (Burns H. Weston ed., 5 vols., 1994) [hereinafter 3 Weston].

[6] Periodization of "cold war" is crucial to any understanding of how the intergovernmental politics of desire pursued its own distinctive itineraries. The "cold war" condenses many a moment of practices of cruelty while simultaneously registering innovation in human rights enunciations.

deeply violative of basic human rights, post-Cold War practices – for example, "ethnic wars" – are no less so.[7]

Still, though not radically ameliorative of here-and-now suffering, international human rights standards and norms empower peoples' movements and conscientious policy-makers everywhere to question political practices. That, to my mind, is an inestimable potential of human rights languages, not readily available in previous centuries. Human rights languages are all that we have to interrogate the barbarism of power, even when these remain inadequate to humanize fully the barbaric practices of politics.

In this essay, I ponder the future of human rights, a future that is periclated by a whole variety of developments in theory and practice. I do so by addressing seven critical themes:

> *first*, the genealogies of human rights, both "modern" and "contemporary," their logics of exclusion and inclusion, and the construction of ideas about "human";
>
> *second*, the realities of the overproduction of human rights norms and standards, and their significance for human rights futures;
>
> *third*, the politics of difference and identity, which views human rights as having not just an emancipative potential but also a repressive one;
>
> *fourth*, the post-modernist suspicion of the power to tell large global stories (the "meta-narratives") which carries the potential of converting human rights languages into texts or tricks of governance;
>
> *fifth*, the resurfacing of arguments about ethical and cultural relativism interrogating the politics of universality of human rights, making possible, in good conscience, toleration of vast stretches of human suffering;
>
> *sixth*, the danger of conversion of human rights movements into human rights markets; and
>
> *seventh*, the emergence, with the forces and relations of "globalization" (attested to by such dominant ideologies as "economic rationalism," "good governance," and "structural adjustment"), of a trade-related, market-friendly paradigm of human rights seeking to supplant the paradigm of the Universal Declaration.

In addressing these themes, I take it as axiomatic that the historic mission of "contemporary" human rights is *to give voice to human suffering*, to make it visible, and to ameliorate it. The notion that human rights regimes may, or ought to, contribute to the "pursuit of happiness" remains the privilege of a miniscule of humanity. For hundreds of millions of the "wretched of the earth,"[8] human rights enunciations matter, if at all, only if they provide shields

---

[7] For an insightful analysis of "ethnic wars" surrounding the former Soviet Union, see Anatoly M. Kazanov, *After the USSR: Ethnicity, Nationalism, and Politics in the Commonwealth of Independent States* (1995).

[8] *See* Frantz Fannon, *The Wretched of the Earth* (1963).

against torture and tyranny, deprivation and destitution, pauperization and powerlessness, desexualization and degradation.

In this connection, contrary to the range of expectations evoked by the title of this essay, I do not make explicit the actual voices of human suffering to assist our sense of the reality of human rights. But I try to do the next best thing: I endeavor to relate the theory and practice of human rights to the endless varieties of preventible human suffering. Recovery of the sense and experience of human anguish provides the only hope that there is for the future of human rights.

Some de-mystifications

Before I address these themes, some approaches to key words may be helpful. I shun the self-proclaimed post-modernist virtue that, even at its best moment, celebrates incomprehensibility as a unique form of intelligibility.

True, the worlds of power and resistance to power are rife with complexity and contradiction. True also, the production of human rights "truths" contesting those of power is marked by a surplus of meaning. For those who suffer violation, an appeal to public virtue, no matter how creatively ambiguous, remains a necessity. In contrast, brutal clarity characterizes regimes of political cruelty.[9] All the same, I also believe that clarity of conviction and communication is a crucial resource for promoting and protecting human rights. Success in this performance is never assured, but the struggle to attain it is by itself a human rights task.

Human rights

The very term "human rights," which I invoke constantly, is itself problematic. The abundance of its meanings may not be reduced to a false totality such as "basic human rights" inasmuch as all human rights are basic to those who are deprived, disadvantaged, and dispossessed. Nor may we succumb to an anthropomorphic illusion that the range of human rights is limited to human beings; the new rights to a clean and healthy environment (or what is somewhat inappropriately, even cruelly, called "sustainable development"[10]) take us far beyond such a narrow notion. Nor should one reduce the forbiddingly diverse range of human rights enunciations or totality of sentiments that give rise to them to some uniform narrative that seeks family resemblance in such ideas as "dignity," "well-being," or human "flourishing." The expression "human rights" shelters an incredibly diverse range of *desire-in-dominance politics* and

---

[9] The "devout" Nazi or contemporary neo-Nazis are rarely affected in their belief or practice, which agonizes human rights intellectuals in each and every direction of the professed "universality," "indivisibility," and "interdependence" of human rights. The esoteric discourse of human rights intellectuals spills *ink*, whereas the perpetrators spill *blood*.

[10] *See* Andrew Rowell, *Green Backlash: Global Subversion of the Environmental Movement* 4–41 (1996). For the extraordinary relation between Nazism and deep ecology, see Luc Ferry, *The New Ecological Order* 91–107 (Carol Volk trans., 1995).

desire-in-insurrection politics. These forms of politics resist encapsulation in any formula. The best one may hope for is to let the contexts of domination and resistance articulate themselves as separate but equal perspectives on the meaning of "human rights."

Discursivity

By "discursivity" I refer to both erudite and ordinary practices of "rights-talk." Rights-talk (or discursive practice) occurs within traditions (discursive formations).[11] Traditions, themselves codes for power and hierarchy, allocate competences (who may speak), construct forms (how one may speak, what forms of discourse are proper), determine boundaries (what may not be named or conversed about), and structure exclusion (denial of voice). What I call "modern" human rights offers powerful examples of the power of the rights-talk tradition.

What I call "contemporary" human rights discursivity illustrates the power of the subaltern discourse. When that discourse acquires the intensity of a discursive insurrection, its management becomes a prime task of human rights diplomacy. Dominant or hegemonic rights-talk does not ever fully supress subaltern rights-talk. Human rights discursivity, to invoke a Filipino template, is marked by complexity and contradiction between the statist discourse of the educated (*illustrados*) and the subversive discourse of the indigenous (*indio*).[12]

Discourse theorists often maintain that discursive practice constitutes social reality; there are no violators, violated, and violations outside discourse. But such discourse theory ignores or obscures non-discursive or material practices of power and resistance. The non-discursive order of reality, the materiality of human violation, is just as important, if not more so, from the standpoint of the violated.[13]

Logics and paralogics of human rights

By the use of the notion of "paralogics," I conflate the notions of logic and rhetoric. Paradigmatic logic follows a "causal" chain of signification to a "conclusion" directed by major and minor premises. Rhetorical logic does not

---

[11] For example, rights-talk (discursive practice) gives rise to distinct, even if related, regimes (discursive formations): the civil and political rights regime in international law is distinct from the social, cultural, and economic rights regime. The ways in which discursive formations occur determine what shall count as a violation of human rights. The prohibition against torture, cruel, inhuman, degrading punishment or treatment in the civil and political rights formation also prohibits rights-talk which equates starvation or domestic violence as a violation of human rights. The latter gets constituted as *violation* only when discursive boundaries are transgressed.

[12] *See* Anthony Woodiwiss, *Globalisation, Human Rights and Labour Law in the Pacific Asia* 104 (1998).

[13] A point cruelly established, for example, by the "productive" technologies entailed in the manufacture and distribution of landmines or weapons and instruments of mass destruction. It would be excessive to say that these are constituted by discursive practices and do not exist outside of these practices. The materiality of non-discursive practices, arenas, and formations is relatively autonomous of discourse theories. It is another matter that human rights discursive practices are able, at times, to highlight victimage caused by the deployment of these technologies as violative of human rights.

regard argument as "links in the chain," but rather, as legs to a chair.[14] What matters in rhetorical logic is the choice of topoi, literary conventions that define sites from which the processes of suasion begin. These sites are rarely governed by any pre-given topoi or ways of reasoning; rather, they dwell in that which one thinks one ought to argue about.[15] "Human rights" logic or paralogics are all about how one may or should construct *"techniques of persuasion [as] a means of creating awareness."*[16]

The human rights "we-ness" that enacts and enhances these techniques of suasion is multifarious, contingent, and continually fragmented. That "we-ness" is both an artifact of power as well as of resistance. Human rights discourse is intensely partisan; it cannot exist or endure outside the webs of impassioned commitment and networks of contingent solidarities, whether on behalf and at the behest of dominant or subaltern ideological practice. Both claim the ownership of a transformative vision of politics, of anticipation of possible human futures. The historic significance of human rights (no matter what we perform with this potter's clay) lies in the denial of administered regimes of disarticulation, even when this amounts only to the perforation of the escutcheon of dispersed sovereignty and state power.

Future of human rights

A sense of unease haunts my heavy invocation of "the future of human rights." In a sense, this future is already the past of human rights time, circumstance, and manner. What may constitute the future history of human rights depends on how imaginatively one defines, both in theory and movement, the challenges posed by the processes of globalization. Already we are urged to appreciate the "need to relocate" human rights in the "current processes of change."[17] From this perspective, what is mandated is the mode of structural adjustment of human rights reflexivity itself. The prospects of recycling the moral languages of human rights appear rather bleak in our globalizing human condition in

---

[14] *See* Julius Stone, *Human Law and Human Justice* 327 (1966).

[15] This is expressed brilliantly by Umberto Eco thus:

> For example, I can argue as follows: "What others possess having taken it away from me is not their property; it is wrong to take from others what is their property; but it is not wrong to restore the original order of property, putting back into my hands what was originally in my hands." But I can also argue: "Rights of property are sanctioned by the actual possession of a thing; if I take from someone what is actually in their possession, I commit an act against the rights of property and therefore theft." Of course a third argument is possible, namely: "All property is *per se* theft; taking property from property-owners means restoring the equilibrium violated by original theft, and therefore taking from the propertied the fruits of their thefts is *not just right but a duty*."

Umberto Eco, *Apocalypse Postponed* 75–76 (Robert Lumley ed., 1994) (emphasis added).

[16] *Ibid.* at 77. I borrow Eco's phrase explaining the task of rhetoric in general (emphasis added).

[17] *The Realization of Economic, Social and Cultural Rights. Final Report on the Question of the Impunity of Perpetrators of Human Rights Violations (Economic, Social and Cultural Rights)*, (prepared by El Hadji Guissé, Special Rapporteur).

ways that they did not to the forerunners and founders of human rights, from Grotius to Gandhi.

A contrasting vision stresses "rooted Utopianism."[18] It conceives of human rights futures as entailing non-technocratic ways of imaging futures. The technocratic imaging takes for granted "the persistence of political forms and structures, at least short of collapse through catastrophe."[19] In contrast, the non-technocratic ways derive sustenance from exemplary lives of citizen-pilgrims "at work amidst us" who embody a "refusal to be bound by either deference or acquiescence to statism" and "relate fulfillment to joy in community, not materialist acquisition."[20]

This essay hovers uncertainly between the globalization (doomsday) anticipation of the human future and the vision of Utopian transformation animated by exemplary lives of countless citizen-pilgrims.[21]

Suffering

Save when expedient, statist human rights discourse does not relate to languages of pain and suffering in its enunciations of human rights. In contrast, peoples' struggles against regimes practicing the politics of cruelty are rooted in the direct experience of pain and suffering.

Even so, it remains necessary to "problematize" notions of suffering. Suffering is ubiquitous to the point of being natural, and is both creative and destructive of human potential. Religious traditions impart a cosmology to human suffering[22] towards which secular human rights traditions bear an ambivalent relationship. Additionally, recent social theory understanding of human suffering evinces many ways of enacting a boundary between "necessary" and "unnecessary" suffering,[23] sensitive to the problematique of the cultural/professional appropriation of human suffering.[24]

Crucial for present purposes is the fact that some human rights regimes enact an hierarchy of pain and suffering. Statist human rights regimes seek to legitimate capital punishment (despite normative trends signaling its progressive elimination); provide for the suspension of human rights in situations of "emergency" (howsoever nuanced); and promote an obstinate division between the

---

[18] Richard Falk, *Explorations at the Edge of Time: The Prospects for World Order* 101–103 (1995).
[19] *Ibid.*   [20] *Ibid.*
[21] Professor Falk mentions Mother Teresa, Bishop Desmond Tutu, Paulo Friere, Lech Walesa, Kim Dae Jung, and Petra Kelly. But alongside these charismatic figures exist "countless other women and men we will never know." Behind every legendary human rights life lie the lives of hundreds of human beings, no less exemplary. The task of historiography of human rights is to roll back the orders of anonymization. This task gets complicated in some troublesome ways by many a media-porous, UN-accredited, and self-certified NGO that obscures from view the unsurpassed moral heroism embodied in everyday exemplary lives. Falk, *supra* note 18.
[22] *See*, e.g., Thomas Aquinas, *The Literal Exposition on Job: A Scriptural Commentary Concerning Providence* (Anthony Damico trans., Martin D. Yaffe Interpretive Essay and Notes, Scholars Press 1989).
[23] Maurice Glasman, *Unnecessary Suffering: Managing Market Utopia* (1996).
[24] *See, e.g., Social Suffering* (Arthur Kleinman et al. eds., 1997).

exercise of civil and political rights, on the one hand, and social, economic, and cultural rights, on the other. Similarly, some global human rights regimes, policing via emergent post-Cold War sanctioning mechanisms, justify massive, flagrant, and ongoing human rights violations in the name of making human rights secure. Even non-statist human rights discursivity (at first sight "progressive") justifies the imposition of human suffering in the name of autonomy and identity movements. The processes of globalization prescribe and apply a new dramaturgy of "justifiable" human suffering.

In sum, relating the future of human rights to human suffering is fateful for the future of human rights.

Two notions of human rights: "modern" and "contemporary"

In this section, the contrasting paradigms of "modern" and "contemporary" human rights are discussed. In many a sense, the distinction between the two masks forms of continuity within the framework of *raison de état*. But critical differences remain.

The basic contrasts seem to me to be four. First, in the "modern" paradigm of rights the logics of exclusion are pre-eminent, whereas in the "contemporary" paradigm the logics of inclusion are paramount. Second, the relationship between human rights languages and governance differ markedly in the two paradigms. Third, the "modern" enunciation of human rights was almost ascetic; in contrast, "contemporary" enunciations present a virtual carnival. Finally, the "contemporary" paradigm inverts the inherent modernist relationship between human rights and human suffering.

The terms I use, *faute de mieux*, may mislead. What I call, "modern" also embraces a Hugo Grotius with his memorable emphasis on *temperamenta belli* (insistence on the minimization of suffering in war) and a Francisco Vittoria who valiantly proselytized, against the Church (to the point of heresy) and the Emperor (to the point of treason), the human rights of the New World. What I call the "contemporary" human rights paradigm is marked in some of its major moments by practices of *realpolitik*, above all the conscripting of human rights languages to brutal ends in former superpower Cold War rivalry and in emergent post-Cold War politics.

In any event, my description of the two paradigms is distinctly oriented to the European imagination about human rights. An adequate historiography will, of course, locate the originating languages of human rights far beyond European space and time. I focus on the "modern" precisely because of its destructive impact, in terms of both social consciousness and organization, on that which may be named – clumsily and with deep human violation – "pre-" or "non-" modern.

The logics of exclusion and inclusion

The notion of human rights – historically the rights of *men* – is confronted with two perplexities. The first concerns the nature of human nature (the *is* question). The second concerns the question: who is to count as human or fully human (the *ought* question). While the first question continues to be debated in both theistic and secular terms,[25] the second – "Who should count as 'human'?" – occupies the center stage of the "modern" enunciation of human rights. The criteria of individuation in the European liberal traditions of thought[26] furnished some of the most powerful ideas in constructing a model of human rights. Only those beings were to be regarded as "human" who were possessed of the capacity for reason and autonomous moral will, although what counted as reason and will varied in the long development of European liberal tradition. In its major phases of development, "slaves," "heathens," "barbarians," colonized peoples, indigenous populations, women, children, the impoverished, and the "insane" have been, at various times and in various ways, thought unworthy of being bearers of human rights. In other words, these discursive devices of Enlightenment rationality were devices of exclusion. The "Rights of Man" were human rights of all *men* capable of autonomous *reason* and *will*. While by no means the exclusive prerogative of "modernity,"[27] the large number of human beings were excluded by this peculiar ontological construction.[28]

Exclusionary criteria are central to the "modern" conception of human rights. The foremost historical role performed by them was to accomplish the justification of the unjustifiable, namely, colonialism and imperialism.[29] That justification was inherently racist; colonial powers claimed a collective human right of superior races to dominate the inferior ones ("the Other"). The Other in many cases ceased to exist before imperial law formulations such as the doctrine of *terra nullius*, following Blackstone's scandalous distinction between the inhabited and uninhabited colonies.[30] Since the Other of European imperialism

---

[25] The theistic responses trace the origins of human nature in the Divine Will; the secular in contingencies of evolution of life on earth. The theistic approaches, even when recognizing the holiness of all creation, insist on Man being created in God's image, and therefore was capable of perfection in ways no other being in the world is; the secular/scientific approaches view human beings as complex psycho-somatic systems co-determined by both genetic endowment and the environment and open to experimentation, like all other objects in "nature." These differences could be (and have been) described in more sophisticated ways, especially by various *ius naturalist* thinkers. *See, e.g.,* Stone, *supra* note 14.

[26] *See* Bhikhu Parekh, "The Modern Conception of Rights and its Marxist Critique", in *The Right To Be Human* 1 (Upendra Baxi et. al eds., 1987). *See also* Raymond Williams, *Keywords* 161–165 (1983).

[27] Religious traditions specialized, and still do, in ontological constructions that excluded, for example, Untouchables, rendering them beyond the pale of the *varna* system. *See* Upendra Baxi, "Justice as Emancipation: The Legacy of Babasaheb Ambedkar" in *Crisis and Change in Contemporary India* 122–149 (Upendra Baxi & Bhikhu Parekh eds., 1995).

[28] *See* Peter Fitzpatrick, *The Mythology of Modern Law* 92–145 (1992); Mahmood Mamdani, *Citizen and Subject: Contemporary Africa and the Legacy of Late Colonialism* 62–137 (1996).

[29] Francisco de Vittoria, remarkably ahead of his times, made out a most cogent case for the human rights of the inhabitants of the "New World." See Francisco De Victoria, *De Indis et de Ivre Belli Relectiones* (J. Bate trans. 1917) (orig. ed. 1557).

[30] See Fitzpatrick, *supra* note 28, at 72–91.

was by definition not human or fully human, it was not worthy of human rights; at the very most, Christian compassion and charity fashioned some devices of legal or jural paternalism. That Other, not being human or fully human, also was liable to being merchandised in the slave market or to being the "raw material" of exploitative labor within and across the colonies. Not being entitled to a right to be and remain a human being, the Other was made a stranger and an exile to the language and logic of human rights being fashioned, slowly but surely, in (and for) the West. The classical liberal theory and practice of human rights, in its formative era, was thus innocent of the notion of universality of rights though certainly no stranger to its rhetoric.

The only *juristic* justification for colonialism/imperialism, if any is possible, is the claim that there is a *natural collective human right* of the superior races to rule the inferior ones, and the justification comes in many shapes and forms. One has but to read the "classic" texts of Locke or Mill to appreciate the range of talents that are devoted to the justification of colonialism.[31] The related but different logics combined to instill belief in the collective human right of the well-ordered societies to govern the wild and "savage" races. All the well known devices of the formative era of classical liberal thought were deployed: the logics of rights to property and progress; the state of nature and civil society; and social Darwinism, combining the infantalization and maturity of "races" and stages of civilization. The collective human right to colonize the less well-ordered peoples and societies for the collective "good" of both as well as of humankind was by definition indefeasible as well, and not in the least weakened in the curious logical reasoning and contradictions of evolving liberalism.

Human rights languages and the power of governance

The languages of human rights often are integral to tasks and practices of governance, as exemplified by the constitutive elements of the "modern" paradigm of human rights – namely, the collective human right of the colonizer to subjugate "inferior" peoples and the absolutist right to property. The manifold though complex justifications offered for these "human rights" ensured that the "modern" European nation-state was able to marshal the right to property, as a right to *imperium* and *dominium*.

The construction of a collective human right to colonial/imperial governance is made sensible by the co-optation of languages of human rights into those of governance abroad and class and patriarchal domination at home. The hegemonic function of rights languages, in the service of governance at home and abroad, consisted in making whole groups of people socially and politically invisible. Their suffering was denied any authentic voice, since it was not

---

[31] Bhikhu Parekh, "Liberalism and Colonialism: A Critique of Locke and Mill", in *The Decolonization of Imagination: Culture, Knowledge and Power* 81–88 (Jan Nederveen Pieterse & Bhikhu Parekh eds., 1995).

constitutive of human suffering. "Modern" human rights, in their original narrative, entombed masses of human beings in shrouds of necrophilic silence.

In contrast, the "contemporary" human rights paradigm is based on the premise of radical self-determination, as we shall see shortly. Self-determination insists that every person has a right to a voice, the right to bear witness to violation, and a right to immunity against "disarticulation" by concentrations of economic, social, and political formations. Rights languages, no longer exclusively at the service of the ends of governance, thus open up sites of resistance.

Ascetic versus carnivalistic rights production

The "contemporary" production of human rights is exuberant.[32] This is a virtue compared with the lean and mean articulations of human rights in the "modern" period. In the "modern" era, the authorship of human rights was both state-centric and Eurocentric; in contrast, the formulations of "contemporary" human rights are increasingly inclusive and often marked by intense negotiation between NGOs and governments. The authorship of contemporary human rights is multitudinous, and so are the auspices provided by the United Nations and regional human rights networks. As a result, human rights enunciations proliferate, becoming as specific as the networks from which they arise and, in turn, sustain. The "modern" notion of human rights forbade such dispersal, the only major movement having been in the incremental affirmation of the rights of labor and minority rights. The way collectivities are now in human rights enunciations is radically different. They do not merely reach out to "discrete" and "insular" minorities;[33] they extend also to wholly new, hitherto unthought of, justice constituencies.[34]

Human suffering and human rights

Even at the end of the Second Christian Century, we lack a social theory about human rights. Such a theory must address a whole range of issues,[35] but for

---

[32] For an insightful overview see Burns H. Weston, "Human Rights", in 20 *Encyclopaedia Britannica* 656 (15th ed., 1997), updated and revised in *Encyclopaedia Britannica Online* (1998), (visited Oct. 30, 1998) www.eb.com:180/cgi-bin/g?DocF=macro/5002/93.htm/

[33] This historic phrase comes from the famous footnote 4 in *Carolene Products v. United States*, 323 U.S. 18, 21 n. 4 (1944).

[34] Contemporary enunciations thus embrace, to mention very different orders by ways of example, the rights of the girl-child, migrant labor, indigenous peoples, gays and lesbians (the emerging human right to sexual orientation), prisoners and those in custodial institutional regimes, refugees and asylum-seekers, and children.

[35] By the phrase "a social theory of human rights," a term frequently invoked in this paper, I wish to designate bodies of knowledge that address (a) genealogies of human rights in "pre-modern," "modern" and "contemporary" human rights discursive formations; (b) contemporary dominant and subaltern images of human rights; (c) tasks confronting projects of engendering human rights; (d) exploration of human rights movements as social movements; (e) impacts of high science and hi-tech on the theory and practice of human rights; (f) the problematic of the marketization of human rights; (g) the economics and the political economy of human rights.

The listing is illustrative of bodies of reflexive knowledges. In select areas these knowledges are becoming incrementally available but remain as yet in search of a new genre in social theory. Even as the era of "grand theory" in the imagination of social thought seems to begin to

present purposes it is necessary only to highlight the linkage between human suffering and human rights.

The "modern" human rights cultures, tracing their pedigree to the Idea of Progress, Social Darwinism, racism, and patriarchy (central to the "Enlightenment" ideology), justified a global imposition of cruelty as "natural," "ethical," and "just." The "modern" liberal ideology that gave birth to the very notion of human rights, howsoever Euro-enclosed and no matter how riven with contradiction between liberalism and empire,[36] regarded the imposition of dire and extravagant suffering upon individual human beings as wholly justified. Practices of politics, barbaric even by the standards of the theological and secular thought of the Enlightenment, were somehow considered justified overall by ideologues, state managers, and the politically unconscious that they generated (despite, most notably, the divergent struggles of the working classes). This "justification" boomeranged in the form of the politics of genocide of the Third Reich, often resulting in cruel complicity by "ordinary" citizens, unredeemed by even Schindler's list, in the worst foundational moments of present-day ethnic cleansing.[37]

In contrast, the post-Holocaust and post-Hiroshima angst registers a normative horror at human violation. The "contemporary" human rights movement is rooted in the illegitimacy of all forms of cruelty politics. No doubt what counts as cruelty varies enormously even from one human rights context/instrument to another.[38] Even so, there now are in place firm *jus cogens* norms of international human rights and humanitarian law which de-legitimate and forbid barbaric practices of power in state as well as civil society. From the standpoint of those

disappear, a return to it seems imperative if one is to make sensible a whole variety of human rights theory and practice. Daunting difficulties entailed in acts of totalization of human rights stand aggravated by this aspiration. But I continue to feel that the endeavor is worthy. Valuable beginnings in some of these directions have been made by Falk, *supra* note 18; Wendy Brown, *States of Injury: Power and Freedom in Late Modernity* (1995); Boaventura De Sousa Santos, *Towards a New Common Sense: Law, Science and Politics in the Paradigmatic Transition* (1995); Roberto Mangabeira Unger, *What Should Legal Analysis Become?* (1996). *See also* Upendra Baxi, *The Future of Human Rights* (forthcoming 1999).

[36] See Uday Mehta, *Liberalism and Empire: a Study in Nineteenth-Century Liberal Thought* (1999).

[37] Is this standpoint any more contestable in the wake of Daniel Jonah Goldhagen, *Hitler's Willing Executioners: Ordinary Germans and the Holocaust* (1996) and Richard Weisberg, *Poethics: and Other Strategies of Law & Literature* (1992).

[38] For example: Is capital punishment in any form and with whatever justification a practice of cruelty? When does discrimination, whether based on gender, class, or caste, assume the form of torture proscribed by international human rights standards and norms? When may forms of sexual harassment in the workplace be described as an aspect of cruel, inhumane, and degrading treatment forbidden under the current international human rights standards and norms? Do non-consensual sex practices within marriage relationships amount to rape? Do all forms of child labor amount to cruel practice, on the ground that the confiscation of childhood is an unredressable human violation? Are mega-irrigation projects that create eco-exiles and environmental destruction/degradation acts of developmental cruelty? Are programs or measures of structural adjustment an aspect of the politics of imposed suffering? This range of questions is vast, and undoubtedly more may be added. For an anthropological mode of interrogation, see Talal Asad, "On Torture, or Cruel, Inhuman and Degrading Treatment", in *Social Suffering*, *supra* note 24, at 285–308.

violated, this is no small gain; the community of perpetrators remains incrementally vulnerable to human rights cultures, howsoever variably, and this matters enormously for the violated. In a non-ideal world, human rights discursivity appears to offer an "ideal" even if "second best" option.

No matter how many contested fields may be provided by the rhetoric of the universality, indivisibility, interdependence, and inalienability of human rights, contemporary human rights cultures have constructed new criteria relative to the legitimation of power. These criteria increasingly discredit any attempt to base power and rule on the inherent violence institutionalized in imperialism, colonialism, racism, and patriarchy. "Contemporary" human rights make possible, in most remarkable ways, discourse on human suffering. No longer may practices of power, abetted by grand social theory, justify beliefs that sustain willful infliction of harm as an attribute of sovereignty or of a good society. Central to "contemporary" human rights discourse are visions and ways of constructing the ethic of power which prevent the imposition of repression and human suffering beyond the needs of regime-survival no matter how extravagantly determined. The illegitimacy of the languages of immiseration becomes the very grammar of international politics.

Thus, the distinction between "modern" and "contemporary" forms of human rights is focused on *taking suffering seriously*.[39] Outside the domain of the laws of war among and between the "civilized" nations, "modern" human rights regarded large-scale imposition of human suffering as just and right in pursuit of a Eurocentric notion of human progress. It silenced the discourses of human suffering. In contrast, "contemporary" human rights are animated by a politics of international desire to render problematic the very notion of the politics of cruelty.

Critiques of "contemporary" human rights

Many critiques of human rights have gained wide currency. Unmitigated skepticism about the possibility and/or desirability of human rights is frequently promoted. Unsurprising when stemming from autocratic or dictatorial leaders or regimes who criticize human rights norms and standards on the grounds of their origin, scope, and relevance (almost always reeking of expediency and bad faith), such critiques, when they emanate from foremost social thinkers, require response.

I sample here two overarching criticisms of the idea of human rights. Talking about "contemporary" human rights in the "normal UN practice," Alasdair MacIntyre says, in his widely acclaimed *After Virtue*, that it thrives on "not giving good reasons for *any* assertion whatsoever";[40] he even is moved to

---

[39] Upendra Baxi, "Taking Suffering Seriously: Social Action Litigation Before the Supreme Court of India", in *Law and Poverty: Critical Essays* 387 (Upendra Baxi ed., 1988).

[40] Alasdair Macintyre, *After Virtue* 69 (1984).

conclude that there are no natural or self-evident human rights and that belief in them is one with belief in witches and unicorns![41] Additionally Zygmunt Bauman asserts that human rights have "become a war-cry and blackmail weapon in the hands of aspiring 'community leaders' wishing to pick up powers that the state has dropped."[42] These eminent thinkers present their *ipse dixit*, however, as manifest truths. In contrast, responsible critiques of human rights are concerned with (a) the modes of production of human rights; (b) the problems posed by the politics of universality of human rights and the politics of identity/difference; and (c) the arguments from relativism and multiculturalism. I examine each of these briefly.[43]

The overproduction of human rights

Is it the case that the late Twentieth Century may be characterized by an overproduction of human rights standards and norms, entailing a policy and resource overload that no government or regime, however conscientious, can bear? Does overproduction entail a belief that each and every major human/social problem is best defined and solved in terms of human rights, in terms of the talismanic property of human rights enunciations? Should concentrations of economic power be allowed to harness these talismanic properties?[44]

I address here only the issue of overproduction. The important question concerns, perhaps not the *quantity* but the *quality* of human rights norms and standards since the Universal Declaration of Human Rights,[45] with insistence on their universality and interdependence. Even more striking is the redefined scope of human rights, which now extends to material as well as non-material needs. This conversion of needs into rights, however problematic, is the hallmark of "contemporary" human rights. It results in waves or "generations" of rights enunciations, at times characterized by a "blue," "red," and "green" rights color scheme.[46] Being color-blind, I do not know which color best signifies the emerging recognition of the collective rights of the foreign investor, global corporations, and international financial capital – in short, of global capitalism. But this much is compellingly clear: the emergent collective human rights of global capital presents a formidable challenge to the human rights paradigm inaugurated by the Universal Declaration of Human Rights.[47]

---

[41] *Ibid.* at 66.   [42] *See* Zygmunt Bauman, *Postmodern Ethics* 64 (1993).

[43] For a fuller elaboration, see *supra* note 35.

[44] As is the case with the assorted interest groups of international airlines, hotels, and travel agents who assiduously lobby the U.N. to proclaim a universal human right of tourism? And when a group of predator investment organizations produce a Draft Multilateral Agreement on Investment (MAI)? *See infra* note 73. Must the aggregations of capital and technology (the propriteriat) always be disabled from acting upon the capitalist belief that the protection of its rights as human rights is the best assurance there is for the amelioration of the life-condition of the proletariat?

[45] The Universal Declaration of Human Rights, *supra* note 5.

[46] *See* Johan Galtung, *Human Rights in Another Key* 151–156 (1994).

[47] The Universal Declaration of Human Rights, *supra* note 5.

The astonishing quantity of human rights production generates various experiences of skepticism and faith. Some complain of exhaustion (what I call "rights-weariness"). Some suspect sinister imperialism in diplomatic maneuvers animating each and every human rights enunciation (what I call "rights-wariness"). Some celebrate human rights as a new global civic religion which, given a community of faith, will address and solve all major human problems (what I call "human rights evangelism"). Their fervor is often matched by those NGOs that tirelessly pursue the removal of brackets in pre-final diplomatic negotiating texts of various United Nations' summits as triumphs in human solidarity (what I call "human rights romanticism").

Some other activists believe that viable human rights standards can best be produced by exploiting contingencies of international diplomacy (what I call "human rights realism"). And still others insist that the real birthplaces of human rights are far removed from the ornate rooms of diplomatic conferences and are found, rather, in the actual sites (acts and feats) of resistance and struggle (what I call "critical human rights realism").

All these ways of "reading" the production of human rights are implicit discourse on "contemporary" human rights. I review, cursorily, five principal approaches.

First, an organizational way of reading this profusion, within the United Nations system, concerns hierarchical control over rights production. Increasing autonomy by agencies within the system is seen as a hazard to be contained, as illustrated by the debate over the right to development.[48] Similarly, the manner in which treaty bodies formulate, through the distinctive device of the "General Comment," somewhat unanticipated treaty obligations upon state parties now begins to emerge as a contested process.

Second, some question the value and the utility of the inflation of human rights. Does this endless normativity perform any useful function in the "real world"? Is there an effective communication (to invoke Galtung's trichotomy) among the norm-senders (the UN system), norm-receivers (sovereign states), and the norm-objects (those for whose benefit the rights enunciations are said to have been made)?[49] Who stands to benefit the most by the overproduction of human rights norms and standards? Is it merely a symptom of a growing democratic deficit, sought to be redressed by "legitimation traffic" between norm-senders (the UN system) and norm-receivers (the member states)?

A third reading, from the standpoint of high moral theory, warns us against the danger of assuming that the languages of human rights are the only, or the very best, moral languages we have. Rights languages, after all, are languages of

---

[48] *See* Philip Alston, "Revitalizing United Nations Work on Human Rights and Development", 18 Melb. U. L. Rev. 216 (1991); Jack Donnelly, "In Search of the Unicorn: The Jurisprudence and Politics of the Right to Development", 15 Cal. W. Int'l L.J. 473 (1985). *But see* Upendra Baxi, "The Development of the Right to Development", in *Human Rights* (Janus Symonides ed., forthcoming 1999: UNESCO).

[49] *See* Galtung, *supra* note 46, at 56–70.

claims and counter-claims that typically entail mediation through authoritative state instrumentalities, including contingent feats of adjudicatory activism. The overproduction of rights locates social movements on the grid of power, depriving human communities of their potential for reflexive ethical action. Being ultimately state-bound, even the best of all rights performances typically professionalize, atomize, and de-collectivize energies for social resistance, and do not always energize social policy, state responsiveness, civic empathy, or political mobilization. Not altogether denying the creativity of rights languages, this perspective minimizes its role, stressing instead the historic role of lived relations of sacrifice, support, and solidarity in the midst of suffering.

A fourth orientation views the production of human rights as perhaps the best hope there is for inclusive participation in the making of human futures. It assumes a world historic moment in which neither the institutions of governance nor the processes of the market, singly or in combination, are equipped to fashion just futures. It thrives on the potential of "peoples' politics" (not as a system but as chaos) which may emerge only by a convergence of singular energies of dedication by (local, national, regional, and global) NGOs. No other understanding of women's movements celebrating the motto "Women's Rights are Human Rights," for example, is possible except the one that regards as historically necessary and feasible the overthrow, by global praxis, of universal patriarchy in all its vested and invested sites. This viewpoint seeks to combat patriarchy, persistent even in the making of human rights, and to explore ways of overcoming the limits of human rights languages that constitute very often the limits of human rights action.

A fifth perspective questions the very notion of the overproduction of human rights norms and standards. Not only does the global enunciation of rights entail a long, often elephantine, gestation period;[50] it also produces mainly "soft" human rights law (exhortative resolutions, declarations, codes of conduct, etc.), that does not reach, or even at times aspire, to the status of operative norms of conduct. The "hard law" enunciations of human rights, which become enforceable norms, are very few and low in intensity of application. Contemporary human rights production remains both sub-optimal (whatever may be said in comparison with the "modern" period) and inadequate. The task is, from this perspective, to achieve an optimal production of internationally enforceable human rights.

These ways of reading the profusion of human rights norms and standards carry within them all kinds of impacts on the nature and future of human

---

[50] As is the case with the Declaration of the Rights of Indigenous Peoples, which emerges as a last frontier of contemporary human rights development. M. Cherif Bassiouni offers a useful approach to the normative stages, which he classifies into the enunciative, declarative, prescriptive, enforcement, and criminalization stages. *See* M. Cherif Bassiouni, "Enforcing Human Rights through International Criminal Law" in *Through an International Criminal Court in Human Rights: an Agenda for the Next Century* 347 (Louis Henkin & John L. Hargrove eds. 1994).

rights. A fuller understanding of these impacts is an important aspect of a social theory of human rights.

Politics of identity/difference

Informed by post-modernist mood, method, and message, critics of "contemporary" human rights, which champions the universality of human rights, are anxious at the re-emergence of the idea of "universal reason," a legacy of the Age of Enlightenment that helped to perfect justifications for classical colonialism and racism and for universal patriarchy.[51] The notion of universality invokes not merely new versions of essentialism about human nature but also the notion of meta-narratives: global stories about power and struggles against power. In both of these tropes, do we return to "totalization" modes of thought and practice?

Critics of essentialism remind us that the notion "human" is not pre-given (if, indeed, anything is) but constructed, often with profound rights-denying impacts. Post-modernist critiques now lead us to consider that the idiom of the universality of human rights may have a similar impact. For example, the motto "Women's Rights are Human Rights" masks, often with grave costs, the heterogeneity of women in their civilizational and class positions.[52] So does the appellation "indigenous" in the search for a commonly agreed declaration of indigenous people's rights.[53] Similarly, the human rights instruments on child rights ignore the diversity of children's circumstances. In many societies, the passage between the first and second childhood or the distinction between "child" and "adult" is brutally cut short, as with child labor, the girl child, or children conscripted into insurrectionist-armed warfare.

Are then identities, universalized all over again in positing a *universal* bearer of human rights, obscuring the fact that identities may themselves be vehicles of power, all too often inscribed or imposed? And do the benign intentions that underlie such performative acts of power advance the cause of human rights as well as they serve the ends of power?

Students of international law, knowingly or not, are familiar with post-modernisms. They know well the problematics of identity as vehicles of power, from the Kelsenite "constitutive" theory of recognition of states (under which states may be said not to exist unless "recognized" by others) to

---

[51] Concerning patriarchy, see Sally Sedgwick, "Can Kant's Ethics Survive the Feminist Critique?" in *Feminist Interpretations of Immanuel Kant* 77–110 (Robin May Schott ed., 1997). See also *Feminists Read Habermas: Gendering The Subject of Discourse* (Johanna Meehan ed., 1995).

[52] *See* Elizabeth V. Spelman, *Inessential Woman: Problems of Exclusion in Feminist Thought*, at ix (1988), who maintains that the endeavors of defining "women as women" or "sisterhood across boundaries" is the "trojan-horse of western feminist ethnocentrism."

[53] *See* The Report of the Working Group on Indigenous Population; Russell Barsh, "Indigenous Peoples in 1990s: From Object to Subject of International Law?", 7 Harv. Hum. Rts. J. 33 (1994); Stephan Marquardt, "International Law and Indigenous Peoples", 3 Int'l J. Group Rts. 47 (1995). See also Draft Declaration on the Rights of Indigenous Peoples, Aug. 26, 1994, U.N. Doc. E/CN.4/1995/2 (1994), reprinted in 3 Weston III.F.4, *supra* note 5.

the travails of the right to self-determination. They know how that "self" is constructed, deconstructed, and reconstructed by the play of global power,[54] with attendant legitimations of enormous amounts of human misery. The evolution of the right to self-determination of states and people signifies no more than the power of hegemonic or dominant states to determine the "self" which then has the right to "self-determination." In sum, that right is only a right to access a "self" pre-determined by the play of hegemonic global powers.

Is it any longer true that, outside the contexts of self-determination, the shackles of state sovereignty no longer determine, even when they condition, the bounds of identity? Increasingly, at the end of the century, the de-territoralization of identity is said to be a *global* social fact or human condition.[55] Identities are becoming fluid, multiple, contingent, perhaps even to the point where an individual (or the subject) is viewed, in Chantal Mouffe's words, as "the articulation of an ensemble of subject positions, constructed within specific discourses and always precariously sutured at the intersection of subject positions";[56] and the community appears as "a discursive surface of inscriptions."[57] There is a great appeal in Mouffe's notion of a "non-individualistic conception of the individual," a notion that rejects, relative to human rights, the idea of the individual in terms of "possessive individualism" and that, furthermore, conceives of the individual as "the intersection of a multiplicity of identifications and collective identities that constantly subvert each other."[58]

In any event, [this] kind of thinking raises several questions from the standpoint of those who are engaged in actual human rights struggles. Four may be noted here.

First, are all the identities being made, by processes of globalization, "fluid," "multiple," and "contingent"? If we were to place ourselves in the (non-Rawlsian) position of a person belonging to an untouchable community (say, in a remote area of Bihar, India), would we agree that caste and patriarchal identity are fluid, multiple, and contingent? As an untouchable, no matter how

[54] *See* Hurst Hannum, "Rethinking Self-Determination", 34 Va. J. Int'l L. 1 (1993). He contrasts effectively the reservation by India confining the right to self-determination in Article 1 of the International Covenant on Civil and Political Rights "only to peoples under foreign rule" with the German objection to it insisting on the availability of this right to "all peoples." The zeal with which the developed countries have sought to expand the range of self-determination rights arises from their unique capability for organizing the collective amnesia of their ruthless prowess in suppressing (not too long ago) even the softest voice urging freedom from the colonial yoke. This said, it also must be said that the Indian reservation based on "national integrity" creatively mimes the very same order of enclosure of the politics of identity and difference, in vastly different postcolonial conditions, and the social imagery of colonial/imperial representation of European nation-states.

[55] For a vivid account of the processes, see Arjun Appadurai, *Modernity at Large: Cultural Dimensions of Globalization* 27–65 (1996).

[56] Chantal Mouffe, "Democratic Citizenship and the Political Community", in *Dimensions of Radical Democracy: Pluralism and Citizenship*, 237 (C. Mouffe, ed., 1992).

[57] Chantal Mouffe, "Democratic Politics Today", in *ibid.*, at 14.

[58] Chantal Mouffe, *The Return of the Political* 97, 100 (1993).

you perceive your identity (as a mother, wife, or daughter), you still are liable to be raped; still will be denied access to water in the high caste village well; still will be subjected to all kinds of forced and obnoxious labor; still have your huts set ablaze; still have your adult franchise regularly confiscated at elections by caste Hindu militia.[59] Human rights logic and rhetoric, fashioned by historic struggles, simply and starkly assert that such imposition of primordial identities is morally wrong and legally prohibited. Discrimination on the grounds of birth, sex, domicile, ethnicity, disability, or sexual orientation, for example, counts as a violation of internationally proclaimed human rights. It is the mission of human rights logics and paralogics to dislodge primordial identities that legitimate the orders of imposed suffering, socially invisible at times even to the repressed. But it is a mission that is fraught with grave difficulties. When the imposition of primordial identities occurs in civil society, human rights logic and rhetoric require the state to combat it, raising liberal anxieties about augmenting the New Leviathan. In addition, the state and the law can oppose such imposition only by a reconstruction of that collective identity. The "untouchables" in India, constitutionally christened the "scheduled castes," will have to be burdened by this reconstitution because, in law and society, they necessarily will be either untouchables or ex-untouchables. Justifications of affirmative action programs worldwide, for example, depend on maintaining the integrity of their narratives of millennial histories of collective hurt. It is true that these narratives essentialize historic identities as new sites of injury. But is there a way out of embattled histories, shaped by the dialectics of human rights?

Second, what is there to subvert if identities are "fluid," "multiple," or "contingent"; if the individual or collective self no longer exists as a unified, discursive, or semiotic object that can be said to be a bearer of human rights? If the subject is no more, and only subject-positions exist, how are we to construct or pursue politics for human rights? Put another way, how may one theorize repression and violation? It would unduly burden this essay to sharpen these questions, attend to their genealogy, and salvage the possibility of conversation about human rights from the debris of post-identity discourse. I attempt it elsewhere.[60]

Third, how does this diaspora of identity narratives empower those who are haunted by practices of flagrant, massive, and ongoing violations of human rights? For the *gurus* of post-modern ethics, this is not a seriously engaged concern compared to the preoccupation of defining and contesting all that is wrong with liberalism and socialism.[61]

---

[59] For a devastatingly accurate account, see Rohinton Mistry, *A Fine Balance* (1996).

[60] *See* Baxi, *supra* note 35.

[61] Jacques Derrida properly assails the heady optimism for liberalism of Fukuyama asking, rightly, whether it is credible to think that "all these cataclysms (terror, oppression, repression, extermination, genocide *and so on*)" constitute "contingent or insignificant limitations for the messianic and triumphant post-cold war moment of liberalism." Jacques Derrida, *Specters of*

Fourth, is this human rights path (requiring us to internalize a primordial identity) counter-productive when, in particular, it casts the state and law "as neutral arbiters of injury rather than themselves invested with the power to injure?"[62] Emancipatory in origin, human rights, in the course of enunciation and administration, may become "a regulatory discourse, a means of obstructing or co-opting more radical political demands, or simply the most hollow of empty promises."[63] It is ironic that "rights sought by a politically defined *group* are conferred upon depoliticized *individuals*; at the moment a particular "we" succeeds in obtaining rights, it loses its "we-ness" and dissolves into individuals."[64] Indeed, in certain moments, human rights development yields itself to tricks of governance; the pillar of emancipation turns out to be the pillar of regulation,[65] as seen in some striking detail in the next section. Were this the only moment of human rights, every triumphal attainment would also be its funerary oration. But does not often a regulatory discourse, at one moment, also become, at another moment, an arena of struggle?

If international human rights lawyers and movement people need to attend to the type of interrogation thus raised, post-modernist ethical thinkers need to wrestle with the recent history of the politics of cruelty, which has constructed, as it were, new primordial communities. These are the communities of the tortured and tormented, the prisoners of conscience across the world, represented with poignancy and unequaled moral heroism by Amnesty International. Would it be true to say that their identity as victims is random, contingent, rather than caused by the play of global politics? Until this question is seriously pursued, can it not be said that human rights enunciations and movements commit no mortal sin of essentialism or foundationalism in insisting upon a universal norm that de-legitimates this invention?

Nor does the post-essentialism that achieves many a rhetorical *tour de force* for a Derrida respond to the problematic posed by the archetypal Aung San Suu Kyi. She embodies human rights essentialism. So do the Afghan women who, under dire straits, protest the Taliban regime. So do UNICEF and Save the Children, which, thanks in part to the globalized media, seek at times to do the

---

Marx: the State of the Debt, the Work of Mourning & the New International, 57 (Peggy Kamuf trans., Routledge 1994) (emphasis added). Note the gesture of exhaustion in the words italicized here! At the same time, Derrida asserts, "[o]ur aporia here stem from the fact that there is no longer any *name* or *technology* for determining the Marxist *coup* and its subject." *Ibid.* at 98. What follows? Derrida, after a fascinating detour on the work of mourning and narcissism, enjoins us thus: "[O]ne must constantly remember that the impossible ... is, alas, possible. One must constantly remember that this absolute evil ... can take place. One must constantly remember that it is even on the basis of the terrible possibility of impossible that justice is desirable ..."; though beyond what Derrida calls "right and law." *Ibid.* at 175.

Who is this "one" addressed by Derrida? The avant-garde theorist or the being of those subjected continually to the absolute order of evil? No doubt, it is important to sensitize theoretical fellow travelers to dangers of amnesia. But what does it or should it mean to the victims of orders of absolute evil?

[62] Brown, *supra* note 35, at 27.   [63] *Ibid.*   [64] *Ibid.* at 98.

[65] I adapt here Santos' analysis of dialectic of regulation and emancipation. *See* Santos, *supra* note 35, at 7–55.

impossible, moving the atrophied conscience of the globalized middle classes to an occasional act of charity, even of genuine compassion, thanks to the unbearable CNN and equivalent depictions of cruelly starved children in Sudan midst a well-earned *aperitif* or first course of dinner.[66] No matter how flawed to the Parisian and neo-Parisian cognitive fashions, human rights discourse furnishes potential for struggle that the post-modernist discourse on the politics of identity as yet does not. These cognitive fashion parades must not be allowed to drain emergent solidarities in struggle unless the post-modernist, anti-essentialist critique demonstrates that human rights are a mistake.

Indeed, engaged human rights discourse makes possible a deeper understanding of the politics of difference insofar as it is an act of suffering rather than sanitized thought. It insists that the Other is *not* dispensable; it sensitizes us to the fact that the politics of Otherhood is not ethically sensible outside the urgency of the maxim: "Ask not for whom the bell tolls; it tolls for thee." It insists, with Rabbi Israeli Salanter, that the "*the material needs of my neighbor are my spiritual needs.*"[67] Critically engaged human rights discourse refuses to de-essentialize human suffering, even under the banner of dispersed identities.

The summons for the destruction of narrative monopolies

The post-modernist critique of human rights further maintains that the telling of large *global* stories ("meta-narratives") is less a function of emancipation as it is an aspect of the politics of intergovernmental desire that ingests the politics of resistance. Put another way, meta-narratives serve to co-opt into mechanisms and processes of governance the languages of human rights such that bills of rights may adorn many a military constitutionalism with impunity and that so-called human rights commissions may thrive upon state/regime sponsored violations. Not surprisingly, the more severe the human rights violation, the more the power elites declare their loyalty to the regime of human rights. The near-universality of ratification of the Convention on the Elimination of Discrimination Against Women (CEDAW), for example, betokens no human liberation of women. Rather, it endows the state with the power to tell more Nietzschean lies.[68]

---

[66] But perhaps suffering as a *spectacle* can do no more. For the very act of mass media introducing the spectacle of suffering needs to divest it of any structural understanding of the reduction of suffering itself. In a way, the community of gaze can be only instantly constructed by the erasure of the slightest awareness of complicity. Thus, the mass media must obscure the fact that "all those weapons used to make far-away homelands into killing fields have been supplied by our own arms factories, jealous of their order-books and proud of their productivity and competitiveness – the life-blood of our own cherished prosperity." Zygmunt Bauman, *Globalization: The Human Consequences* 75 (1998).

[67] *Cited in* Emmanuel Levinas, *Nine Talmudic Readings* 99 (Annette Aronwicz trans., 1991) (emphasis added).

[68] "State is the name of the coldest of all cold monsters. Coldly, it tells lies, too; and this lie grows out of its mouth: 'I, the state, am the people'." Walter Kaufmann, *The Portable Nietzsche* 160–61 (1954).

All too often, human rights languages become stratagems of imperialistic foreign policy through military invasions as well as through global economic diplomacy.[69] Superpower diplomacy at the United Nations is not averse to causing untold suffering through sanctions whose manifest aim is to serve the future of human rights.[70] The United States, the solitary superpower at the end of the millennium, has made sanctions for the promotion of human rights abroad a gourmet feast at the White House and on Capitol Hill.

What is more, the post-modernist critique may rightly insist that the classic paradigm of universal human rights contains contradictory elements. The Universal Declaration of Human Rights provides for the protection of the right to property[71] and thereby makes possible its conversion, in these halcyon days of globalization, into a paradigm of trade-related, market-friendly human rights (beginning its career with the World Trade Organization (WTO),[72] now maturing in obscene progression in the Multilateral Agreement on Investment (MAI) of the Organization for Economic Cooperation and Development[73] (OECD)). Global trade relations now resonate with the moral rhetoric of human rights (witness, for example, the discourse on the "social clauses" of the WTO as well as many a bilateral/regional economic/trade arrangement). More to the point, many southern NGOs that merely critiqued globalization now look upon international financial institutions as instrumentalities of deliverance from the pathologies of the nation-state.

The range and depth of post-modernist critiques of human rights is not dissimilar to Karl Marx's critique *On the Jewish Question*,[74] though the unique idiom of post-modernism was not historically available to him. The summons for the destruction of "narrative monopolies"[75] in human rights theory and practice is of enormous importance, as it enables us to recognize that the authorship of human rights rests with communities in the struggle against illegitimate power formations and the politics of cruelty. The "local," not the "global," it needs to be emphasized, remains the crucial locus of struggle for the

---

[69] See Noam Chomsky, "Great Powers and Human Rights: The Case of East Timor", in Noam Chomsky, *Powers and Prospects: Reflections on Human Nature and the Social Order* 169–221 (1996). *See also* Chandra Muzaffar, *Human Rights and the New World Order* (1993).

[70] *American Association for World Health, Denial of Food and Medicine, the Impact of the U.S. Embargo on Health and Nutrition in Cuba* (visited Oct. 24, 1998) www.usaengage.org/studies/cuba.html.

[71] Article 17 protects individual as well as associational rights to property, a provision which for all practical purposes negates the radical looking assurances in Articles 23–26. Not surprisingly, intellectual property rights are fully recognized in Article 27(2).

[72] Agreement Establishing the World Trade Organization, Apr. 15, 1994, *reprinted in* 33 I.L.M. 1144; 4 *International Law & World Order: Basic Documents* IV.C.2a (Burns H. Weston ed., 5 vols., 1994–) [hereinafter 4 Weston].

[73] The text of the MAI is available on the OECD web page (visited Oct. 24, 1998) www.oecd.org/daf/cmis/mai/maitext.pdf. *See also supra* note 44.

[74] For a post-modernist revisitation, see Brown, *supra* note 35, at 97–114.

[75] Lyotard insists: "Destroy all narrative monopolies ... Take away the privileges the narrator has granted himself." Jean Francois Lyotard, *The Lyotard Reader* 153 (Andrew Benjamin ed., 1989).

enunciation, implementation, and enjoyment of human rights. Almost every global institutionalization of human rights has been preceeded by grassroots activism.[76]

From this perspective, claims of "Western" authorship of human rights are sensible only within a meta-narrative tradition that in the past served the domineering ends of colonial/imperial power formations and that now serve these ends for the Euro-Atlantic community or the "triadic states" (the USA, the EC, and Japan). In this dominant discourse, both "modern" and "contemporary" notions of human rights emerge, though in different modes, as a "vision of a *novus ordo selcorum* in the world as a whole."[77] And this discourse prevents recognition of the fact that communities in struggle are the primary authors of human rights. As the golden dust of Universal Declaration festivities settles, no task is more important than tracing the history of human rights from the standpoint of communities united in their struggle midst unconscionable human suffering.

Various feminists have rightly contested the destruction of meta-narratives as inimical to the politics of difference.[78] At the same time, they maintain that the telling of stories of everyday violation and resistance that recognize the role of women as authors of human rights is more empowering in terms of creating solidarity than weaving narratives of universal patriarchy or theorizing repression only as a discursive relation.[79] The feminization of human rights cultures begins only when one negotiates this conflict between meta- and micro-narratives of women in struggle. One may even call the task or mission as one of *humanizing human rights* – going beyond rarefied discourse on the variety of post-modernisms and post-structuralisms to histories of individual and collective hurt. Narratives of concrete ways in which women's bodies are

---

[76] To quote myself, immodestly:

> After all it was a man called Lokmanya Tilak who in the second decade of this century gave a call to India: *swaraj (independence) is my birthright and I shall have it*, long before international human rights proclaimed a right to self-determination. It was a man called Gandhi who challenged early this century racial discrimination in South Africa, which laid several decades later the foundations for international treaties and declarations on the elimination of all forms of racial discrimination and apartheid. Compared with these male figures, generations of legendary women martyred themselves in prolonged struggles against patriarchy and for gender equality. The current campaign based on the motto "Women's Rights *Are* Human Rights" is inspired by a massive history of local struggles all around.

> Upendra Baxi, "The Reason of Human Rights and the Unreason of Globalization", Address at the First A.R. Desai Memorial Lecture (1996). "The historic birthplaces of all human rights struggles are the hearth and the home, the church and the castle, the prison and the police precinct, the factory and the farm." *See ibid.*

[77] Jacobson *supra* note 4, at 1.

[78] *See* Christine Di Stefano, *Dilemmas of Difference in Feminism & Postmodernism* 76 (Linda Nicholson ed., 1990).

[79] *See* Ernesto Lacalu & Chantal Mouffe, *Hegemony and Socialist Strategy: Towards a Radical Democratic Politics* 87–88, 115–116 (1985).

held *in terrorem*[80] do not preeminently feature or figure in human rights theory, and theorizing repression does not, to my mind, best happen by contesting a Lacan, a Derrida, or a Foucault; it happens when the theorist shares both the nightmares and dreams of the oppressed. To give language to pain, to experience the pain of the Other inside you, remains the task, always, of human rights narrative and discourse. If the varieties of post-modernisms help us to accomplish this, there is a better future for human rights; if not, they constitute a dance of death for all human rights.

Arguments from relativism

"Contemporary" human rights paradigms invite post-modernist interrogation when they stress the universality of human rights. But no recourse to a grand theory or to a whole variety of "post-isms" or endologies[81] is required to maintain a just anxiety about the universality of human rights. Any international human rights lawyer worth her or his calling knows the riot of reservations, understandings, and declarations that parody the texts of universalistic declarations.[82] The "fine print" of reservations usually cancels the "capital font" of universality. In this sense, claims concerning the universality of human rights are diversionary, embodying the politics *of*, rather than *for*, human rights. What is universal about human rights is the logic of aspiration, not the reality of attainment.

This logic, however, is at the heart of the "contemporary" relativism/universalism controversy and polemic. Not surprisingly no such controversy afflicted "modern" human rights enunciations that enacted, cruelly, many a variety of exclusionary theory and practice. The "modern" epoch of human rights enunciation was unabashedly relativistic; it claimed individual and collective rights for some peoples and regimes and denied them wholesale to others. Human rights universalism began somehow to become problematic at the very time the Universal Declaration of Human Rights was enunciated[83] and as human rights norms and standards proliferated, extending to the collective rights of de-colonized states and peoples, from the Resolution of Permanent Sovereignty

---

[80] Mary Jo Frug, "A Postmodern Feminist Legal Manifesto", in *After Identity, a Reader in Law and Culture* 7–23 (Dan Danielson & Karen Engle eds., 1995). The lived reality of sex-trafficking, sweat-labor, agrestic serfdom, workplace discrimination, sexual harassment, dowry murders, rape in peacetime as well as in war as a means of doing "politics," torture of women and medicalization of their bodies – all these and related devices of state and society – present problems of routinization of terror. While feminist scholarship has demonstrated the power of story-telling, social theory of human rights has yet to conceive of ways and means of investing individual biographies of the violated with the power of social texts.

[81] *See* FHR II, p. 244.

[82] Upendra Baxi, "'A Work in Progress?': Reflections on the United States Report to the United Nations Human Rights Committee", 36 Ind. J. Int'l L. 34 (1996); Elizabeth Ann Meyer, "Reflections on the Proposed United States Reservations to CEDAW", 23 Hastings Const. L.Q. 727–823 (1996).

[83] *See* Executive Board, American Anthropological Association, "Statement on Human Rights", in 49 *American Anthropologist* 539 (1947).

over Natural Resources[84] (to take a long leap!) to the Declaration on the Right to Development.[85]

Absolute v. universal

Many confusions and anxieties surround the notion of the universality of human rights. To begin, the claim of universality often is confused with the absoluteness of rights. But nothing about the logics of universality renders human rights absolute, and for several reasons, the most obvious being that my right to do or have or be x (or be immune from y) is limited by your similar right to x (and immunity from y).[86] If human rights release individual energies, talents, and endowments to pursue individual or collective life projects, they also set bounds upon them. Human rights thus make sense only within the texture of human responsibilities. The logics of universality entail the interdependence of human rights; every human being is entitled to an order of rights because every other person or human being is likewise entitled to it. If this were not so, human rights would cease to have any ethical justification whatsoever.

This was not always the case. "Modern" human rights logics were absolutist, not universal. "Contemporary" human rights are, in contrast, universal precisely because they deny the absoluteness of any positing of rights. Some human rights are said to be "near absolute," as is the case with a handful of often contested *jus cogens* human rights norms, and the logic of universality is constantly bedeviled by the "utilitarianism of rights," that is, by arguments from consequences.[87]

Thus, the universality of human rights symbolizes the universality of collective human aspiration to make power more accountable, governance progressively just, and state incrementally more ethical. I know of no "relativist" line of thought that contests this *desideratum*.

Multi-culturalism

In complete disregard of the fact that contemporary human rights are not monologically but are dialogically produced and enacted (and stand brokered and mediated by global diplomacy), it still is maintained that human rights enunciations ignore cultural and civilizational diversity. This is bad, even wicked, sociology. The pro-choice women's groups at Beijing, for example, confronted by His Holiness the Pope's Open Letter to the Conference, or the participants at the Cairo summit on population planning, know this well.

The enactment of human rights into national social policies is even more heavily mediated by the multiplicity of cultural, religious, and even civilizational

---

[84] G.A.Res. 1803, U.N. GAOR, 17th Sess., Supp. No. 17, U.N.Doc. A/5217 (1962) reprinted in 4 Weston IV.F.l, *supra* note 49.

[85] G.A. Res. 41/128, U.N. GAOR, 41st Sess., Supp. No. 53, art. 1, at 186, U.N. Doc. A/41/53 (1986), reprinted in 3 Weston III.R.2, *supra* note 5.

[86] *See* Alan Gewirth, *The Community of Rights* 47–48 (1996).   [87] *Ibid.* at 44–54.

traditions. The American feminists on every anniversary of *Roe v. Wade*[88] know this. So does the African sisterhood modulating public policy on female genital mutilation, and the Indian sisterhood in their efforts to outlaw dowry murders. No engaged human rights theory or practice, to the best of my knowledge, pursues universal human rights without regard for cultural or religious traditions. Nor does it succumb, to the virtues and values of ethical relativism.

In ways that relativist arguments do not, the logic of the universality of rights is one that opens up for interrogation settled habits of representation of "culture" and "civilization." It makes problematic that which was regarded as self-evident, natural, and true, and makes possible a friendly human rights reading of tradition or scripture[89] and indeed, the claim that some contemporary human rights were anticipated by them.

Of course, conflicts over the interpretation of tradition are conflicts not just over values but about power as well. In turn, both the fundamentalists and the human rights evangelists become prisoners of a new demonology. Both tend to be portrayed, in the not always rhetorical warfare[90] that follows, as fiends, not fully human, and therefore unworthy of the dignity of discourse. The politics of intolerance begin to thrive all around. The politics of solidarity among human rights activists, national and transnational, begin to be matched by powerful networks of power and influence at home and abroad. The politics of the universality of human rights becomes increasingly belligerent. And the martyrdom count of human rights activists registers an unconscionable increase, at which point the universality of human rights ceases to be an abstract idea with its history of doctrinal disputations, but, instead, a living practice, a form of struggle, a practice of transformative vision. Its truths of resistance, in constant collision with the truths of power, seek to universalize themselves. And its truths are formed not in the comfort of contemplative life but in and through the gulags.

In other words, the claim to the universality of human rights signifies an aspiration and movement to bring new civility to power among states and human societies. Does the dialogue over relativity of values matter much when so much is at stake?

---

[88] 410 U.S. 113 (1973).

[89] Readings of scriptural traditions yield repressive as well as emancipative consequences. As is well-known (or ought to be), long before feminism happened the Koranic verse on polygamy generated a two century old debate (before the doors of *itjehad* were declared to be closed in 10th century A.D.), on the verse on polygamy which was construed to prohibit the practice of polygamy which it, on established reading, permitted. Similarly, rights to sexual orientation – friendly readings have been discovered in major religious texts of the world by the hermeneutic labors of human rights praxis.

[90] Those who proselytize "radical" readings of the scriptural traditions, though no longer burned at the stake, are relentlessly subjected to territorial and even extra-territorial repression and punishment.

Westoxification

Third, although the complex history of the notion of "Westoxification" cannot be pursued here,[91] the critique insists that human rights enunciations and cultures represent secular versions of the Divine Right to rule the "unenlightened." It demonstrates that the West seeks to impose standards of right and justice, which it has all along violated in its conduct towards Islamic and other societies and states.[92] It rejects the notion that the outpourings and actions of the U.S. Department of State and their normative cohorts are exhaustive of the totality of "contemporary" human rights discourse. It seeks to locate the politics of human rights within the tradition of the *shari'a* and other such sacred phrases.[93] As Muhammad Shykh Fadalla has stated: "As Moslems, we consider politics to be part of our whole life, because the Koran emphasizes the establishment of justice as a divine mission … *In this sense, the politics of the faithful is a kind of prayer.*"[94] At the heart of the critique is the epochal politics of difference, which of course does not regard Islam, in the image of "the recurrent Western myth," as a "monolithic" tradition.[95]

Responsible "Westoxification" notions seek to bring an element of piety within the logics and paralogics of the theory and practice of human rights. If the politics for human rights is a kind of "prayer of the faithful" for pious Muslims, so is it also for the secular congregation of a civic religion called "human rights." The contribution that this kind of understanding brings for the future of human rights (of a very different order than that provided by post-modernisms or recrudescent forms of relativism) calls for inter-faith dialogue. A dialogue that will yield a sense of justice to the worlds of power provides invaluable resource to the universalization of human rights.

What is living and dead in relativism?

Relativism, a coat of many colors,[96] indicts the logic of the universality of human rights on the grounds that different cultural and civilizational traditions have diverse notions of what it means to be human and for humans to have rights. While true, this does not make impossible cross- or inter- or trans-cultural understandings. Human rights enactments vouchsafe otherwise, as anyone familiar with the African, Arab, Asian, and Latin American charters or conventions on human rights will testify. To the extent these processes command significance for human futures, arguments from relativism are

---

[91] For a rich account of the history of origins, see John L. Esposito, *The Islamic Threat: Myth or Reality?* 188–253 (2nd ed. 1995).

[92] *See* Muzaffar, *supra* note 69.

[93] *See* the recent *Cairo Declaration on Human Rights in Islam*, in 11 *Human Rights: a Compilation of International Instruments* 478–484 (1997). Quoted in Esposito, *supra* note 91, at 149 (emphasis added).

[94] Quoted in Esposito, *supra* note 91, at 149 (emphasis added).   [95] *Ibid.* at 201.

[96] *See* the superb analysis in Christopher Norris, *Reclaiming Truth: Contribution to a Critique of Cultural Relativism* (1996).

altogether unhelpful, excepting as *realpolitik* which it is the task of "contemporary" human rights to render problematic.

What, perhaps, is helpful in relativism regarding the "contemporary" human rights movement is the notion that human suffering is not wholly legible outside cultural scripts. Since suffering, whether defined as individual pain or as social suffering is egregious, different religions and cultural traditions enact divergent hierarchies of "justification" of experience and imposition of suffering, providing at times and denying at others, language to pain and suffering. The universality of human rights, it may be argued, extravagantly forfeits cultural understanding of social suffering[97] and alienates human rights discourse from the lived experience of culturally/civilizationally constituted "human-ness."

Even so, one may distinguish here the pursuit of suffering as an aspect of a self-chosen exercise of human rights norms and standards (that is, practices of sado-masochism within the human right to "privacy," assuring a right to self-exploitation by way of "victimless crime") from non-consensual and therefore illegitimate orders of pain and suffering imposed by the civil society and the state. Responsible and responsive relativism must be confronted with a human rights ethic that teaches us that the buying and selling of women as chattels in the marketplace, harnessing children in blood sports (like camel riding), or the conscription of children into state armies or mercenary forces is not justified by any serious understanding of culture or tradition.

What we need, is a human right-responsive relativism, one that interrogates the "contemporary" human rights paradigm in its endless renegotiations of its own foundations.[98] This is, as yet, not in sight. The moral invention of the past half-century of human rights theory and practice consists in contesting human suffering here-and-now, and the *nirvana* that contemporary human rights seek is therefore sometimes said to suffer from a relatively impoverished cosmology. However, human rights activism has its own *dharma*, which is the performance of righteous deeds (*karma*) which, too, earn merit (*punnya*) to redeem the "soul."

While the praxis of human rights needs no such eschatology, it simply insists on the development of a theory about secular evil, seeking to place the prerogative of the construction of this evil beyond the hands of those who have the power to inflict it. The maxim of the powerful is "*De Minimis Non Curat Praetor.*"[99] The imperatives of human rights enunciations and movements insist that neither human suffering nor human dignity is *de minimis*. Nor is it the mission of human rights enunciations to make this maxim a legitimate basis for power in state or society.

---

[97] Asad, *supra* note 38.

[98] Stanley E. Fish, "Doing What Comes Naturally: Change, Rhetoric, and Theory", in *Literary and Legal Studies* 29 (1989).

[99] The Praetor has no time for little things or little people.

Yet even in such a moral hierarchy, the universality of human rights elevates the discourse. It does so by (a) creating ethical benchmarks for unjustified and unjustifiable forms of suffering; (b) raising important questions concerning the justification of imposition or acceptance of suffering both at the site of power and of resistance to power;[100] and (c) outlawing practices of the imposition of surplus repression and suffering in ways that put to the test claims to legitimacy of power in states and human communities to account for the imposition of suffering. Post-modernists and relativists are innocent of even a modest reading of the Grotian doctrine of *temperamenta belli.*[101]

All the same, subjection of the notion of human suffering to an ethical relativist standpoint helps us to question human rights holism by alerting us to the fact that all forms of human rights praxis entail the construction of a hierarchy of suffering or evil; and it is difficult to privilege one hierarchy over the other.[102] It summons both human rights theory and practice to a new and higher order of reflexivity.[103]

Human rights movements and human rights markets

Human rights movements as social movements

Human rights struggles are among the most defining characteristics of the second half of the Christian Twentieth Century; indeed, more often than not, we think of human rights praxis in terms of social movements. But the notion of social movement raises many perplexing issues concerning how one may define, classify, and evaluate them, and all remain apposite to a social theory

[100] See the interesting, though not wholly persuasive, analysis in Robert A. Friedlander, "Terrorism and National Liberation Movements: Can Rights Derive from Wrongs?" 13 Case W. Res. J. Int'l L. 281 (1981).

[101] That doctrine renders ethically problematic the practices of total war or total sanctions, which erase the crucial distinction between the regime and the people, combatants and civilians. So does the great *jusnaturalist tradition* in Karl Marx's corpus and the classical Hindu doctrine of *dharama yuddah (just war).*

[102] The way in which human rights mandates are fashioned or formed within the United Nations agencies and across the NGOs illustrates this problem rather strikingly. As concerns the former, it often is argued that specialized agencies claim a version of human rights for themselves rather than for the violated. Katarina Tomaševski has shown recently that much of the discourse of the UNHCR has been focused on the *right of access* by intergovernmental agencies to victims of "wars of hunger," rather than of the human right of access by the violated to ameliorative agencies. Katarina Tomaševski, "Human Rights and Wars of Starvation", in *War & Hunger: Rethinking International Response to Complex Emergencies* 70–91 (Joanna Marae & Anthony Zwi eds., 1997). As concerns the NGO sculpting of human rights mandates, the activist grapevine all too often condemns Amnesty International for focusing too heavily on violations of civil and political rights, in the process failing to fully understand the importance of the protection of economic, social, and cultural rights. Human rights NGOs who adopt a special mandate for themselves (*e.g.,* "sustainable development," "population planning") often are charged with neglecting other bodies of crucial human rights. It is pointless to multiply instances. In each such situation, the criticism is justified only from the standpoint of different constructions of hierarchy of suffering or evil, rarely made theoretically explicit.

[103] *See* Falk, *supra* note 18, at 14–16.

of human rights yet in its infancy. Among the first necessary steps is a fuller grasp of the potential benefits and costs of exploring human rights movements as social movements. How the former define their identity, their antagonists, and their teleology (visions of transformation)[104] shape the future of human rights as a whole. Social theory about social movements stresses the importance of either the Weberian value neutrality or the postmodern suspicion of "predetermined directionality." Thus writes Manuel Castells:

> Social movements may be socially conservative, socially revolutionary or both or none. After all, we now have concluded (and I hope for ever) that there is no predetermined directionality in social evolution, that the *only sense of history is the history we sense*. Therefore, from an analytical perspective, there are no "bad" and "good" social movements. They are all symptoms of our societies and all impact social structures, with variable intensities and outcomes that must be established by social research.[105]

Human rights movements demand such research.[106] But a social theory of human rights may have considerable difficulty with the perspective that demands that even the manifestly rights-denying or rights-diminishing social or human rights movements should escape moral evaluation pending social research. A willing suspension of ethical beliefs, deferring human rights action to sustained social science research, can have impacts on the power of human rights movements to name an evil and to create public concern and capacity to contain or eliminate it. For example, some social movements may defend as just traditions that confine women to home and hearth, or may find justifications for reinventing apartheid and genocide. Indeed, they may claim the protection of extant human rights regimes to do so. Hate speech missionaries seek to "justify" racism as an aspect of freedom of speech and expression. The protagonists of human life invoke the fetal human right to life even to justify aggression on abortion clinics and professionals. The recent Rawlsian notion valorizing the defense of "well-ordered societies" is eminently suitable to justify regimes of military intervention or superpower sanction against the less well-ordered societies.[107]

Such movements turn upside down the very power of human rights rhetoric to identify certain regimes of human rights! The power of human rights discourse to name an order of evil is used to name human rights as the very order of evil! Perhaps, to evoke Castells' phrase, this standpoint emerges as a "symptom" of our societies. No doubt, as he says, these symptoms "impact social structures, with variable intensities and outcomes,"[108] inviting a prolific

---

[104] *See* Manuel Castells, *The Power of Identity* 71 (1997).   [105] *Ibid.* at 70 (emphasis added).

[106] Upendra Baxi, "The State and Human Rights Movements in India", in *People's Rights: Social Movements and the State in the Third World* 335–352 (Manoranjan Mohanty et al. eds., 1998).

[107] John Rawls, "The Law of Peoples", in *On Human Rights: The Oxford Amnesty Lectures* 1993, at 41 (Stephen Shute et al. eds., 1993).

[108] Castells, *supra* note 104.

growth of cognitive social science knowledge to empower us with some understanding. At the same time, human rights praxis (whether through movements
or markets) may generate scientific knowledge rather than await it; the history
of human rights praxis, from Mohandas Gandhi to Nelson Mandela, from Joan
of Arc to Petra Kelly, is truly prefigurative of future knowledges about freedom
and fulfillment.

A social theory of human rights must find bases for ethical judgment concerning "good" and "bad" social movements; howsoever contestable, human
rights movements cannot take as axiomatic the notion that "the only sense of
history is the history we sense." It must seek to provide a "predetermined
directionality" in human social development by articulating an ethic of
power, whether in state, civil society, or the market. It must contest the notion
that certain human interactions and transactions constitute moral free zones.[109]

From "movements" to "markets"

Increasingly, human rights movements organize themselves in the image of
markets. Of course, the use of terms like "market" and "commoditization" may
be deeply offensive to human rights practitioners, and the analogy with markets
may turn out, on closer analysis not to be too strong. Moreover, we should
distinguish between the discourse of social movements and the "social processes
with which they are associated: for example, globalization, informationalization,
the crisis of representational democracy, and the dominance of symbolic politics
in the space of media."[110] From this standpoint, and quite rightly so, "movements" are analytically distinguishable from "markets." A reductionist analysis,
which disregards the relative autonomy of movements from markets, does not
advance clarity or conviction. At the same time, the idiom of the "market" brings
more sharply into view the complexity and contradiction of human rights
movements.

Human rights markets consist of a network of transactions that serve the
contingent and long term interests of human rights investors, producers, and
consumers. These transactions rely upon the availability, which they in turn
seek to reinforce, of symbolic capital[111] in the form of international human
rights norms, standards, doctrines, and organizational networks. Furthermore,
since grids of power are globalized, human rights markets also create and
reinforce global networks, each of which seek to influence the conduct of
those actors who violate human rights norms and standards and the behavior
of those who resist such violations. Human rights market rationality requires
the production and re-production of human rights skills and competences,
which enable negotiation of tolerably acceptable outcomes between and among

---

[109] David Gauthier, *Morals by Agreement* 13, 83–112 (1986).
[110] *See* Castells, *supra* note 104, at 70.
[111] *See generally* Pierre Bourdieu, *The Field of Cultural Production: Essays on Art and Literature*
73–142 (1993); Pierre Bourdieu, *Outline of a Theory of Practice* (R. Nice trans., 1977).

the violators and the violated such that market failures do not erode the legitimacy of the network of overall transactions. Human rights markets thus share the salient features of service industries.

The investor and consumer markets in human rights

Human rights movements at all levels (global, regional, national, and local) have tended to become "capital-intensive." That is, the praxis of protecting and promoting human rights now entails entrepreneurship in raising material resources, including funding, from a whole variety of governmental, inter-governmental, and philanthropic sources. These sources are organized in terms of management imperatives, both of line-management and upward accountability. Any human rights NGO or NGI (nongovernmental individual) currently involved in programs for the celebration of the golden jubilee of Universal Declaration of Human Rights surely knows this! The protection and promotion of human rights is an enterprise that entails access to organized networks of support, consumer loyalty, efficient internal management, management of mass media, and public relations and careful crafting of mandates.

A full analysis of these variables would unconscionably burden this essay; but it needs to be acknowledged that both consumer NGOs and funding agencies compete *inter se* for scarce resources and that this scramble for support generates forms of investor rationality, which generally may be defined as seeking a tangible return on investment.[112] That rationality must negotiate the Scylla of mobilization of support of governmental, corporate, and community conscience-money contributions and the Charybdis of their "legitimation" in host societies and governments. This negotiation, in turn, requires the marshaling of high entrepreneurial talent suffused with a whole range of negotiating endowments. Understandably, investor rationality in human rights markets is constantly exposed to a crisis of "nervous rationality." Both the "inputs" and "outputs" in human rights portfolio investment protection remain indeterminate; nevertheless, these must be ledgered, packaged, sold, and purchased on the most productive terms.

The crisis of "nervous rationality" is replicated in consumer rationality. Human rights NGOs, especially in the Third World, must negotiate the dilemmas of legitimacy and autonomy. The ever so precarious legitimacy of human rights networks seems forever threatened by allegations of foreign funding orchestrated both by interested governments and by rival NGOs that want to do better than their "competitors." There exists, too, competition to capture the beneficiary groups who measure the legitimacy of human rights networks not in terms of any "cargo cult" or messianic rationality but according to what these networks bring to people in terms of here-and-now accomplishments or results.

---

[112] *See* David Gillies, *Between Principle and Practice: Human Rights in North-South Relations* (1996); Katarina Tomaševski, *Between Sanctions and Elections: Aid Donors and Their Human Rights Performance* (1997).

At the same time, NGOs seek a free enterprise market relative to the agenda of their semi-autonomous human rights concerns. They seek to define their markets for human rights promotion and protection not merely in terms of what the markets of human rights investment will bear at any given moment but also in terms of how these markets may be re-orientated in terms of consumer-power. This may partly explain the populous presence and participation of the best and the brightest of NGOs and NGIs in this decade and half of the United Nations summits: Vienna, Cairo, Copenhagen, Beijing, and Istanbul. By their determined participation at these summits (and the inevitably mandated "plus-5" meetings), they seek to re-orient the global investment markets in human rights. The interests of civil servants (national and global) intermesh, in this process, with those of the NGOs and the NGIs.

Techniques of commodification of human suffering

The raw material for human rights investment and consumer markets is provided by here-and-now human misery and suffering. However morally deplorable, it is a social fact that the overall human capacity to develop a fellowship of human suffering is awesomely limited. It is a salient fact about the "contemporary" human scene that individual and associational life-projects are rarely disturbed, let alone displaced, by the spectacle of human suffering or human suffering as a spectacle. In such a milieu, human rights markets, no matter whether investor or consumer, are confronted with the problem of "compassion fatigue." This is a moral problem, to be sure, but it is also a material problem. Of necessity, markets for human rights concentrate on this aspect of the problem if only because, when compassion fades, the resources for the alleviation of human suffering through human rights languages are depleted. This intersection registers the necessity for human rights entrepreneurs to commodify human suffering, to package and sell it in terms of what the markets will bear. Human rights violations must be constantly commoditized to be combated. Human suffering must be packaged in ways that the mass media markets find it profitable to bear overall.

But the mass media can commodify human suffering only on a dramatic and contingent basis. Injustice and human rights violations are headline news only as the porn of power and its voyeuristic potential lies in the reiterative packaging of violations that titillate and scandalize, for the moment at least, the dilettante sensibilities of the globalizing classes. The mass media plays also a creationist role in that they "in an important sense 'create' a disaster when they decide to recognize it ... [T]hey give institutional endorsement or attestation to bad events which otherwise will have a reality restricted to a local circle of victims."[113] Such institutional endorsement poses intractable issues for the marketization of human rights. Given the worldwide patterns of mass

---

[113] Jonathan Benthall, *Disasters, Relief and the Media* 3–4 (1993); quoted in Stanley Cohen, *Denial and Acknowledgment: The Impact of Information About Human Rights Violations* 90 (1995).

media ownership, and the assiduously cultivated consumer cultures of "info-entertainment," the key players in human rights markets need to manipulate the media into authentic representations of the suffering of the violated. They must marshal the power to mold the mass media, without having access to resources that the networks of economic/political power so constantly command, into exemplary communicators of human solidarity. So far, this endeavor has rested in the commodification of human suffering, exploiting the markets for instant news and views.

In a germinal monograph, Stanley Cohen has brought home the daunting tasks entailed in the commodification of human suffering. The commodification of human suffering has as its task (according to Cohen, with whom I agree) the conversion of the "politics of denial" into that of the "politics of acknowledgment." Cohen brings to attention an entire catalogue of perpetrator-based techniques of denial of human violation and the variety of responses that go under the banner of "bystanderism," whether internal or external.[114]

The various techniques of marketing human suffering in the name of "human rights" succeed or fail according to the standpoint one chooses to privilege. Efficient market rationality perhaps dictates a logic of excess. The more human rights producers and consumers succeed in diffusing horror stories, the better it is, on the whole, for the sustenance of global human rights cultures. The more they succeed in establishing accountability institutions (truth commissions, commissions for human rights for women, indigenous peoples, children, and the urban and rural impoverished) the better commerce there is. Giving visibility and voice to human suffering is among the prime functions of human rights service markets. But it is an enterprise that must overcome "compassion fatigue"[115] and an overall desensitization to human misery. When the markets are bullish, the logic of excess does seem to provide the most resources for the disadvantaged, dispossessed, and deprived human communities. But in situations of recession, serious issues arise concerning the ways in which human suffering is or should be merchandized; and when those who suffer begin to counter these ways, we witness crises in human rights market management.

Human rights markets are crowded with an assortment of actors, agencies, and agendas. But they seem united in their operational techniques. A standard technique is that of reportage: several leading organizations specialize in services providing human rights "watch" and "action alerts." A related market technique is that of lobbying, whereby official or popular opinion is sought to be mobilized around human rights situations, events, or catastrophes.

---

[114] These consist in: (a) denial of injury; (b) denial of victims; (c) denial of responsibility; (d) condemnation of the condemners; and (e) appeal to higher loyalty. These "neutralization" techniques are firmly in place and violators only play variations on a theme. Professor Cohen also offers a typology of bystander passivity or effect, consisting of (a) diffusion of responsibility; (b) inability to identify with the victim; and (c) inability of conceiving an effective intervention. *See* Cohen, *supra* note 113, at 32–35.

[115] *Ibid.* at 89–116.

A third technique is that of cyberspace solidarity, spectacular uses of instant communication networks across the world. Manuel Castells has recently provided stunning examples of how cyber-technologies have made a dramatic difference in networking solidarities; but, as his analysis itself suggests, these solidarities may work for human rights advancement (as in the case of the Zapatistas) or, more importantly, against the nascent human rights cultures (as in the case of the American militia or Japanese *Aum Shinrikyo* movements).[116] Apparently the days of the pre-cyberspace creation of mass movement solidarity are numbered or over, at least if one is to believe that the cyberspace markets for human rights provide the only or best creative spaces. In any case, once we recognize the danger of an historical cyberspace romanticism, it remains a fact that cyberspace offers a useful marketing technique. A fourth technique consists in converting the reportage of violation in the idiom and grammar of judicial activism. An exemplary arena is provided by the invention of social action litigation, pursuant to which Indian appellate courts, including the Supreme Court of India, have been converted from the ideological and repressive apparatuses of the state and global capital into an institutionalized movement for the protection and promotion of human rights.[117] The resonance of this movement extends to many a third world society.

A fifth technique is to sustain the more conventional networks of solidarity of which the facilitation of inter-NGO dialogue is a principal aspect. Usually done through conferences, colloquia, seminars, and the facilitation of individual visits by victims or their next of kin, this technique has in recent times extended to the holding of hearings/listenings of victim groups, a device that seeks to bring unmediated the voices and texts of suffering to empathetic observers across the world. The various U.N. summits have provided a spectacular illustration of this technique, but there are more institutionalized arrangements as well. All bring the raw material of human suffering for further processing and packaging in the media and related human rights markets.

A sixth technique is rather specialized, comprising various acts of lobbying of the treaty bodies of the United Nations. This form of human rights marketing specializes in providing legislative or policy inputs in the norm creation process, with NGO entrepreneurs assuming the roles of quasi-international civil servants and quasi-diplomats for human rights, although it is the thinking and conduct of the *de jure* international diplomats and civil servants that they seek to influence. By this specialized intervention, this activity runs the risks of co-optation and alienation from the community of the violated, especially when the NGO activity becomes the mirror-image of inter-governmental politics. However, this sort of intervention does offer, when invested with integrity, substantial gains for the progressive creation of human rights norms.

A seventh, and here final, technique is that of global direct action against imminent or actual violations of human rights. Apart from the solitary though

---

[116] *See* Castells, *supra* note 104, at 68–109.   [117] *See* sources cited *supra* notes 39 and 106.

splendid example of Greenpeace, however, this technique is not considered sustainable by the leading global and regional NGOs. Of course, there are less spectacular and sustained examples furnished in the narratives of resistance to such global events, such as the G-7 and Asia–Pacific Economic Cooperation (APEC) conferences where methods of "citizen arrest" of global leadership are enacted, or when celebrations of the golden jubilee of international financial institutions are sought to be converted into events of embarrassment. Not to be ignored in this context are recourses to direct action by the Argentine mothers against "disappearances" or of the British women's movements against the sites of civilian or military nuclear operations. At the end of the day, however, the dominant market cost-benefit rationality does not legitimate such recourse to direct action in the dramaturgy of human rights.

This sort of illustrative listing is to suggest the variety and complexity of human rights market initiatives, which entail high quotients of managerial and entrepreneurial talent and the ability to boost market or investor confidence in human rights ventures. It also is partly my intention to suggest that the "science" of risk-analysis and risk-management is as relevant to the markets of promotion and protection of human rights as it is to those that perpetrate violations.

It is true that as human suffering intensifies, markets for human rights grow. But to say this does not entail any ethical judgment concerning the commodification of human suffering, although the reader may feel justified in treating some anguished sub-texts in this paper as warranting a wholesale moral critique of human rights markets. The future of human rights praxis is linked with, as always, the success or failure of human rights missions and their latent or patent capability to scandalize the conscience of humankind. The modes of scandalization will, of course, remain contested among the communities of the violators and the violated. The task for those who find the commodification of human suffering unconscionable lies in the contested ways of its accomplishment, not in lamenting the global fact of the very existence of human rights markets.

The problem of "regulation" of human rights markets

State regulation of human rights markets is fraught with complexities. When may it be said to be invasive of human rights? How far, if at all, should states regulate the very existence or modes of operation of the NGOs involved? Should the regime of accreditation of NGOs in the United Nations system be liberal or conservative? How and by whom is this process to be determined?

The problem of regulation of human rights markets is not just state-centric. Human rights investors as well as consumer communities are stakeholders, with investor-based regulation taking myriad forms of channeling and controlling human rights agendas and transactions, generating a product mix that is the very essence of an audit culture (of upward accountability and line management). But the investors in human rights themselves may be regulated and, in this regard, must establish their legitimacy with the host society and government in ways that are propitious for cross-border markets in human rights promotion and protection.

The operators of the local/global human rights markets, primarily NGOs, confront related but distinct problems in devising self-regulatory and other-oriented regulatory frameworks. Self-regulatory frameworks must address the crises of investor rationalities in a highly competitive scramble for resourcing. Other-directed regulatory approaches are no less complex. On the one hand, there is a need to maintain acceptable patterns of consumer solidarity in the global investor markets; on the other hand, there exists the historic need, from the standpoint of the ultimate beneficiaries, to keep a watch on sister NGOs that are exposed to corruption, co-optation, or subversion by the forces of global capitalism, a problem recently illustrated in the now happily aborted case of the Bangla Desh Grameen Bank which initially proposed a "deal" with Monsanto for their terminator seed technology. If there is no peer group regulation of occasions of co-optation, human rights markets can undergo substantial downturns.

But forms of peer-group regulatory interventions raise difficult, if not intractable, issues. When are NGO communities entitled to sound the alarm? Which modes of alleviation of human suffering are more progressively "just" from the standpoint of human rights communities that otherwise do not contest the existence of human rights markets in the name of human suffering? What supererogatory ethics is at play here? Put another way, what standards of critical morality are furnished by extant human rights instruments (addressed primarily to state morality) for NGO critiques of sister NGOs? Are human rights markets per se more sensibly moral than all other markets?

Just as surely as there is an ideology of human rights, abundantly illustrated by the discourse on human rights, so is there a materiality to it, ever present in cross-border transactions in the symbolic capital of human rights. The usefulness of the market metaphor therefore should be apparent.

The emergence of an alternate paradigm of human rights

The paradigm shift

My thesis herein requires a brutally frank statement. I believe that the paradigm of the Universal Declaration of Human Rights is being steadily supplanted by a trade-related, market-friendly, human rights paradigm. This new paradigm reverses the notion that universal human rights are designed for the dignity and well being of human beings and insists, instead, upon the promotion and protection of the collective rights of global capital in ways that "justify" corporate well-being and dignity over that of human persons. The Universal Declaration of Human Rights model assigned human rights responsibilities to states; it called upon the state to construct, progressively and within the community of states, a just social order, both national and global, that could meet at least the basic needs of human beings.

The new model denies any significant redistributive role for the state. It calls upon the state (and world order) to free as many spaces for capital as possible, initially by fully pursuing the "Three-Ds" of contemporary globalization: deregulation, denationalization, and disinvestment. Putting an end to national regulatory and redistributive potentials is the *leitmotif* of present-day economic globalization, as anyone who has read several drafts of the Multilateral Agreement on Investment (MAI) knows.[118] But the program of rolling back the state aims at the same time for vigorous state action when the interests of global Capital are at stake. To this extent, de-regulation signifies not an end of the nation-state but an end to the redistributionist state.[119]

Recent history has shown that multinational capital needs at one and the same time a "soft" state and a "hard" one.[120] The production of soft states is a high priority for multinational capital and its normative cohorts, as exemplified by the continuing reports of Ms. Fatima-Zohra Ksentini, Special Rapporteur to the Commission on Human Rights, on the adverse effect of the illicit movement and dumping of toxic and dangerous wastes on the enjoyment of human rights.[121] The biggest waste exporters are, of course, the most "developed" countries, and wastes continue to be dispatched to regions lacking the political and economic power to refuse it.[122] This deficit is not innate but caused, in the last instance, by the formations of the global economy.

All kinds of unfortunate business practices abound: use of falsified documents; bribing of officials in the "country of origin, the transit country, or … the country of final destination,"[123] and private contracts "between Western companies and African countries whereby the companies paid a pittance for the land on which to dump toxic products …"[124] The latter scandal brought forth an anguished resolution from the Organization of African Unity a decade ago, declaring toxic dumping to be a "crime against Africa and African people."[125] The Special Rapporteur had no difficulty in cataloging a large number of violations that these practices knowingly – and criminally – entail.[126] Soft states and regimes need to be continually constituted for the benefit of global capital, benefiting a few communities of people. That this imposes the cost on incredible human suffering of the impoverished nations[127] is irrelevant to the ruling

---

[118] *See* Multilateral Agreement on Investment, *supra* note 73.

[119] *See* Jane Kelsey, *The New Zealand Experiment: A World Model for Structural Adjustment?* (1995).

[120] *See* Gunnar Myrdal, *Asian Drama: An Inquiry into the Poverty of Nations* (1968). Myrdal's concern was to portray South Asian states as lacking in social or institutional discipline and vulnerable to high levels of corruption.

[121] *Adverse Effects of the Illicit Movement and Dumping of Toxic and Dangerous Products and Wastes on the Enjoyment of Human Rights*, U.N. Comm. on H.R., U.N. Doc. E/CN.4/1998/10 (1998).

[122] *Ibid.* at paras. 54 and 56.   [123] *Ibid.*   [124] *Ibid.*   [125] *Ibid.* at para. 57.

[126] *Adverse Effects of the Illicit Movement and Dumping of Toxic and Dangerous Products and Wastes on the Enjoyment of Human Rights, supra* note 121, at paras. 77–107 (1998).

[127] If you find this too metaphorical, please recall children being exposed to radiation by playing on irradiated nuclear waste dump sites in Marshall Islands or the victims of Bhopal still suffering from the lethal impact of catastrophic exposure of 47 tons of MIC.

standards of global capital, which must measure the excellence of economic entrepreneurship by standards other than those provided by seemingly endless human rights normativity.

The context of this enterprise bids a moment of reflection. The multinational corporations may not perform toxic dumping projects, for example, without the active support of the international financial institutions, and such support causes some Third World countries, ridden by "over-indebtedness and collapse of raw material prices," to view the import of hazardous wastes as "attractive" as a last resort to improve their liquidity.[128] In this context, one is talking about no more bad business practice that international codes of conduct may prohibit but, rather, of genocidal corporate and international financial institutional regimes of governance. These are, to coin a neologism (a barbarism in language that is insufficient to cope with the savagery of the "free market"), *rightsicidal* practices of management of governance.

Hardheaded international business practices require also proliferation of "hard" states and regimes which must be market-efficient in suppressing and de-legitimating human rights practices of resistance or the pursuit of alternate politics. Rule of law standards and values need to be enforced by the state on behalf and at the behest of formations of the global economy and global technology. When, to this end, it is necessary for the state to unleash a reign of terror, it must be empowered, locally and globally, to do so. The state must remain, at all times, sufficiently active to ensure maximal security to the global or foreign investor, who has corresponding duties to assist the state in managing or refurbishing any democratic deficit that might thus arise. The flagrant, massive, and ongoing violations of human rights thus entailed must be denied a voice by state-of-the-art management of public and political opinion, nationally and globally.

The new paradigm will succeed if it can render problematic the voices of suffering. This occurs primarily through "rationality reform" – that is, by the production of epistemologies that normalize risk (there is no escape from risk), ideologize it (some grave risks are justified for the sake of "progress," "development," and "security"); problematize causation (in ways that the catastrophic impacts may not be traced to the activity of global corporations); raise questions (so dear to law and economics specialists concerning the efficiency of legal regimes of liability); and interrogate even a modicum amount of judicial activism (compensating rights-violation and suffering, favoring unprincipled and arbitrary extra-judicial settlement when risk management and damage containment strategies fail). It is not surprising that some of the most important questions in globalization discourse relate to how we conceptualize "victim," who may authentically speak about victimage and what, indeed, may be said to constitute "suffering."

---

[128] *See Adverse Effects, supra* note 121, at para. 57.

The new paradigm asks us to shed the fetishism of human rights and to appreciate that, in the absence of economic development, human rights have no future at all. Some behavioral scientists urge us to believe in a quantitative methodology that "produces results," (certainly for them), that demonstrates a positive co-relation between foreign direct investment, multinational capital, and the observance of human rights. It is easier to combat dictatorial regimes that suspend human rights on the grounds of priority of economic development than to contest the gospel of economic rationalism, which is mystified by a new scholasticism with the assertion that, for example, "meso-development" is best promoted under conditions of authoritarianism. *Faute de mieux*, human rights communities must now work within the languages and imperatives of "economic rationalism"; they need to focus not on a conceptually elevated plateau of post-modern political theory, but, rather, on the new institutional economics, maintaining at the same time constant conversation with human suffering.

The paradigms in conflict

The paradigm of universal human rights has progressively sought normative consensus on the integrity of human rights, albeit expressed in different idioms. The diverse bodies of human rights found their highest summation with the Declaration on the Right to Development,[129] insisting that the individual is a subject of development, not its object.

The emergent paradigm reverses this trend. It seeks to make not just the individual human being but whole nations into the objects of development, as defined by global capital embodied in the "economic rationalism" of the suprastatal networks of the World Bank and the IMF, which are not democratically composed nor accountable to any constituency save investors. Their prescriptions for re-orientating the economic structures and policies of indebted and impoverished Third World societies, far from being designed to make the world order equitable, are addressed to the overall good of the world's hegemonic economies, in all their complexity and contradiction. Prescriptions of good governance are discriminatorily – and viciously – addressed only to states and communities outside the core Euro-Atlantic states. Even so, good governance is articulated as a set of arrangements, including institutional renovation, that primarily privileges and disproportionately benefits the global producers and consumers.

The paradigm of universal human rights enabled the emergence of the United Nations system as a congregation of faith. Regarded as no omnipotent deity but only as a frail, crisis-ridden arena, it became the privileged historic site for co-operative practices of reshaping the world through the idiom and grammar, as well as the vision, of human rights. This arena is being captured by the votaries of economic globalization who proselytize that free markets offer the best hope for human redemption. But the residue of the past cultures of

---

[129] *See* Declaration on the Right to Development, *supra* note 85.

universal human rights remains nonetheless, as recently manifested in a U.N. document that dares to speak about perverse forms of globalization, namely, those that abandon any degree of respect for human rights standards and norms.[130] A moment's reflection on the WTO agreements and the proposed Multilateral Agreement on Investment (MAI)[131] should demonstrate the truth of this assertion. But, of course, no United Nations formulation would go this far, given its own diplomacy on resourcing the system and emerging global economic realities. The Vienna Conference on Human Rights summed it all up with its poignant preambulatory reference to "the spirit of our age" and the "realties of our time."[132] The "spirit" is human rights vision; the "realities" are furnished by the headlong and heedless processes of globalization that are creating in their wake cruel logics of social exclusion and enduring communities of misfortune.

Of course, the continuing appropriation by the forces of capital of hard-won human rights for its own ends is not a *sui generis* event. Long before slavery was abolished and before women won the right to contest and vote at elections, corporations had appropriated rights to personhood, claiming due process rights for regimes of property but denied to human beings. The unfolding of what I call "modern" human rights is the story of the near-absoluteness of the right to property, as a basic human right. So is the narrative of colonization/ imperialism which began its career with the archetypal East India Company (which ruled India for a century) when corporate sovereignty was inaugurated. Politics was commerce and commerce became politics.

So, it may be said, is this the case now. Some would even maintain that it was the case even during the halcyon days of human rights enunciations (from the Declaration on Permanent Sovereignty over Natural Wealth and Resources[133] to the Declaration on the Right to Development[134]). Peel away the layers of human rights rhetoric, they would maintain, and you will find a core of historic continuity where heroic assertions of human rights remained, in fact and effect, the insignia of triumphant economic interests.

This continuity thesis deserves its moment. It directs attention to facts and feats of global diplomacy over human rights in ways that moderate or even cure the celebrationist approach to human rights (whether human rights romanticism, mysticism, triumphalism, or hedonism). It alerts us to the fact that within the modalities of human rights enunciation beats the regular heartbeats of hegemonic interests. It directs us towards a mode of thought that relocates the authorship of human rights away from the politics of inter-governmental desire to the multitudinous struggles of people against human violation.

---

[130] *See Adverse Effects, supra* note 121.
[131] *See* proposed Multilateral Agreement on Investment, *supra* note 73.
[132] *See* Upendra Baxi, "'The Spirit of Our Age, The Realities of Our Time': The Vienna Declaration on Human Rights", in *Mabrino's Helmet? Human Rights for a Changing World* 1–18 (1994).
[133] *Supra* note 84.   [134] *Supra* note 85.

If all this be so, is there a paradigm shift or merely an extension of latent capitalism that always has moved (as the readers of *Das Kapital* surely know) in accordance with bourgeois human rights trajectories? This is an important and difficult question raised by Burns Weston in his indefatigable editorial labors. My short answer for the present is that, while the appropriation by the capital of human rights logic and rhetoric is not a distinctively contemporary phenomenon, it is the scale of reversal now manifest that marks a radical discontinuity. Global business practices cancel, for example, many normative gains of the "contemporary" human rights movement through techniques of dispersal of these evils. The exploitation of child and sweat labor through free economic zones, and accompanying sex-based discrimination even in subsistence wages, is the hallmark of contemporary economic globalization. So is the creation of a "global risk society"[135] through hazardous industry and the very legible scripts of "organized irresponsibility" and "organized impunity" for corporate offenders, of which the Bhopal catastrophe furnishes a mournful reminder.[136]

What distinguishes the paradigm shift is the "legitimation" of extraordinary imposition of human suffering in the cause and the course of the present contemporary march of global capital. In the "modern" epoch of human rights, such suffering was considered *per se* legitimate. "Contemporary" human rights logics and paralogics challenged, and at times denied, this self-evident axiom. The paradigm shift seeks to cancel the historic gains of the progressive universal human rights movement in seemingly irreversible ways. It seeks to mute the voices of suffering and, in the process, regress human rights futures.

Toward a conclusion?

History, especially current history, presents always confused pathways. It is difficult to foretell with any degree of assurance, despite advances in futurology, where the future of human rights or indeed any future may lie. In this situation, the only reflexive task open to human rights communities consists in "planning ahead." The CEOs of leading multinationals are preoccupied with planning the futures of global capital movements in 2025 A.D. even as, remarkably, they confine the energies of human rights activists to perfidious instances of the "local-in-the-global" causation of human suffering (as, for example, in Bhopal and Ogoniland). The *fin-de-siecle* need and ordeal for human rights communities, worldwide, is to develop an agenda of action to arrest the paradigm-shift, without them converting themselves into new bureaucrats or technocrats of human suffering. To some, this may seem an insensible challenge, as nothing seems more ludicrous than sailing against the wind. What is necessary is to combat this kind of mind-set. Human rights futures, dependent as they are

---

[135] *See* Ulrich Beck, *The Risk Society: Toward a New Modernity* (1992).

[136] *See* Upendra Baxi, Introduction to *Valiant Victims and Lethal Litigation: The Bhopal Case* (Upendra Baxi & Amita Dhandha eds., 1990).

upon imparting an authentic voice to human suffering, must engage in a discourse of suffering that moves the world.

Over a century and half ago, Karl Marx put the notion of human futures presciently when he urged that they are best born when the following twin tasks occur: when suffering humanity reflects and when thinking humanity suffers. I know of no better way to unite the future of human rights to human suffering.

5.3 Rights and "development"

(a) "Development", "terror" and the posthuman world*

Understanding the relationship between human rights and human/social development remains a daunting task, indeed. Chapter 3 of this work, in over-viewing the dominant notions of development suggests that the notions of development (rather of reading and writing development) vary within and across human societies and inescapably raise questions of justice, systematically underprivileged in the practices of "developmentalism". By this, I here signify an ideological practice in which the *developers* (key political actors animated by a wide range of strategic interests) decide what is, or may constitute, "good" for the *developees* (the subjects and objects of development) in the short or long term, and in the name of that "good" relentlessly enforce decisions which usually entail imposition on the worst-off humans a disproportionate sharing of costs of development. Whether approaches to justice are necessarily integral to the politics of human hope that sustain alternative visions of humane development remains an open question. One way to address this is to foreground the question of justice both as a kind of Levinasian responsibility to the other and a kind of Foucaldian [sic] notion of "the care of self", as enhancing the forms of contemporary development ethic. Amidst all this, the idea of a human *right* to development now gets translated into new philosophic and ethical "universal" languages, posing in the process at least the question: What is lost in this translation/transgression?

It is in this context that Chapter 4 addresses the dilemmatic character of the much vaunted rights-based approaches to development. How these may after all proceed in the face of insistent claims that most realms of governance ought to remain human rights-neutral? On this register, no longer may any bright lines be drawn between human rights-friendly, and unfriendly, forms of governance. How far then may we understand the diverse quests towards identifying the component rights for the overarching values enshrined in the United Nations Declaration on the Right to Development as the best possible move ahead at a normative level? I say "normative" because it is now eminently clear that the contemporary processes of economic globalization and the accompanying

---

* This passage contains an outline of the themes developed in Ch 3–6 of *Human Rights in a Posthuman World* (2007) Preface at ix–xiii. This, and the excerpts in (b) and (c) are reproduced here by kind permission of Oxford University Press, New Delhi.

ideology of "neoliberalism" are beginning to render the institutionalization of the component rights almost *improbable*. In a strange, though not unanticipated inversion, the *right* to development increasingly tends to become, in effect, instruments shaping the contours of hegemonic global social *policy*. All this, put differently, raises the question: how may we convert old habits of "rethinking development" to some new ways of thought, at least a little more propitious and congenial to the tasks of emancipatory or transformative politics in the next few difficult decades of the 21st century?

This large question invites attention to at least two different orders of global social reality. First, we need to explore new forms of the post-Cold War practices of belligerence made cruelly legible by the two contemporary "terror" wars: the wars *of* and *on* terror. Second, the discourse of the emergent posthuman condition deserves anxious attention because it so fully both dissipates as well as reconstitutes the "human" self as a bearer of rights.

Chapter 5 seeks to decipher the rhetoric and the reality of the two "terror wars" that now so fully achieve what Immanuel Levinas precociously named as the "suspension of the ethical" in the ethical obscenity of war. Not merely the relation between the two "wars" remains staggeringly vast and complex but also understanding "terror" remains a difficult task, aggravated further by the newly emergent post-Cold War forms, of global McCarthyism, all too disposed to suspect and even punish any serious effort at understanding and evaluation. Clearly, any sustained intellectual effort unravelling the complex understanding of "justifications" – both principled and expedient for recourse to insurgent terror and for counter-terror measures – these insurgent and state-sponsored forms of "terrorisms" – remains a difficult pursuit, given the new "medievalism" that now "polices" even punishes, the acts of thought.

At the same moment, the wars *on, or against* "terror" now promote the emergence of some new conceptions of the global governance (to adapt the words of George Deleuze and Felix Guttari) as a "nomadic war machine". In this zodiac, the re-silencing of human rights voices now becomes a quotidian performance of global and international policy of collective security networks. Increasingly, emergent judicial globalization fosters some uncommon learning, conscripting in the process adjudicatory policies to the newly-fangled tasks of celebration of the virtue of "constitutional patriotism" and development of new techniques of production of judicial indifference towards human rights. I do not address this thematic directly but engagement with it reconfigures the futures of human rights values, standards, and norms as we know these.

Moving to a different trajectory, Chapter 6 attempts an understanding of the new discourse concerning the "posthuman", which now furiously develops apace. Nurtured initially and notably by science fiction, films, and related popular/populist culture industries, the posthuman now acquires an edge of a serious philosophical enterprise in the wake of astonishing developments in artificial intelligence, bio-, nano-, technologies, and the Star Wars genre of military technologies. The distinction between *homo sapiens* and *robo sapiens* (as Katherine Hayles so often painstakingly reiterates)[1] now constantly diminishes. The new contexts of global circumstances of justice require some sustained understandings of the dynamic relationship between contemporary forms of technoscience, and associated aspects of technopolitics, with accompanying forms of techno-narcissisms.

We may not any longer confidently rely upon *the* faculty of human or divine Reason as a sovereign constituent marker of differentiation between humans and machines. Developments in artificial intelligence reprogramme the very idea of being human; we all tend increasingly to become cyborgs, a new digitalized incarnation of the classical mermaid figurations. Developments in genomic sciences, variously decoded by the Human Genome projects, now fully suggest that human life is no more than a code, or a series of complex flows, of genetic information, ever-ready for a cascading variety of genomic, and related technoscientific orders of mutations, via the extraordinary prowess of bio-, nano-, and biomedical neuro-technologies. All these, more or less, deprive us of the old "consolations of philosophy" that once-upon-a-time enabled us somehow to draw some bright lines demarcating sharply the human species from the animal, and objects in nature, as well as from the machinistic species; in sum, the privileging of the distinctively "human".

Biomedical sciences, neurobiology, and pharma-global industries now proceed apace with the practices and techniques of disembodiment/re-embodiment. This, for the present purposes, means at least four things. First, the human body is no longer conceivable in sacred terms as a unique gift of God or as a terminal point of evolution. Second, the body itself may be reprogrammed in terms of a "body without organs" or "organs without bodies". Third, at best remains contingent the notion that the human body may provide seat and source of a distinctive "human" self, identity, and human agency. Thus, the previously unheard genre of "bioethics" and "genethics" now crowds the landscape of normative ethical theory promoting in troubled ways some approaches towards posthuman moral/ethical theory and politics which render somewhat already obsolescent the otherwise freshly minted notions of biopolitics. Fourth, developments in neurosciences and artificial intelligence suggest some new ways of conceiving human agency and responsibility, beyond the conventional discourses of free will and forms of "compatibilism" between the "hard" and "soft" determinisms, entirely unanticipated by salient postmodernist critiques of the European project of the Enlightenment and of the notions of subjectivity it so fully fostered.

In the posthuman epoch, now upon us, the place of human rights as we have known them since the Universal Declaration of Human Rights (UDHR) becomes, to say the least, parlous. Some pioneering thinkers even suggest that

---

[1] N. Katherine Hayles, *My Mother was a Computer: Digital Subjects and Literary Texts* (2005) Chicago: Chicago University Press.

the "posthuman" may help us redefine some of our notions of human freedom and "dignity". The air is already promise-crammed, as Lord Hamlet would say.

Clearly, relating the posthuman discourse to theory of classical and contemporary human rights remains a formidable task, in itself deserving at least a series of separate volumes. In this sense, [this] work registers a preliminary effort, carrying a simple message: the tasks of understanding the "human rights" in the discourse of the posthuman may not any longer be "safely" deferred, at least by theorists of and about human rights. Some may even say that it [is] too *late* in the day to now address these concerns. I venture to disagree.

(b) Gandhi and development*

If we must put individual names contributing to these mutinous acts of authorship, the name Mohandas Gandhi clearly compels a whole range of acknowledgements.[1] There is no reason whatsoever to orphan development discourse by the erasure of this name; Gandhi's *Hind Swaraj*, preceding by several decades the Truman enunciation, provides the still live forms of legacy for its critique. Development, for him, did not primarily signify economic growth and wealth-maximization, mindless emulation of structures, institutions, process of liberal governance, and the notion of human rights at least as celebrative of the classical rights of contract and property, or adoption of Marxian critique of the bourgeois state-ways. Development, for the Mahatma, meant *Swaraj* (a protean word in Gandhi's discourse not open to any singular summative narrative). Swaraj meant first of all a cosmopolitan republic of ideas, based deeply on understanding one's own traditions, combined with a sincere respect for the traditions of the other. It further meant placing all forms of power at the service of the impoverished. Political power and economic wealth comprised moral assets or public goods only in so far as "owners" of power and wealth regarded themselves as trustees of the "poorest of the poor". Swaraj also signified non-

---

* From *Human Rights in a Posthuman World* (2007) at 98–99.

[1] The literature celebrating and critiquing Gandhi here remains vast indeed. See, for example, Robert Young, *Postcolonialism: An Historical Introduction* (Oxford: Blackwell, 2001) at 317–59; Thomas Pantham, "Habermas' Practical Discourse and Gandhi's *Satyagraha*", in Bhikhu Parekh and Thomas Pantham (eds.), *Political Discourse: Explorations in Indian and Western Political Thought*, 292 (New Delhi: Sage publications, 1987); R. Sundara Rajan, *Towards a Critique of Cultural Reason* (New Delhi: Oxford University Press, 1987); Lloyd I. Rudolph and Susanne H. Rudolph, *The Modernity of Tradition: Political Development in India* (Chicago: University of Chicago Press, 1967); and their *Postmodern Gandhi and Other Essays* (New Delhi: Oxford University Press, 2006); Bhikhu Parekh, *Gandhi: A Very Short Introduction* (Oxford: Oxford University Press, 2001); Upendra Baxi, "Justice as Emancipation: The Legacy of Babasaheb Ambedkar" in Upendra Baxi and Bhikhu Parekh (eds.), *Crisis and Change in Contemporary India* 122–49 (New Delhi: Sage Publications, 1995).

I must here add that my reading stems from a Gujarati text of Mohandas Gandhi, *Mara Swapnanu Bharat* ("Bharat of my Dreams") (Ahmedabad: Navjeevan Trust, 1963; compiled by R. K. Prabhu).

violent forms of emancipatory praxes directed at righting ancient wrongs (mainly untouchability but also open to a contemporary reading inclusive of gender-based discrimination and violence, xenophobia, and related forms of social and cultural intolerance). Gandhi insisted that the Idea of Development (vikas) ought to set ethical boundaries to forms and scales of destructive developmental interventions and change (vinash). He also fashioned an extra-ordinary constellation of ideas and practices of, and for, Swaraj in terms of freedom as a code of social responsibility; not for him was ethically valid the notion that rights (including human rights) which assured various degrees of social freedom remain bereft of the distinction he variously made between just *freedom* and *just* freedom. The exercise of *just* freedom consists in its non-violent exercise relative to others. Gandhi presaged richly practices and tech-nologies of thought which non-violently seek to combat what now passes by as forms of the politics of global *misrecognition* and *maldistribution*.[2] Above all, Gandhi also exemplified the uses of his body as a fecund site of non-violent struggles against imperialism as well as for Swaraj-based practices of social regeneration, and even renaissance. Even this barebones, a non-hagiographic narrative of Gandhian notion of development should at least suggest that his relevance to the theory and practice of contemporary development remains inexhaustible.[3] I desist here from saying more save to add that the dominant development discourse understandably pursues the marginalization of his life and thought.

(c) Time and development: The Millennium Development Goals*

(i) Obligations to minimize human suffering emerge in contemporary human rights discourse as slow motion, rather than as fast-forward, kind of state and public policy orientations. The generative grammars, as it were, of human rights dissipate human and social suffering, at times to a point of social illegibility. The most stunning example stands furnished by the recent (23 September 2004) Independent Experts Report to the United Nations Secretary General concerning the implementation of the Millennial Goals. It, understandably, sets the most meagre standards, slated for

---

[2] To appropriate here in a different context Nancy Fraser's celebrated formulations, see, Nancy Fraser, "Social Justice in the Age of Identity Politics" in Nancy Fraser and Axel Honneth (eds.), *Redistribution or Recognition? A Political-Philosophical Exchange*, 7–109 (London: Verso, 2003). And see, Bouaventura de Sousa Santos, "Neustra America: Reinventing a Subaltern Paradigm of Recognition and Redistribution", *Theory, Culture and Society* 18 (2–3), 185–217 (2001).

[3] This remains true even when, as we ought to, re-situate Gandhi with other, more or less contemporary, postcolonial figurations, fully with Robert Young, *Postcolonialum*, Part IV, at 159–334, entitled, "Theoretical Practices of the Freedom Struggles". See also Young's discussion of "Marxism in India", at 311–16.

* (i) From *The Future of Human Rights* (2nd edn., 2006) Preface at p.xvi and (ii) *Human Rights in a Posthuman World* (2007a) at pp. 82–83.

attainment by 2015, for access to the basic minimum needs for the poorest of the poor of the world. The wise women and men, acting as *loco parentes* for the "wretched of the earth", speak thus guardedly only to the distant future for the here-and-now rightless peoples for whom international human rights enunciations appear as a series of callous governance tricks and subterfuges. Even amidst the "war *on* terror", against the nomadic multitudes[1] that now wage myriad "wars *of* terror", the portfolio of the "progressive implementation" of the social and economic remains cruelly the same as ever before. In the meantime, innumerable histories of human suffering criss-cross and co-mingle with the historicity of the pre-9/11 and the post-9/11 Grounds Zero.

(ii) *The time dimension*: How may the sacrificial time of development be "legitimately" constructed by the classes of *developers*? Sacrificial because the classes *of developers* always ask the *developees* that they should bear their present generational sufferings in good grace (that is without recourse to practices of collective militant political violence) as custodians of better life-prospects for their children and grandchildren. Even as a tiny percentage of multimillionaires grow (and now it is considered an indicator of development in the globalizing South to have its own share in the annual list of millionaires), masses of impoverished peoples are constantly exhorted to accept the various versions of trickle-down economic growth and development. Not all "civil society" "stakeholders" challenge this notion of sacrificial time within and across human societies. The trickle-down time at one level presents visions of the so-called "enduring time" of "development"; in turn it remains exposed to characterization in terms of "deceptive time", "erratic time", "cyclical time", "retarded time", "time in advance", "alternating time", and "explosive time" of development.[2] For millions of impoverished across the world, for example, the Millennial Development Goals and Targets, and related texts of international development policy, mark forms of deceptive, erratic, retarded, and even cyclical time.[3] Moving a bit further, the question is: how may we address the intransigently difficult distinction between "time-as-a measure" and time as a "collective substance"?[4]

---

[1] To adapt the figure so congenial to Michael Hardt and Antonio Negri (2002) *Empire* (London: Routledge).

[2] Alfred Gell, *The Anthropology of Time*, 62–8 (Oxford: Berg, 2001).

[3] See Upendra Baxi, "A Report for all Seasons? Small Notes Towards Reading the Larger Freedom", in C. Raj Kumar and Dhirendra Srivastava (eds.), *Human Rights and Development: Law, Policy, and Governance*, 495–514 (Hong Kong: Butterworths Lexis/Nexis, 2006). The Millennial Development Goals, for example, now provide for halving by 2015 the absolute numbers of starving, homeless, destitute, and unhealthy global impoverished! [See also Chapter 5 of *Posthuman*].

[4] See Antonio Negri, *Time for Revolution* (London: Continuum Books, 2003). Relating Negri to the discourse of development raises at least a germinal question: "When the entire time of life has become the time of production, *who measures whom?*" (emphasis added, at 29). The time of

5.4. Suggestions for further reading[1]

The Future of Human Rights (2nd edn., 2006) and *Human Rights in a Posthuman World: Critical Essays* (2007a) bring together Baxi's main writings on human rights since 1998. His *festschrift* "Upen Baxi – A Celebration" was published in the tenth issue of *Law, Social Justice and Global Development Journal* (LGD), an e-journal published by the University of Warwick Law School (www2.warwick.ac.uk/fac/soc/law.elj/lgd/2007). It contains further biographical and bibliographical data.

development, to here adapt Negri, is the "*constitution of time as the collective essence, as the machine constitutive of the subject*" (at 58), this subject being conceived as a "collective substance ... a *multiplicity of antagonisms*" reduced however and presented "within an *equilibrium* for capitalism that reduces the dialectical possibilities to a zero" (at 40). The contrast between the notion of "timeless time" of development as globalization and Antonio Negri cannot be any more profoundly presented.

[1] For full references, see the Bibliography (below pp. 222ff.).

6

Conclusion

The purpose of this book is to make the views of four jurists more accessible to Anglophone audiences and to provide material for reflection and discussion about important issues in human rights theory. It is not my role as editor to analyze or criticize their views in detail. However, it may be helpful to provide some suggestions about how they relate to each other, where they fit into a broad picture of scholarship about human rights, and how the project of making the ideas of "Southern" thinkers better known might be extended. A symposium in Belfast about this project and Dembour's framework for comparing human rights theories provide two convenient starting points for this purpose.

A symposium on "Human Rights: Southern Voices" was held at the Transitional Justice Institute (TJI) in Jordanstown, County Antrim in June 2008. All four of the subjects of this book attended and for two days discussed their ideas on human rights and debated with each other. They were known jocularly as "the four tenors", but they did not sing from a single hymn sheet. Indeed, this occasion brought out rather clearly some significant differences in perspectives and emphasis of four human rights scholars and activists, who all belong to the same post-Independence generation and whose early development involved similar traditions of legal education and shared reactions against colonialism, racism, and injustice.[1]

Some of the themes that emerged from very wide-ranging discussions and informal conversations deserve comment.

First, not surprisingly, there was some discussion of the word "Southern" in this context. When they first heard the title, some people in Belfast thought that it referred to the Republic of Ireland. Similarly, it was later pointed out that in

---

[1] All four are law-trained and belong to the post-Independence generation of public intellectuals in their own country or region. India became independent in 1946, in Baxi's eighth year; the Sudan in 1956, when Deng and An-Na'im were still at school; Kenya became independent in 1963, the year that Ghai took up his first teaching post at Dar-es-Salaam, where Tanzania had attained Independence two years earlier. For each of them, local, regional, and international post-Independence politics formed a crucial part of the context of their intellectual development. See further above pp. 1–2.

the United States the title, read out of context, might be taken to refer to the American Deep South. Of course, the point of this project is to counter such parochialism. More seriously, some have suggested that "South" should not be interpreted geographically, but should be taken to refer to any situation or condition or context in which there is serious poverty, deprivation, or inequality. Amartya Sen has argued that in respect of both identity and ideas, talk of East–West, North–South divides often obscures both the variety within particular regions and commonalities across them.[2] Others have pointed out that not all "Southern" countries are poor and that there are many poor people in "the North". However, most agree that phrases such as "The Global South" or "the North–South divide" have significance in the context of concerns about development, justice, and human rights, provided that they are not taken too literally or precisely. "Southern" in this context does not refer to a place – rather to what Upendra Baxi calls "geographies of injustice".[3] I have stuck with the title, because no better alternative has been suggested and, taken in context, it has some resonance.

There was also some discussion about the idea of "voice". None of the four contributors claimed to *represent* a constituency or to be in some special way *typical* of any group or culture. Indeed all are individual public intellectuals who deserve to be heard because each has something quite distinctive to say. Each *represents* ideas and perspectives that relate to "the South", but we should not expect a consensus or a single voice within particular traditions or cultures. In fact, at the symposium all four claimed to be "cultural hybrids".

Two other themes about "voice" emerged in discussion. First, as is apparent from earlier chapters, one of the main functions of the language of human rights is to "give voice to", and thus to empower, those with interests, concerns, or beliefs that deserve a better hearing.[4] Human rights advocacy may be used to express a distinctive identity or concerns, but we were reminded that it can also be a vehicle for demanding fair and equal treatment in respect of interests that are not culturally or ideologically specific, such as food, shelter, and freedom of expression. Conversely, human rights discourse may not always be the most appropriate or comfortable language for articulating such concerns.

A second theme related to silences. There are, of course, barriers to having opportunities to "give voice", such as lack of access to print or online outlets,

---

[2] E.g. Sen (2005) Ch. 13, discussing the reach of reason and cultural divides in relation to the East–West distinction.

[3] At the symposium Baxi argued forcefully that the South is not a place, but a system marked by systematic violations. "Southern voices" articulate experiences of suffering anywhere.

[4] In addition to human rights discourse serving as a direct expression of claims, some scholars serve as a bridge to the outside world as interpreters of attitudes and practices regarding human rights in particular countries and cultures. Albert Chen of Hong Kong was cited as an example in respect of the People's Republic of China. See Chen (1993), (2006) and his numerous contributions to the *Hong Kong Law Journal*.

inhibitions on free speech and other political deprivations; there are linguistic and educational barriers; and there are other reasons why potential voices go unheard.[5] One must listen for silences as well as being open to hearing unfamiliar voices.

Closely related to this are issues of gender. As should be clear from earlier chapters, all four contributors are strongly committed to gender equality. However, we were conscious from the start that they are all male. Rather than add one or two token female voices, it was felt that it would be better to have at least one separate volume devoted to gender issues and feminist perspectives and this project is being pursued.[6]

Naturally the question arose: who else might have been included or merits attention in future initiatives of this kind? This project was consciously narrowly focused on jurists writing in English about human rights theory whose views ought to be better known in Anglo-American legal circles. I selected these individuals as contemporaries with whose work and background I was already familiar. The project could, of course, be extended in other directions to include other areas of law,[7] relevant scholarly writings by non-lawyers,[8] writings in other languages, writings that do not claim to be scholarly, public expressions of views other than through print media, other audiences, and so on. The possibilities are almost endless. Here I shall restrict my comments to writings in English that are directly relevant to this book. Even here one has to be highly selective.

Even among those who write in English, there are many other individuals and groups who deserve attention. For instance, two Nobel Prize winners, Aung San Suu Kyi and Shirin Ebadi might help to right the gender balance.[9] There are other contemporary authors from outside Europe who have written about human rights. Some, such as Nelson Mandela,[10] Amartya Sen,[11] and Mr. Justice Christie Weeramantry,[12] are world famous. So are successive Secretary-Generals of the United Nations, who have spoken on human rights,

---

[5] For further ideas concerning themes of translation, silencing, and "de-silencing" human rights voices see Baxi (2007) and (2008).

[6] At the TJI Symposium Radhika Commaraswamy's "To Bellow Like a Cow: Women, Ethnicity and the Discourse of Rights" (1994) was included in the conference pack. Useful feminist anthologies (not entirely "Southern") are Cook (1994) and Wing (2000). See further below n. 9.

[7] E.g. there is an extensive literature on international law from non-Western points of view. For example, see Rajagopal (2003); Onuma (2000); Sornarajah, M (1997); D'Asprement (2008). I am grateful to Jean D'Asprement for some of these references.

[8] There are, of course, anthologies and commentaries on the ideas of contemporary Muslim thinkers who are not jurists, for example Cooper, Nettler, and Mahmoud (eds.) (2000), Esposito and Voll (eds.) (2001), Kamrava (ed.) (2006). See also the writings of Tariq Ramadan, especially Ramadan (2004). For an interesting commentary on Muslim intellectuals in Europe, see Jenkins (2007a) esp. Ch. 6; cf. Bowen (2005).

[9] See Aung San Suu Kyi (1991) and the Nobel Lecture by Shirin Ebadi (2003).

[10] E.g. Mandela (1965).

[11] Especially Sen (1999) and (2004), discussed by Baxi (2007) Ch. 2 and Twining (2009) at pp. 219–24.

[12] Weeramantry (1997).

including U Thant, Boutros Boutros Ghali, Kofi Annan, and Ban Ki-moon.[13] Other jurists, such as Issa Shivji of Tanzania,[14] several Latin American jurists,[15] or the late Neelan Tiruchelvam of Sri Lanka,[16] are well known in their own regions and in specialist circles. There is a younger generation of scholars who are coming into prominence, some of whom are quite sceptical about rights.[17] There is an extensive literature on Islam, human rights, and law reform.[18] And, of course, if one goes back in time, one can include Mahatma Gandhi or B.R. Ambedkar among others,[19] to say nothing of the rich heritage of literatures of non-Western religious and legal traditions.

At the symposium there was an interesting discussion of the Universal Declaration of Human Rights (UDHR) led by David Kretzmer.[20] It is striking that all four contributors still treat it as an important reference point that is of much more than historical interest. Critics have pointed to significant omissions or silences, about the responsibilities of non-state actors, the environment, minorities, for example. Some speak harshly of its failure to stress international obligations.[21] Commentators differ as to whether its focal concept, "dignity", has any substantive meaning and whether it is sensible to seek for a consensus about its content and philosophical basis.[22] The document was drawn up in a particular historical context and inevitably involved some compromises. There is also disagreement about whether the claim that it was a genuinely cross-cultural creation is no more than a front for another hegemonic imposition of Western liberal values. Despite these reservations and controversies, the UDHR seems to survive as a living document that represents not only a bold starting point for the modern development and evolution of human rights, but also as a succinct, powerful, inclusive, inspirational statement that still projects a vision that has very widespread support. It has not been entirely superseded by the Covenants and it is still sometimes

---

[13] There are also influential writings on human rights and development by leading figures in international organizations, e.g. Ul Haq (1995) (UNDP), Shihata (1991) (IBRD).

[14] E.g. Shivji (1989), (1993).

[15] See, for example, Nino (1991) and (1998), Escobar et al. (eds.) (2004), Guardiola-Rivera (2008). Boaventura de Sousa Santos, although Portuguese, has developed themes relating to "globalization from below" largely from a Latin American perspective, e.g. Santos (2002) and Santos and Rodríguez-Gavarito (2005).

[16] Baxi dedicated The Future of Human Rights to Neelan Tiruchelvam, a Sri Lankan human rights scholar and activist, who was assassinated by a suicide bomber in Colombo in 1999. See Munger (2001).

[17] For example, Makau Mutua (2002), Mahmood Mamdani (2000), and Balakrishnan Rajagopal (2003). On Latin American "voices", mainly of the same generation, see above.

[18] See above Ch. 3.   [19] See above pp. 207–8.

[20] For general discussions of the UDHR see Wagner and Carbone (eds.) (2001) and Sweet (ed.) (2003).

[21] Ghai expressly dissents from these criticisms and treats dignity as a powerful concept (see further Cottrell and Ghai on the UDHR and the Millennium Development Goals (2009) forthcoming). On silences about international obligations see Baxi (2007a) pp. 42–4.

[22] E.g. Kretzmer and Klein (eds.) (2002), Maritain (1951); McCrudden, (2008), Deng above in Chapter 2 at pp. 12–15, 41–3.

invoked in legal argument and it has value in states which have not signed other major human rights conventions.

The UDHR is an important reference point for all four contributors, but each of them has also emphasized the importance of the local: Deng argues that the specific meanings of human rights have to be grounded in local culture; An-Na'im similarly stresses adaptation to local circumstances and implementation; in his praxis and writings about constitution-making Ghai has regularly insisted on "grassroots" participation in constitutive processes by people at local levels;[23] one of Baxi's central themes is that the basis of human rights is the experiences and struggles of particular human beings in specific historical contexts. None of them sees human rights merely as aspiration or abstract ideas.

Interestingly, there was little discussion at the symposium of "rights-based approaches to development". But "development" features in all the texts. Deng writes interestingly about Dinka responses to the idea in relation to their perceived conservatism;[24] An-Na'im stresses the importance of economic, social, and cultural rights; Ghai appears to be a late convert to the idea of a "right to development"; Baxi writes sceptically about development discourses and is sharply critical of the Millennium Development Goals.[25] An unanswered question is whether any of them would support a strong "rights-based approach" to strategies for poverty reduction.[26]

Naturally, one persistent theme raised by their presence as much as by what they said related to the similarities and differences between our four contributors. I have already commented on some similarities in their backgrounds.[27] But readers of the writings in Chapters 2–5 often express surprise that they seem to be very different. One can point to differences in ethnicity,[28] mother tongue (English was for each of them a second or third language), attitudes to religion,[29] professional fields of specialization,[30] the arenas in which they have been activists, and the historical events they have witnessed. By and large they have read different things.[31] These points do indeed matter, even if, in the

---

[23] E.g. Cottrell and Ghai (2007).   [24] Above pp. 24–30 and 50–1.   [25] See above pp. 208–9.

[26] See, however, Ghai (2006) and (2007), favouring a quite strong "rights-based approach" to constitution-making. On "rights-based approaches" generally, see Alston (2005) and Twining (2009) Ch. 10.

[27] See further above at Chapter 1.

[28] Ethnically Deng is Nilotic, An-Na'im is Northern Sudanese (Arab), Ghai is Kenyan Asian (Hindu), Baxi is Indian (also Hindu background).

[29] An-Na'im is a committed Muslim.

[30] Each has somewhat different specialisms: Deng in ethnography, international relations, and diplomacy; An-Na'im in Islamic theology and public international law; Ghai in public law and constitutionalism (and to a lesser extent public international law); Baxi in Indian law, especially public law, and recently environmental protection and responses to terrorism. All converge under the umbrella of "law and development", but with different perspectives.

[31] Ghai and Baxi are well read in both Marxist theory and Anglo-American jurisprudence; Deng and An-Na'im less so. Although some of An-Na'im's ideas seem to echo liberal thinkers such as Rawls (overlapping consensus, public reason), or Habermas (deliberative democracy, ideal

present context, one may interpret the main differences in their treatment of human rights as relating to concerns, emphasis, and style. But, one may ask, do these surface differences mask any more profound disagreements?[32] That is a question of interpretation for readers of this book to reflect on and debate, but it may be useful to give some pointers.

First, there were a few explicit disagreements and differences between the four speakers. For example, Baxi and Ghai both commented on the strong emphasis on the individual in An-Na'im's position and pointed out that there is a distinct trend in international law towards a greater emphasis on community, as exemplified by the right to development, people's rights, and language rights. Baxi expressed reservations about the emphasis placed on the international law regime by Ghai and An-Na'im. More generally, one difference that was commented on was the extent to which there were variations in their focus on human rights law as opposed to human rights as moral and political ideas and as a form of discourse.[33]

There was a temptation to categorize Baxi and Ghai as pessimists and Deng and An-Na'im as optimists, but that on its own is probably too simple. Some other differences on specific points have been noted in earlier chapters. There are, of course, significant variations between them in respect of perspectives, focus, and style. Nevertheless, for at least some of those who attended the symposium the overwhelming impression was that these quite different thinkers are essentially allies in the cause of furthering the development and implementation of human rights values in this era of globalization.

In recent years their ideas seem to have converged in some significant ways. Three aspects of this deserve emphasis. First, all four are acutely aware that we live in a world characterized by a diversity of beliefs, both within and across national boundaries, and that this creates profound problems of co-existence and co-operation. None sees much prospect of papering over such differences. Francis Deng's writings evoke a cosmology and way of life that is beyond the experience and imagination of most of us. Much of Ghai's practice has been concerned with reaching constitutional settlements and handling conflicts in

speech situation), he denied having read them before he developed his own ideas (interview with author). None is an out-and-out post-modernist, but Baxi has flirted with post-modernism and is much more familiar with modern Continental European ideas than the others.

[32] Baxi's criticism of Ghai, and Ghai's exchange with An-Na'im about the role of judiciaries in protecting economic, social, and cultural rights, seem to me to involve relatively minor differences.

[33] At one end of the spectrum Deng compares Dinka traditional values with those underlying the UDHR. Although law-trained, his main career has been in international diplomacy and he disclaims being a legal scholar. Baxi is a public lawyer and legal theorist. He has had interests in Indian constitutional law and aspects of public international law, he has been active in public interest litigation, but his main perspective on human rights is political and moral. Although An-Na'im insists that his project is essentially religious, a great deal of his writing about human rights refers to international law and specific domestic fields such as family law, crime, and constitutional law. Ghai also has some interest in public international law, but his main work has been on constitutional law and domestic bills of rights. On the relationship between human rights law and human rights as moral and political rights, see above p. 3 and Twining (2009) pp. 178–83.

multi-ethnic societies in which civil strife and protection of minorities are acute problems. The difficulties of achieving consensus by reflection, persuasion, negotiation, public debate, or struggle are a recurrent theme in this book. So far as I can tell, each of them would opt for what Patrick Glenn calls "sustainable diversity"[34] rather than some bland homogenization in which one size is made to fit all.

Secondly, all four emphasize the importance of local particularities. Oscar Guardiola-Rivera has suggested that emphasis on place and locality is significant in respect of the idea that human rights are a general intercultural creation of mankind involving the interplay of local reactions to injustice and appeals to universal values: "[This] points towards a tradition – old, venerable and thoroughly inter-cultural – that has suggested that there is a strong relationship between place (land) and human nature."[35] But are these tendencies to emphasize local conditions, culture, and context based on shared assumptions?

Thirdly, the fact of pluralism (of beliefs, cultures, traditions) raises issues that are fashionably discussed in terms of universalism versus cultural relativism. My sense is that all four are impatient about such debates. Each steers a path between strong versions of universalism and particularism. In interpreting them, it is important to distinguish between four different meanings of universalism: (i) *formal universalisability*, as embodied in Kant's categorical imperative or the Golden Rule; (ii) *empirical universalism*, the position that human nature and systems of belief grounded in this nature are in their essentials universal or near-universal and that this can form the basis for an over-arching metaphysics of humanism. This view that has gone out of fashion in anthropology and most social sciences, which tend to emphasize the diversity, plasticity, and contingency of social cultures and belief systems. But it still finds some, but by no means overwhelming, support among geneticists, socio-biologists, and more "hard-wired" perspectives on the human psyche; (iii) *ethical universalism*, the position that there are universal moral principles, including principles underpinning human rights, that apply to all persons at all times and in all places; and (iv) *procedural universalism*, the hope that despite diversity of beliefs and conflicting interests, humankind can through reasonable dialogue and negotiation construct sufficient consensus to ground stable institutions and practices to sustain co-existence and co-operation.

On my interpretation, all four are quite close to each other on these points. All appear to accept formal universalism and to reject strong empirical claims to universality of cultures and beliefs; in other words, they accept diversity of beliefs as a psychological and social fact. On ethical universalism, their positions are somewhat different: all four are politically committed to fighting for the

---

[34] Glenn (2004) Ch. 10.
[35] Oscar Guardiola-Rivera, citing "mainly Aristotelian precedents" (Communication to Editor, December 2008). This links directly to Baxi's argument about the importance of local struggles as a crucial part the genealogies of human rights (e.g. pp. 183–4 above).

basic values embodied in the UDHR.[36] An-Na'im comes close to espousing a religion-based form of ethical universalism; Deng in all of his writings emphasizes human dignity as a basic value, but seems to use international human rights documents as consensual working premises rather than as embodying a single set of universal moral precepts; Ghai and Baxi pragmatically plugged into human rights discourse quite late in their careers, because it was so dominant in the spheres in which they operated. Ghai sees it as a historically contingent workable framework for negotiating constitutional and political settlements and developing constitutions through genuinely democratic constitutive processes, but he emphasizes material interests rather than cultural differences as the main recurrent basis of conflict. Baxi also treats human rights as a form of discourse and emphasizes its potential for abuse and obfuscation, passionately arguing for it to be allowed to be the medium for expressing "voices of suffering", especially of the half of the world that is deprived of food, water, health, education, and other necessities for a life worth living.

All four reject strong cultural relativism. They respect cultural diversity and value tolerance, but this involves no commitment to "tolerating the intolerable". Each believes in the value of dialogue, but with different emphases: Deng, the diplomat, has always relied on persuasion and mediation;[37] An-Na'im stresses the importance of internal dialogue; Ghai points to the value of human rights discourse as a framework for political negotiation and compromise between people with different interests, concerns, and ethnicities; Baxi, more pugnacious, sees dialogic human rights as the gentler part of struggle.

Many readers may feel that this catalogue of similarities and differences does not adequately explain the profoundly different impressions given by the four lots of readings. Could it be that these are significantly different kinds of thinker? Professor Marie-Bénédicte Dembour analyzes Western human rights theories in terms of four "schools" that cut across academic disciplines and differ from each other in respect of the origin, universality, possible realization, and legal embodiment of human rights as follows:

"*Natural scholars*" conceive of human rights as *given*;
"*Deliberative scholars*" conceive of human rights as *agreed*;
"*Protest scholars*" conceive of human rights as *fought for*;
"*Discourse scholars*" conceive of human rights as *talked about*.[38]

This scheme is elaborated in Table I. Classifying thinkers is a dangerous enterprise. So this kind of scheme needs to be treated with care. Dembour stresses that her categories are Weberian ideal types to which any individual human

---

[36] None of them treats the fact of pluralism of beliefs as a ground for abdicating moral commitments or refusing to criticize particular cultural practices.

[37] He calls this the Dinka way. See further *Talking it Out: Stories in Negotiating Human Relations* (2006).

[38] Dembour, *Who Believes in Human Rights?* (2006) Ch. 8 and developed in "What are Human Rights? Four Schools of Thought" (2010).

rights theorist more or less approximates. Members of the same school may disagree with each other and may not like to be bracketed together. The ideas and positions of individual thinkers develop over time: some may shift between or straddle different schools; some may adopt different perspectives in different contexts. However, the scheme does help to explain broad differences between human rights theories and it has some support in psychological research into patterns of shared understandings of human rights.[39]

Readers may find it helpful to use this scheme as a basis for comparing and contrasting the ideas about human rights embodied in the texts presented here. Such an exercise is of interest in testing Dembour's schema and applying it to "Southern" thinkers, albeit that these ones are acknowledged hybrids. First impressions might suggest that each belongs to a different school as follows:

Natural An-Na'im and Deng
Deliberative[40] Ghai
Protest Baxi
Discourse none[41]

Since the category of "protest theorist" was partly built on the writings of Baxi,[42] he fits the category fairly squarely. How the others fit these categories is more problematic. It depends in part on interpretation of their writings. But there are also questions whether these categories capture or explain similarities and differences between them. For example, all four assert that human rights should apply to all human beings, that the relationship between human rights morality and law are complex and problematic, and that economic, social, and cultural rights are human rights. All four steer a path between universalism and particularism and, in different ways, stress the importance of dialogue and persuasion. On the other hand, they differ on the significance of "culture" and material interests, and on several specific issues. And there remains the question: are there distinctively "Southern" aspects of their views which fall outside Dembour's categories for Western rights theorists?

---

[39] Paul Stenner, "Subjective Dimensions of Human Rights: What do Ordinary People Understand by 'Human Rights'"? (forthcoming) citing an earlier study by Rex Stainton-Rogers and Celia Kitzinger (1986). These psychological studies into subjective meanings of human rights emphasize that the patterns are more like *gestalts* than abstract theories: "[T]he basic procedure involves having a small and strategically sampled cohort of participants sort a large number of thematically related propositions into a meaningful holistic pattern according to some criterion of subjective judgement" (p. 4).

[40] Dembour uses "discourse theorists" to refer to thinkers, who some would label "human rights sceptics". Thus theorists such as Derrida and Sen are categorized as "deliberative theorists", although they treat human rights as a kind of discourse and emphasize rational public debate as the main means to constructing consensus. Ghai, who is sceptical about such classifications in the context of the complexities of human rights, suggests that he is more "deliberative" in respect of constitution-making, emphasizes struggle much more in respect of poverty, but he does not feel that these categories are helpful in interpreting his work.

[41] Or is Baxi a sceptic as well as a protest theorist?

[42] Dembour also includes Jacques Derrida, Neil Stammers, and June Nash among protest theorists.

I am personally sceptical about the value of classifying individual thinkers other than in very broad terms, and I am only slightly less cautious about classifying particular texts. However, readers may find the schema helpful as a framework for comparing and contrasting the readings in Chapters 2–5 and relating them to broad patterns in "Western" human rights theory.[43]

Finally, why do these authors deserve our attention? They are prolific writers whose works contain many prticular insights and arguments. Apart from that, it may be as dangerous to look for one essential message as it is to pigeon hole thinkers. But I venture to suggest an answer:

- For a case study of the relationship between an exotic traditional nomadic culture and the international human rights regime, read Francis Deng.
- If you wish to learn how a devout Muslim scholar has developed a strategy for reconciling Islamic beliefs with Western liberal democratic ideals, read Abdullahi An-Na'im.
- If you are interested in a pragmatic, materialist argument about the practical value of using human rights discourse to reach political settlements and compromises in multi-ethnic or other conflicted societies, and its role in constitution-making more generally, read Yash Ghai.
- And, if you are interested in an impassioned plea that human rights discourse should first and foremost be interpreted and used to further the interests of the worst off, read Upendra Baxi.

---

[43] Anyone attempting this exercise should consult Dembour's writings, which give a more detailed explanation of the categories. My own views on human rights are set out in my *General Jurisprudence* (2009) Ch. 5–7.

Table 1: Systematic comparison of human rights' schools[44]

Schools of thought (orientation) Human rights (HR)	Natural school (HR orthodoxy)	Deliberative school (HR secularism)	Protest school (HR dissidence)	Discourse school (HR nihilism)
Are conceived, in short, as	A given	Agreed	Fought for	Talked about
Consist in	Entitlements (probably negative at their core)	Principles	Claims/Aspirations	Whatever you put into them
Are for	Every single human being	Running the polity fairly	First and foremost those who suffer	Should be, but are not, for those who suffer
Can be embodied in law?	Definitely – this is the aim	Yes, law is their typical if not only mode of existence	Should be, but law too often betrays the HR idea	HR law exists but does not embody anything grand
See HR law since 1948 as progress?	Yes*	Yes	No	No
Are based on	Nature/God/Universe/Reason [with legal consensus acting as a fallback for many]	A consensus as to how the polity should be run [with reason in the background]	A tradition of social struggles [but with a yearning for the transcendental]	Language
Are realizable?	Yes, through individual enjoyment (and good substantive laws)	Yes, through political organization (and good processual laws)	No, they require a perpetual struggle (and implementing laws risk being an abject deformation of their ideal)	No, unsurprisingly, they are a failure
Are universal?	Yes – definitely, they are part of the structure of the universe (even if they get translated in practice in slightly different forms)	Potentially – if the consensus broadens	At source, yes, if only because suffering is universal	No – their supposed universality is a pretence

*Notes** Though exceptionally a natural scholar will reject the present form of human rights law as not embodying human rights.

44 From Dembour (2010) reproduced with permission. See the earlier version in Dembour, *Who Believes in Human Rights?* (2006) at p. 255.

Bibliography

This selective bibliography contains the references to works cited in Chapters 1 and 6 and the Introductions to Chapters 2–5. It also contains a selection of those writings of the four contributors that are relevant to themes in this book. All four are prolific authors who have written on a wide range of other topics. Works cited in the readings in Chapters 2–5 are not listed here.

Abdelkader, Deina (2000) *Social Justice in Islam* Herndon, VA: IIIT.

Abimbola, Wande and Kola Abimbola (2007) *Orisa: Yoruba Religion and Culture in Africa and the Diaspora* Birmingham: Iroko Academic Publishers.

Adelman, Sammy and Abdul Paliwala (eds.) (1993) *Law in Crisis in the Third World* London: Hans Zell.

Ahmed, Khurshid (2003) "The Challenge of Global Capitalism: An Islamic Perspective" in Dunning (ed.) Ch. 8.

Alston, Philip (ed.) (1999) *Promoting Human Rights Through Bills of Rights: Comparative Perspectives* Oxford: Oxford University Press.

Alston, Philip (2005) "Ships Passing in the Night: The Current State of the Human Rights and Development Debate Seen Through the Lens of the Millennium Development Goals" 27 *Human Rights Quarterly* 755.

Al-Turabi, Hassan (2006) "Sudanese Scholar Hassan Al-Turabi Elaborates on his Revolutionary *Fatwa*" www.memritv.org/Transcript.asp?P1=1112

An-Na'im, Abdullahi (1990) *Toward an Islamic Reformation: Civil Liberties, Human Rights and International Law* Syracuse, NY: Syracuse University Press, Preface by John Voll.

An-Na'im, Abdullahi (ed.) (1992) *Human Rights in Cross-Cultural Perspectives: A Quest for Consensus* Philadelphia: University of Pennsylvania Press.

An-Na'im, Abdullahi (1993) "Toward an Islamic Reformation; Responses and Reflections" in Lindholm and Vogt (eds.) Ch. 6.

An-Na'im, Abdullahi (1999) "Promises We Should All Keep in Common Cause" in Okin *et al.*

An-Na'im, Abdullahi (2001) "Human Rights in the Arab World: A Regional Perspective" 23 *Human Rights Quarterly* 701.

An-Na'im, Abdullahi (2002) *Islamic Family Law in a Changing World: A Global Resource Book* London: Zed Books.

An-Na'im, Abdullahi (ed.) (2003) *Human Rights Under African Constitutions: Realizing the Promise for Ourselves* Philadelphia: University of Pennsylvania Press.

An-Na'im, Abdullahi (2004a) "The Future of Shari'ah Project" (Memo).

An-Na'im, Abdullahi (2004b) "To Affirm the Full Human Rights Standing of Economic, Social and Cultural Rights" in Ghai and Cottrell (eds.) p. 7.

An-Na'im, Abdullahi (2005a) *The Future of Shari'a Project* (unpublished manuscript; see now An-Na'im (2008)).

An-Na'im, Abdullahi (2005b) "The Interdependence of Religion, Secularism and Human Rights" 11 *Common Knowledge* 56–80 (Symposium on Talking Peace with Gods).

An-Na'im, Abdullahi (2006) *African Constitutionalism and the Role of Islam* Philadelphia: University of Pennsylvania Press.

An-Na'im, Abdullahi (2008) *Islam and the Secular State: Negotiating the Future of Shari'a* Cambridge, MA: Harvard University Press.

An-Na'im, Abdullahi and Francis Deng (eds.) (1990) *Human Rights in Africa: Cross-Cultural Perspectives* Washington, DC: Brookings Institution.

An-Na'im, Abdullahi, Jerald Gort, Henry Jansen, and Hendrik Vroom (eds.) (1995) *Human Rights and Religious Values: An Uneasy Relationship?* Amsterdam: Editions Rodopi (Vol. 8 of *Currents of Encounter*).

Andreassen, Bård-Anders and Stephen Marks (eds.) (2006) *Development as a Human Right: Legal, Political and Economic Dimensions* Cambridge, MA: Harvard School of Public Health/Harvard University Press.

Aung San Suu Kyi (1991) *Freedom from Fear and other Writings* Michael Aris (ed.) New York: Penguin.

Barak-Erez, Daphne and Aeyal Gross (eds.) (2007) *Exploring Social Rights* Oxford: Oxford University Press.

Baxi, Upendra (ed.) (1989) *Law and Poverty: Critical Essays* Bombay: N. M. Tripathi.

Baxi, Upendra (1994a) *Inhuman Wrongs and Human Rights: Some Unconventional Essays* New Delhi: Har Anand.

Baxi, Upendra (1994b) *Mambrino's Helmet?: Human Rights for a Changing World* New Delhi: Har Anand.

Baxi, Upendra (1996a) "'A Work in Progress?': The United Nations Report to the United Nations Human Rights Committee" 38 *Indian Journal of International Law* 34.

Baxi, Upendra (1996b) "'Global Neighbourhood' and the 'Universal Otherhood': Notes on the Report of the Commission on Global Governance" 21 *Alternatives* 525.

Baxi, Upendra (1996c) "The 'Reason' of Human Rights and the 'Unreason' of Globalization" University of Bombay, The First A.R. Desai Memorial Lecture.

Baxi, Upendra (1999a) "Voices of Suffering, Fragmented Universality and the Future of Human Rights" in Burns H. Weston and Stephen P. Marks (eds.) *The Future of International Human Rights* 101 New York: Ardsley, Transnational Publishers (also in *Transnational Law and Contemporary Problems* 125).

Baxi, Upendra (1999b) "From Human Rights to the Right to be a Woman" in Dhanda and Prasher (eds.) pp. 275–90.

Baxi, Upendra (2000a) "Constitutionalism as a Site of State Formative Practices" 21 *Cardozo Law Review* 1183.

Baxi, Upendra (2000b) *Mass Torts, Multinational Enterprise Liability and Private International Law* The Hague: Martinus Nijhoff.

Baxi, Upendra (2001a) "What Happens Next is up to You: Human Rights at Risk in Dams and Development" 16 *American University International Law Review* 1507.

Baxi, Upendra (2001b) "From Human Rights to Human Flourishings: Julius Stone, Amartya Sen and Beyond?" (Julius Stone Lecture, University of Sydney, 2001; forthcoming 2009).

Baxi, Upendra (2001c) "Too Many or Two Few Human Rights?" *Human Rights Law Review* 1.

Baxi, Upendra (2001d) "Geographies of Injustice: Human Rights at the Altar of Convenience" in Scott (ed.) 197–202.

Baxi, Upendra (2002) *The Future of Human Rights* (2nd edn. 2006) New Delhi: Oxford University Press.

Baxi, Upendra (2003a) Comment on the UN Draft Code of Conduct of Transnational Corporations and Businesses.

Baxi, Upendra (2003b) *Memory and Rightlessness* (15th J. P. Naik Memorial Lecture) New Delhi: Centre for Women's Development Studies.

Baxi, Upendra (2003c) "'A Known but an Indifferent Judge': Situating Ronald Dworkin in Contemporary Indian Jurisprudence" 1 *International Journal of Constitutional Law (ICON)* 557.

Baxi, Upendra (2003d) "Toward a General Assembly of Peoples: Notes for a Conversation" 13 *Widener Law Review* 401.

Baxi, Upendra (2005) "Protection of Human Rights and Production of Human Rightlessness in India" in Peerenboom, Petersen and Chen (eds.) Ch. 13.

Baxi, Upendra (2006) "A Report for all Seasons? Small Notes Towards Reading the Larger Freedom" in Kumar and Srivastava (eds.) 495.

Baxi, Upendra (2007a) *Human Rights in a Posthuman World* New Delhi: Oxford University Press (*Posthuman*).

Baxi, Upendra (2007b) "Failed De-Colonization and Future of Social Rights" in Barak-Erez and Gross (eds.).

Baxi, Upendra (2007) "Re-Silencing Human Rights" in Bhambra and Shillman (eds.).

Baxi, Upendra (2008) "Translating Terror: Siting Truth, Justice and Rights Amidst the Terror Wars" in E. Bielsa and C. W. Hughes (eds.) *Globalization, Political Violence and Translation* New York: Palgrave MacMillan, Ch. 2.

Baxi, Upendra and Oliver Mendelsohn (eds.) (1994) *The Rights of Subordinated Peoples* New Delhi: Oxford University Press.

Baxi, Upendra and Kenny Ikeman (2006) *The People's Report on Human Rights Education* New York: People's Decade for Human Rights Education (available at www.pdhre.org).

Bhambra, Gurminder K. and Robbie Shillman (eds.) (2007) *Silencing Human Rights* Cambridge: Cambridge University Press.

Bowen, John R. (2003) *Islam, Law and Equality in Indonesia: An Anthropology of Public Reasoning* Cambridge: Cambridge University Press.

Bowen, John R. (2005) "Pluralism and Normativity in French Islamic Reasoning" in Hefner (ed.) 326–46.

Bowen, John R. (2007) *Why the French Don't Like Headscarves: Islam, the State and Public Space* Princeton: Princeton University Press.

Cauquelin, Josiane, Paul Lim, and Birgit Mayer-König (eds.) (1998) *Asian Values: An Encounter with Diversity* Richmond: Curzon Press.

Chen, Albert H.Y. (1993) "Developing Theories of Rights and Human Rights in China" in Wacks (ed.) Ch. 5.

Chen, Albert H.Y. (2006) "Comparative Reflections on Human Rights in Asia" in Peerenboom, Petersen, and Chen (eds.) Ch. 16.

Cohen, Roberta and Francis Deng (1998) *Masses in Flight: The Global Crisis of Internal Displacement* Washington, DC: The Brookings Institution.

Commaraswamy, Radhika (1994) "To Bellow Like a Cow: Women, Ethnicity, and the Discourse of Rights" in Cook (ed.) Ch. 2.

Commission on Global Governance (1995) *Our Global Neighbourhood* New York: Oxford University Press (The Brandt Report).

Cook, Rebecca J. (ed.) (1994) *Human Rights of Women: National and International Perspectives* Philadelphia: Pennsylvania University Press.

Cooper, John, Ronald Nettler and Mohamed Mahmoud (eds.) (2000) *Islam and Modernity: Muslim Intellectuals Respond* London: Tauris.

Cottrell, Jill and Yash Ghai (2007) "Constitution-making and democratization in Kenya (2000–2005)" 14 *Democratization* 1.

D'Asprement, Jean (2008) "International Law in Asia: The Limits to Constitiutonalist and Liberal Doctrines" 13 *Asian Yearbook of International Law*.

Dembour, Marie-Bénédicte (2006) *Who Believes in Human Rights? Reflections on the European Convention* Cambridge: Cambridge University Press.

Dembour, Marie-Bénédicte (2010) "What are Human Rights? Four Schools of Thought," *Human Rights Quarterly*.

Deng, Francis (1971) *Tradition and Modernization: A Challenge for Law Among the Dinka of the Sudan* New Haven: Yale University Press. (Paperback, 1986; 3rd edn. 2004, Washington, DC: Kush Inc.).

Deng, Francis (1972) *The Dinka of the Sudan* New York: Holt, Reinhart and Winston (2nd edn. 1984, 3rd edn. 1986) Prospect Heights, ILL: Waveland Press.

Deng, Francis (1973) *The Dinka and their Songs* Oxford: Clarendon Press.

Deng, Francis (1974) *Dinka Folktales: African Stories from the Sudan* New York: African Publishing Co.

Deng, Francis (1978) *Africans of Two Worlds: The Dinka in Afro-Arab Sudan* New Haven: Africana Publishing Co.

Deng, Francis (1980) *Dinka Cosmology* London: Ithaca Press.

Deng, Francis (1986a) *Seed of Redemption: A Political Novel* New York: Lilian Barber Press.

Deng, Francis (1986b) *The Man Called Deng Majok: A Biography of Power, Polygyny and Change* New Haven: Yale University Press.

Deng, Francis (1989) *Cry of the Owl* New York: Lilian Barber Press (novel).

Deng, Francis (1993) *Protecting the Dispossessed: A Challenge to the International Community* Washington, DC: The Brookings Institution.

Deng, Francis (1995) *War of Visions: Conflict of Identities in the Sudan* Washington DC: Brookings Institution.

Deng, Francis (1998) "The Cow and the Thing Called 'What': Dinka Cultural Perspectives on Wealth and Poverty" 52 *Journal of International Affairs* 101.

Deng, Francis (1998) "Traditional Institutions and Participatory Democracy in Africa" *Sudan Democratic Gazette*, April.

Deng, Francis (1998) "Globalisation and Localisation of Democracy in the African Context" *Sudan Democratic Gazette*, May.

Deng, Francis (1998) "Universalism versus Relativism in Cultural Contextualisation of Human Rights" *Sudan Democratic Gazette*, June.

Deng, Francis (1998) "Cultural Constraints on the Universality of Human Rights" *Sudan Democratic Gazette*, August.

Deng, Francis (1998) "Dinka Values and Human Rights Principles" *Sudan Democratic Gazette*, September.

Deng, Francis (1999) "Further Perspectives on Dinka Perceptions of Property and Wealth" *Sudan Democratic Gazette*, June.

Deng, Francis (1999) "Dinka Perspectives VI – Modernity and Diminishing Self-image" *Sudan Democratic Gazette*, October.

Deng, Francis (2006) *Talking it Out: Stories in Negotiating Human Relations* London: Kegan Paul.

Deng, Francis (2008) *Identity, Diversity and Constitutionalism in Africa* Washington, DC: United States Institute for Peace.

Deng, Francis (2009) *Customary Law in the Cross-fire of Sudan's War of Identities* Washington, DC: United States Institute for Peace.

Deng, Francis and Adbdullahi An-Na'im (eds.) (1990) *Human Rights in Africa: Cross-Cultural Perspectives* Washington, DC: The Brookings Institution.

Deng, Francis and Roberta Cohen (eds.) *The Foresaken People: Case Studies of the Internally Displaced* Washington, DC: The Brookings Institution.

Deng, Francis and Roberta Cohen (1998) *Masses in Flight: The Global Crisis of Internal Displacement* Washington, DC: The Brookings Institution.

Deng, Francis and Terrence Lyons (1998) *African Reckoning: A Quest for Good Governance* Washington, DC: The Brookings Institution.

Dhanda, Amita and Archana Prasher (eds.) (1999) *Engendering Law: Essays in Honour of Professor Lotika Sarkar* Lucknow: Eastern Book Co.

Dunning, John H. (ed.) (2003) *Making Globalization Good* Oxford: Oxford University Press.

Ebadi, Shirin (2003) Nobel Lecture (available at www.nobel.se./peace/laureates).

El-Gamal, Mahmoud A. (2006) *Islamic Finance: Law, Economics and Practice* Cambridge: Cambridge University Press.

Escobar, Arturo *et al.* (eds.) (2004) *The World Social Forum: Challenging Empires* New Delhi: Viveka.

Esposito, John L., and John H. Voll (eds.) (2001) *Makers of Contemporary Islam* New York: Oxford University Press.

Gearty, Conor (2006) *Can Human Rights Survive*? (Hamlyn Lectures) Cambridge: Cambridge University Press.

Ghai, Dharam and Yash Ghai (1971) *Asians in East and Central Africa* London: Minority Rights Group (reprinted in Ben Whitaker, *The Fourth World* (1974)).

Ghai, Yash (1967) "Independence and Safeguards in Kenya" (1967) *East African Law Journal* 177–217.

Ghai, Yash (1986) "Legal Radicalism, Professionalism and Social Action: Reflections on Teaching Law in Dar-es-Salaam" in Shivji (ed.) Ch. 3.

Ghai, Yash (ed.) (1991) *Put Our World to Rights* London: Commonwealth Human Rights Initiative.

Ghai, Yash (1993a) "Asian Perspectives on Human Rights" 23 *Hong Kong Law Journal* 342.

Ghai, Yash (1993b) "The Rule of Law and Capitalism: Reflections on the Basic Law" in Wacks (ed.) 203.

Ghai, Yash (1995) "The Politics of Rights in Asia" in Wilson (ed.) Ch. 13.

Ghai, Yash (1997) "Sentinels of Liberty or Sheep in Woolf's Clothing? Judicial Politics and the Hong Kong Bill of Rights" 60 *Modern Law Review* 459.

Ghai, Yash (1998a) "Human Rights and Asian Values" 9 *Public Law Review* 168.

Ghai, Yash (1998b) "Rights, Duties and Responsibilities" in Cauquelin, Lim and Mayer-Konig (eds.) Ch. 2.

Ghai, Yash (1999a) *Hong Kong's New Constitutional Order* (2nd edn.) Hong Kong: Hong Kong University Press.

Ghai, Yash (1999b) "The Kenyan Bill of Rights: Theory and Practice" in Alston (ed.) Ch. 6.

Ghai, Yash (ed.) (2000a) *Autonomy and Ethnicity: Negotiating Competing Claims in Multi-ethnic States* Cambridge: Cambridge University Press.

Ghai, Yash (2000b) "Universalism and Relativism: Human Rights as a Framework for Negotiating Interethnic Claims" 21 *Cardozo Law Review* 1095.

Ghai, Yash (2005) "A Journey Around Constitutions" (Beinart Lecture, University of Capetown, 2002) 122 *South African Law Journal* 804.

Ghai, Yash (2006) "Redesigning the State for Right Development" in Andreassen and Marks (eds.) Ch. 8.

Ghai, Yash (2008) "Understanding Human Rights in Asia" above Chapter 4.3 and in Krause and Scheinin (eds.).

Ghai, Yash (2008) "Constitutionalism and Diversity" in Heckman, James, Robert Nelson, and Lee Cabatinga *Global Perspectives on the Rule of Law* London: Routledge.

Ghai, Yash (2009) "The Challenge of Creating a Constitutional Order in African States: Some Perspectives from Kenya" (forthcoming).

Ghai, Yash and Jill Cottrell (eds.) (2004) *Economic, Social and Cultural Rights in Practice* London: Interights.

Ghai, Yash and Jill Cottrell (forthcoming) *MDGs through Socio-Economic Rights: Constitution Making and Implementation* (UNDP).

Ghai, Yash and Patrick McAuslan (1970) *Public Law and Political Change in Kenya: A Study of the Legal Framework of Government from Colonial Times to the Present* Nairobi: Oxford University Press.

Ghai, Yash, Mark Lattimer, and Yahia Said (2003) *Building Democracy in Iraq* (Report) London: Minority Rights Group International.

Glenn, H. Patrick (2004) *Legal Traditions of the World* (revised edn.) Oxford: Oxford University Press.

Guardiola-Rivera, Oscar (2008) *Being Against the World: Rebellion and Constitution* London: Routledge.

Halme, Miia (2008) *Human Rights in Action* Helsinki: Helsinki University Press.

Hefner, Robert (ed.) (2005) *Remaking Muslim Politics* Princeton: Princeton University Press.

Horowitz, Donald L. (1994) "The Qu'ran and the Common Law: Islamic Law Reform and the Theory of Legal Change", 42 *American Journal of Comparative Law* 233 and 543.

Ishay, Micheline (2004) *The History of Human Rights: From Ancient Times to the Globalization Era* Berkeley: University of California Press.

Jenkins, Philip (2007a) *God's Continent: Christianity, Islam and Europe's Religious Crisis* Oxford: Oxford University Press.

Jenkins, Philip (2007b) *The Next Christendom: the Coming of Global Christianity* (revised edn.) Oxford: Oxford University Press.

Kamrava, Mehran (ed.) (2006) *The New Voices of Islam: Reforming Politics and Modernity* London: Tauris.

Karst, Kenneth (2000) "The Bonds of American Nationhood" 21 *Cardozo Law Review* 1095.

Krause, Catarina and Martin Scheinin (eds.) (2008) *International Protection of Human Rights: A Textbook* Turku: Institute for Human Rights, Åbo Akademi University.

Kretzmer, David and Eckart Klein (eds.) (2002) *The Concept of Human Dignity in Human Rights Discourse* The Hague: Kluwer Law International.

Kumar, Raj and D.K. Srivastava (eds.) (2006) *Human Rights and Development: Law, Policy and Governance* Hong Kong: Lexis-Nexis.

Kung, Hans (2007) *Islam, Past, Present and Future* (trs. John Bowden) Oxford: One World.

Lindholm, Tori and Kari Vogt (eds.) (1993) *Islamic Law Reform and Human Rights; Challenges and Rejoinders* Copenhagen: Nordic Human Rights Publications, Oslo.

Mamdani, Mahmood (2000) *Beyond Rights Talk and Culture Talk: Comparative Essays on the Politics and Rights and Culture* New York: St Martin's Press.

Mandela, Nelson (1965) *No Easy Walk to Freedom: Articles, Speeches and Trial Addresses* (ed. Ruth First) New York: Basic Books.

Maritain, Jacques (1951) *Man and the State* Chicago: University of Chicago Press.

Mayer, Ann E. (1991) *Islam and Human Rights: Tradition and Politics* (3rd edn. 1999) Boulder, COL: Westview Press.

Mayer, Ann E. (1993) "A Critique of An-Na'im's Assessment of Islamic Criminal Justice" in Lindholm and Vogt (eds.) Ch. 3.

Mayer, Ann E. (1994) "Universal Versus Islamic Human Rights: A Clash of Cultures or a Clash with a Construct?" 15 *Michigan Journal of International Law* 307.

McCrudden, Christopher (2008) "Human Dignity and Judicial Interpretation of Human Rights" 20 *European Journal of International Law* 1.

Menski, Werner (2003) *Hindu Law: Beyond Tradition and Modernity* New Delhi: Oxford University Press.

Menski, Werner (2006) *Comparative Law in a Global Context: The Legal Systems of Asia and Africa* (2nd edn.) Cambridge: Cambridge University Press.

Munger, Frank (2001) "Inquiry and Activism in Law and Society" 35 *Law and Society Review* 1 (Presidential address).

Mutua, Makau (2002) *Human Rights: A Political and Cultural Critique* Philadelphia: University of Pennsylvania Press.

Nino, Carlos (1991) *The Ethics of Human Rights* Oxford: Oxford University Press.

Nino, Carlos (1998) *The Constitution of Deliberative Democracy* New Haven: Yale University Press.

Nyerere, Julius (1966) *Freedom and Unity* (selected speeches and writings) Dar-es-Salaam: Oxford University Press.

Okin, Susan Moller with respondents (1999) *Is Multiculturalism Bad for Women?* Joshua Cohen, Matthew Howard and Martha C. Nussbaum (eds.) Princeton, NJ: Princeton University Press.

Onuma, Yasuaki (2000) "In Quest of Intercivilizational Human Rights: 'Universal' vs. 'Relative'" 1 *Asia-Pacific Journal on Human Rights and Law* 53.

Peerenboom, Randall, Carole J. Petersen and Albert H.Y. Chen (eds.) (2006) *Human Rights in Asia* London: Routledge.

Rajagopal, Balakrishnan (2003) *International Law from Below: Developing Social Movements and Third World Resistance* Cambridge: Cambridge University Press.

Ramadan, Tariq (2004) *Western Muslims and the Future of Islam* Oxford: Oxford University Press.

Ramadan, Tariq (2007) *The Messenger: The Meanings of the Life of Muhammed* London: Allen Lane.

Rawls, John (1999) *The Law of Peoples* Cambridge, MA: Harvard University Press.

Ryle, John *et al.* (1982) *Warriors of the Nile: The Dinka* Amsterdam: Time-Life Books.

Santos, Boaventura de Sousa (2002), *Toward a New Legal Common Sense: Law, Globalisation and Emancipation* (2nd edn.) London: Butterworth.

Santos, Boaventura de Sousa and César Rodríguez-Garavito (2005) *Law and Globalization from Below: Towards a Cosmopolitan Legality* Cambridge: Cambridge University Press.

Scott, Craig (ed.) (2001) *Torture as Tort: Comparative Perspectives on the Development of Transnational Human Rights Litigation* Oxford: Hart.

Sen, Amartya (1997) "Human Rights and Asian Values: What Lee Kuan Yew and Li Peng Don't Understand about Asia" (14 and 21 July) *The New Republic* 33.

Sen, Amartya (1999) *Development as Freedom* Oxford: Oxford University Press.

Sen, Amartya (2004) "Elements of a Theory of Human Rights" 32 *Philosophy and Public Affairs* 315.

Sen, Amartya (2005) *The Argumentative Indian* London: Penguin.

Sharma, Arvind (2004) *Hinduism and Human Rights: A Conceptual Approach* New Delhi: Oxford University Press.

Shihata, Ibrahim F. (1991) *The World Bank in a Changing World* Dordrecht: Martinus Nijhoff.

Shivji, Issa (ed.) (1986) *The Limits of Legal Radicalism* Dar-es-Salaam: University of Dar-es-Salaam.

Shivji, Issa (1989) *The Concept of Human Rights in Africa* London and Dakar: Codesria.

Shivji, Issa (1993) "Rights-struggle, Class-struggle and the Law: Reflections on Experiences in the University of Dar-es-Salaam" in Adelman and Paliwala (eds.) Ch. 6.

Siddiqi, Muhammad Nejatullah (1997) *Banking Without Interest* (revised edn.) The Islamic Foundation.

Simpson, A.W. Brian (2001) *Human Rights and the End of Empire* Oxford: Oxford University Press.

Sornarajah, M. (1997) "Power and Justice in International Law" 1 *Singapore Journal of International Law* 28.

Stainton-Rogers, Rex and Celia Kitzinger (1986) "Human Rights: Bedrock or Mosaic?" 9 *Operant Subjectivity* 123–30.

Steiner, Henry J., Philip Alston and Ryan Goodman (2008) *International Human Rights in Context: Law, Politics, Morals* (3rd edn.) Oxford: Oxford University Press.

Stenner, Paul (forthcoming) "Subjective Dimensions of Human Rights" Presentation given at the International Workshop on Sociology and Human Rights, Onati, Spain, May 2007.

Sweet, William (ed.) (2003) *Philosophical Theory and the Universal Declaration of Human Rights* Ottawa: University of Ottawa Press.

Tabandeh, Sultanhussein (1970) *A Muslim Commentary on the Universal Declaration of Human Rights* London: Goulding.

Taha, Mahmoud Mohamed (1987) *The Second Message of Islam* (trs. with an Introduction by Abdullahi An-Na'im) Syracuse: Syracuse University Press.

Taylor, Charles (2007) *A Secular Age* Cambridge, MA: Belknap Press.

Tibi, Bassam (1993) "Islamic Law/Shar'ia and Human Rights: International Law and Relations" in Lindholm and Vogt (eds.) Ch. 5.

Twining, William (1975) "The Contemporary Significance of Bentham's *Anarchical Fallacies*" 61 *Archiv fur Rechts – und Sozialphilosophie* 325.

Twining, William (2000) *Globalisation and Legal Theory* Evanston, ILL: Northwestern University Press (*GLT*).

Twining, William (2006) "Human Rights: Southern Voices" (MacDonald lecture, University of Alberta) 11 *Review of Constitutional Studies* 203 (reprinted in Twining (2009) Ch. 13).

Twining, William (2009) *General Jurisprudence: Understanding Law from a Global Perspective* Cambridge: Cambridge University Press (*GJP*).

Ul Haq, Mahbub (1995) *Reflections on Human Development* New York: Oxford University Press.

Wacks, Raymond (ed.) (1993) *Hong Kong and China 1997* Hong Kong: Hong Kong University Press.

Wagner, Teresa and Leslie Carbone (eds.) (2001) *Fifty Years after the Declaration* Lanham: University Press of America.

Weeramantry, Christopher G. (1997) *Justice Without Frontiers: Furthering Human Rights* The Hague: Kluwer Law International.

Widner, Jennifer A. (2001) *Building the Rule of Law: Francis Nyalali and the Road to Judicial Independence in Africa* New York: Norton.

Wilson, Geoffrey P. (ed.) (1995) *Frontiers of Legal Scholarship* Chichester: Chancery Lane Publishing.

Wing, Adrien K. (ed.) (2000) *Global Critical Race Feminism: An International Reader* New York: New York University Press.

Zubaidi, Sami (2003) *Law and Power in the Islamic World* London: Tauris.

Index